WOMEN'S WORK IN THE UNORGANISED SECTOR

This book probes into the beedi industry, a highly gendered and class-divided unorganised sector in India. It introduces an analysis of the lives, health status, and work of the Indian women and girl children in the industry and discusses the role of gender constructions, global capitalism, and global racism in shaping the ideologies and conceptions about men and women at work.

The volume presents a gendered postcolonial perspective on women's employment in the context of social and economic processes that are critical to globalisation. It focuses on Telangana's Nizamabad district – where a majority of the women population are employed in the beedi industry. Through detailed surveys and case studies, the author analyses different aspects of exploitation of these women such as poor working conditions, income inequalities, health risks, and the realities of child labour in the process of beedi making.

Richly detailed, this book will be of great interest to students, researchers, and teachers of geography, particularly human geography and feminist geography, women and gender studies, feminism, labour economics, capitalism, development studies, political sociology, and cultural studies. It will also be of interest to gender and feminist geographers, occupational health professionals, NGOs, and those interested in the issues of gender and development.

Rekha Pande is Professor of History and Women's Studies. She is Professor Emeritus at Henry Martin Institute, International Centre for Research, Interfaith Relations and Reconciliation, Hyderabad. She is the former Head at the Centre for Women's Studies and former Head in the Department of History, University of Hyderabad, India.

WOMEN'S WORK IN THE UNORGANISED SECTOR

Issues of Exploitation and Globalisation in the Beedi Industry

Rekha Pande

Routledge
Taylor & Francis Group
LONDON AND NEW YORK

Designed Cover image: Getty Image

First published 2023
by Routledge
4 Park Square, Milton Park, Abingdon, Oxon OX14 4RN

and by Routledge
605 Third Avenue, New York, NY 10158

Routledge is an imprint of the Taylor & Francis Group, an informa business

British Library Cataloguing-in-Publication Data
A catalogue record for this book is available from the British Library

ISBN: 978-1-032-26155-3 (hbk)
ISBN: 978-1-032-33056-3 (pbk)
ISBN: 978-1-003-31794-4 (ebk)

DOI: 10.4324/9781003317944

Typeset in Bembo
by codeMantra

CONTENTS

FIGURES

TABLES

PREFACE

Women and girls who produce beedis are among India's most exploited workers in the unorganised sector. In India, an indigenous cigarette known as a beedi is made by rolling tobacco in a leaf and tying it with cotton thread. Most of the women working in this profession come from the most disadvantaged areas of society and are forced to work in this field because they have no other options. With the advent of globalisation, today these women are at cross roads. The awareness related to tobacco and the demand to ban these products has had an impact on their diminishing livelihood option and has rendered them very vulnerable. The women are working here on a per-piece rate and they are home-based female workers with very low incomes. They are rarely offered the status as employees. Since most of this work is done at home, children, especially girls, become an easy prey. Often these girls drop out of school and help the mothers in making beedis or provide assistance in housekeeping. Beedi making is highly labour intensive and a health hazard for workers. These women work from home and are to a great deal shaped by conceptions about women's work in the domestic sphere, and at the same time they produce for and take part in the capitalist market. This antagonism is exploited by capitalistic forces within the Indian society to keep wages low. These women often earn very small incomes and the girl children add a little to it. Beedi making is regarded as women's work and only women and girls make beedis, and men and boys if involved in this industry are employed in the factory in packaging and in transportation. In India, the beedi industry employs over 5 million workers, of whom 90% are women and girls. This industry can be found in different states like Madhya Pradesh, Karnataka, Odisha, Kerala, Andhra Pradesh, and Telangana. By this study of Telangana beedi workers, we hope to bring out some of the hitherto unknown aspects of this industry at large because the reality of beedi making is similar all over India.

Women's work has traditionally been represented as inferior to men's work. This has shaped women's work as low status with low pay and insecure terms of employment. Gender constructions shape norms and conceptions about what is possible behaviour of men and women at home and at work. Global capitalism exploits naturalised assumptions about women by using gendered and raced ideologies to create women's work and to generate increased profits. Patriarchy and global racism thereby become effective structures to supply cheap labour. Traditional male labour unions also profit by women's insecure work within the informal sector, as women are temporarily hired as extra workers during peak seasons and are laid off during low seasons. Thereby the income of the male workers is secured and they can avoid overtime work during peak seasons. Women must bear the cost of flexibility, insecurity, and bad working hours. At the same time, it is in the interest of capitalism that women are gainfully employed and earn their own money and maybe possibilities of work can create greater liberty of action among those women who traditionally are placed in the domestic sphere doing domestic work and mainly handling childcare. Employment can increase the possibilities of economic independence among women who conventionally are dependent on husband, brother, or father. Accordingly, capitalism and patriarchy both collaborate and have conflicting interests. These conflicting interests shape possibilities for women to act and organise themselves as workers and women. Women's work and organisation threatens patriarchy and at the same time patriarchy and global capitalism, with its international division of labour, profit on Third World women as a cheap labour force.

The global economy has undergone significant transformations as a result of economic restructuring brought about by globalisation. The developing world has been affected by these economic, social, and political changes in a variety of ways. Globalisation's logic may be traced back to neo-liberalism and modern capitalism; however, different thinkers have their own theories about what that means. A large part of the expansion of transnational production relies on subaltern women as cheap factory workers or subcontracted home workers, transforming them into flexible global categories of workers with low wages and uncertain employment terms, making them simple to fire when needed. As a result, the global division of labour is more dependent on ideological ideas of women's work, while at the same time creating Third World and immigrant women as a low-cost and adaptable workforce in the West.

Women's work is never recognised by policy makers and statisticians and by and large their work remains invisible. Women are usually portrayed as nimble, docile, and submissive workers naturally and especially suited for static, monotone, unskilled, and repetitive tasks such as beedi making. These workers are not naturally suited for this kind of work, but rather their vulnerable position as poor, subaltern women without education or bargaining power leaves them few other possibilities than taking up the job they often inherited. This position of the poor justifies, creates, and guarantees low labour costs for these workers and helps employers make great profits at low costs and few liabilities. Hence, the beedi industry attracted our attention for there were two very neat divisions of women's work and men's work. There are an estimated 4.5 million workers in beedi, according to the government. Because many beedi employees do not have official identification cards, trade unions and non-governmental organisations (NGOs) believe that the true number of rollers is substantially higher. Since it's nearly impossible to police, contractors who provide the raw materials for beedis made at home typically pay less than half of the legal minimum wage. Despite this, beedi manufacturing is an essential source of income for the poorer rural households because women's earnings from beedi making account for a large amount of household's revenue. Because of this, the beedi workers provide an intriguing study subject of women's work.

ACKNOWLEDGEMENTS

At first glance, a historian's investigation into the history of women's labour in the beedi sector may raise a number of issues. This research is the result of a long-standing interest in women's and children's concerns, both academically and in the actual world. Understanding how women's subordination and oppression has been perpetuated and replicated in the past has been a major focus for historians. These concerns and awareness are directly linked to the academic discipline interest in women and girls in contemporary times. To understand the multiple facets of a problem, one must first understand the problem itself, which is why researching women's challenges and problems can't just be a theoretical and academic exercise. It is because of these issues and my expertise with feminist research methodology that I am able to transcend beyond my profession and take on projects that would fall within the scope of sociology, child development, or economics. Thank you to the field of Women's Studies for giving me an interdisciplinary viewpoint on this and other projects. For their friendship and moral support and a cross-disciplinary approach, I'd like to express my gratitude to my colleagues in the Women's Studies Centers and Cells.

The book's roots can be found in a project we did in the 1990s on child labour in the Beedi industry, which was funded by the Ministry of Labour. For this I would like to thank the Ministry of Labour. I want to give Prof. Susheela Kaushik and Dr. Nijhawan my special thanks for all their support during this period. I would like to thank Dr. A. Padma and Dr. M.C. Raja for helping me with this project. My thanks also to P. Pulliah, Janardhan Reddy, Babu Rao, Ramesh, and Srinivas who helped in collection of data and Sri Lakshmi who worked as Research Officer in the latter half of the project.

At that time in the field the realisation dawned that this was a very complicated issue and there was a need to study the women too. However, my day-to-day responsibilities at the work place never gave me a window to go back to the field.

However, in 2018, through the University with a potential of excellence Project, I could once again take up this work and go back to the field and expand the scope of this work. For this I would like to thank my University, the University of Hyderabad. Not much had changed in the field during these three decades, except the fact that salary was slightly increased. We also expanded the scope of the work to include Hyderabad. I would like to thank Rashmi Batchu who worked as a research assistant and Abhishek, a Ph.D. student of economics who helped me with the analysis of the data and making the charts and diagrams. Surya Pratap Singh also came to my assistance with the figures and data analysis, and I thank him for sparing his valuable time. I would also like to thank Urvija P. my Ph.D. scholar who went through the rough drafts of this manuscript and made valuable suggestions.

I started working on this project report to convert it into a book during the period of 2019 and the pandemic period from 2020 onwards gave me a considerable amount of time. I also thank Mr. Arif who is the owner of a beedi factory, for allowing me to enter into this world to understand the issue. My long conversations with him have really helped me get a lot of clarity on this industry. He was very much available during the pandemic period to answer to all my queries. Many thanks also to Ankit Chauhan who has helped with the data analysis. A big thank you to him and his team.

I would also like to thank the University of London for providing the Birkbeck fellowship. This gave me time to spend the summer of 2019 working in the British Library at London and have access to a large number of resources that were available, and this made my task a little easy. My discussions with Rebecca Darley, in the University of London, and one who takes a lot of interest in India, have gone a long way in clarifying many issues.

I would also like to thank my husband, Dr. Suresh Pande, who was never very demanding on my time, during the course of my several trips to the field area. But for his cooperation and managing the house in my absence, I could never have carried out my field work. This book has taken shape due to the free time that I have found from the day-to-day mundane affairs of managing the house with all its day-to-day details and this has been possible because he has shared a large amount of the household responsibilities with me. He has also contributed his valuable inputs to my manuscript. My elder son, Sankalp, and my daughters-in-law, Nidhi and Geetakshi, and my twins, Tarun and Varun, have always been my anchor and the wind beneath my wings. Both Tarun and Varun have been very enthusiastic in helping with the data and analysing it. You are the rock that binds me. To you all a big thank you.

Finally, but for the cooperation extended to us in the research area by all our respondents the thousands of beedi workers of Nizamabad in Pipri, Armoor, Balkonda, Kisanagar, Nizamabad and Gopanpally village, and the Hyderabad area the project could not have been completed. I owe a great obligation to the women and children who have taught me more about life in a short period of time than all the literature combined.

Rekha Pande

PART A
The background

1

INTRODUCTION

The business of making beedis is a home-based enterprise in the unorganised sector that employs a large number of women and children. Beedis are cheroots formed from tendu leaves rolled in tobacco dust, which women and girls make by hand, using a putting-out procedure in their houses. About 90% of the workers in this industry are women who collect raw materials and deliver finished beedis to subcontractors who set up units (*karkhanas)* in the villages. It takes a woman about eight to ten hours to roll about 800 beedis, but because they mix this job with domestic and reproductive chores in their houses, this beedi-making activity spills over into their other household tasks and draws on the efforts of other family members, particularly female children. Beedis are popular in both rural and urban regions, accounting for nearly half of all tobacco consumption in India. This industry, which has been around for over a century, coexists alongside agricultural labour and other non-farm enterprises.

Women who make beedis live and work in a male-dominated industry, where the manufacturer, contractor, and customer are all men, with just the real beedi worker being a woman. Most of these women handle all of their household tasks and work 11–14 hours a day for a pittance. When making beedi, workers are continually exposed to tobacco dust, which might cause health problems. The producer of the beedi is constantly exposed to tobacco dust, which is a workplace health danger. Women and girls here face health risks not because they use the beedis, but because they make them in the absence of any other means of income.

When it comes to India's unorganised sector or "informal sector", beedi is one of the most important industries. Large numbers of women and girls are employed throughout India, which allows the owner to reap great profits with minimal risk and liability. In the states of Karnataka, Kerala, Madhya Pradesh, West Bengal, Andhra Pradesh, and Telangana, the facts are all the same. Because

DOI: 10.4324/9781003317944-2

it's in the unorganised market, it's vulnerable to abuse (ILO, 1972). In Andhra Pradesh and Maharashtra, women outnumber men by 77.3% and 66.35%, respectively, in the sweated industries (Toward Equality, 1974).

In a survey conducted, the ILO pointed out that there are at least 450 million (Rs. 340 crores) worth of beedis which are produced annually in India, but only about 160 million of these go to the beedi workers as wages. The ILO study shows that the contractors who supply the material for manufacturing beedis in homes rarely pay more than the equivalent of half the statutory minimum wages since this is almost impossible to enforce (ILO, 1972). The minimum wages are set by the states to include a monetary value equal to the basic needs of employees and their families for their consumption. And this monetary value does not take into account the age and years of worker experience, and thus, for all purposes, all entry-level and exit-level salaries are minimum wages. Without legislative social security for jobs in the informal sector, minimum wages are the only means of subsistence for wage earners and their families. A minimum daily wage can only provide subsistence for a day and has no certainty for the days to come for casual daily workers with little job security (Satpathy et al., 2020). Yet beedi making is an important source of income for the poorer rural households, and women's earnings from beedi making constitute on an average 45–50% of the total income.

Beedi is an indigenous cigarette, which is mostly made at home by women and children by rolling tobacco into a dried tendu leaf (Coromandal Ebony, Persimmon; Latin Name, *Diospyros melanoxylon* Roxb). A woman must pick up a pinch of tobacco grains and arrange it on the leaf for each beedi prepared. She holds the leaf in her left hand and spreads the tobacco with her right hand's fingers. As a result, her fingers are constantly in contact with the tobacco. Cotton thread is then used to bind it. Beedi is connected with the working class in the popular imagination, as opposed to the cigarette-smoking elite class. The majority of the women here are from disadvantaged backgrounds, posing occupational health risks. The women and girls here are exposed to health risks not because they smoke, but because they make these beedis.

India is the world's second-largest tobacco producer, with an estimated 800 million kg of annual production. Tobacco occupies a meagre 0.24% of the total arable land area of the country. It is grown mainly in semi-arid and rain-fed areas where it is economically unviable to cultivate alternative crops. India produces 4.2 lakh tons of tobacco, or 430 million kg. Tobacco cultivation in Andhra Pradesh in 2.02 lakh hectares of land is under way. Only a small portion of this is used by direct employees in the organised sector to prepare cigarettes, with the rest done outside as beedis, resulting in a big workforce of home workers. Tobacco is grown in India in the following 12 states: Assam, Bihar, Chhattisgarh, Gujarat, Karnataka, Madhya Pradesh, Maharashtra, Odisha, Tamil Nadu, Telangana, Uttar Pradesh, and West Bengal.

China was the largest producer of tobacco in 2013. This continued till 2020, when China was the world's greatest tobacco producer, accounting for 39.06%

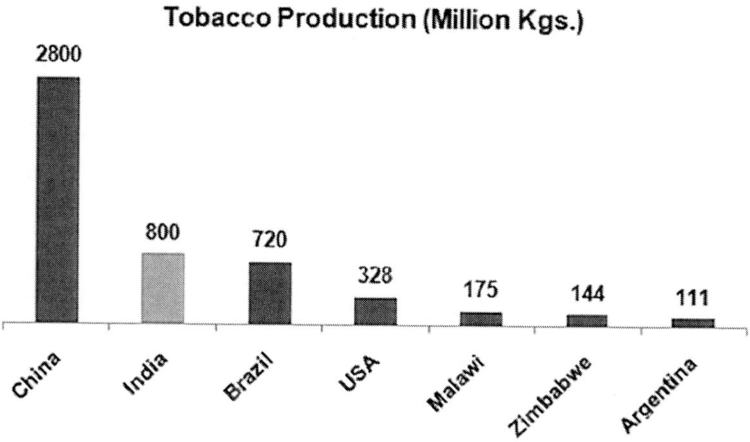

FIGURE 1.1 UN Trade database (2013).
Source: Universal Leaf Tobacco.

of global tobacco output, followed by India with 12.3%, Brazil with 11.51%, and Zimbabwe with 3.81% (Cook, 2022).

Despite the fact that tobacco products such as cigarettes, beedis, and chewing leaves are widely used in India, the country imposes very minimal tariffs on the substance itself. Tobacco uses also contributes significantly to the death toll. In India, the number of people dying from tobacco-related causes is on the rise, accounting for around one-sixth of the global total. More than a million Indians died from heart disease, cancer, respiratory sickness, and tuberculosis in the early 2010s because of smoking. By the year 2020, this number is expected to have grown dramatically. Rs 36.9 billion in tax income and the lives of 15.5 million beedi smokers will be saved if beedi prices are raised to Rs 98 per 1,000 sticks (John et al., 2010). According to World Health Organization (WHO) representative in India Dr. Roderico H. Ofrin, healthcare costs related with tobacco smoking have increased by 21% between 2011 and 2018. This consumes a significant portion of the government's investment in health, including efforts to achieve universal health coverage. Indians can save millions of lives by implementing a comprehensive set of measures that will reduce the detrimental impact of smoking on society and economy, according to this analysis. In response to the globalisation of the tobacco pandemic, the WHO Framework Convention on Tobacco Control (FCTC) was created. The tobacco epidemic's spread is aided by a number of complex cross-border factors, such as trade liberalisation and foreign investment, globalisation, direct investment, and other activities, such as promotion, marketing, and international tobacco advertising and sponsorship, as well as the global movement of cigarettes that are illegal or counterfeit. The WHO FCTC is an evidence-based treaty that affirms all people's rights to the best possible level of health (WHO FCTC, 2003).

The demands in foreign countries have stimulated beedi production in India. As per a report in one of the local English dailies, *Deccan Chronicle,* Indian beedis brands such as Kailas, Shivasagar, Ganesh, and Parchan have also been given a place today in the US Marlboro, Camel, and Rothman. These beedis, which come in an attractive pink box and in flavours like strawberry, raspberry, vanilla, chocolate, and even blueberry, have carved out a niche for themselves among American youths. Five years ago, Los Angeles was the first city to get beedis smuggled from India, but it has been a regular sight since then (Sen, 1999). According to a *Massachusetts Health Department survey,* many American young people are addicted to rolled beedis by hand. This study found that 40% of the 642 teenagers in the city of Boston smoked a beedi, 16% also smoked the beedi, and almost 8% were actively active in smoking this hand-rolled blunt cigarette, most of whom smoked more than 100 beedis. Many of these adolescents, the study reports, considered the beedi to be very good with less nicotine and tar than the standard cigarette (Sen, 1999). In another survey of 461 high school students, 40% of respondents had been smoking beedis for more than a year, and nearly 50% of this sample claimed that beedis did not cause any harm, as it contained only tobacco and not the toxic tar and nicotine (Sen, 1999). The study concludes that it was found on the examination of the beedi's contents that the beedi's apparently innocent leaf wrapped look could contain five times the tar and three times the traditional cigarette's nicotine content. Health officials say that there is around 8% nicotine in a single beedi, which is four times more than the regular American cigarette.

Tobacco-related disease

Three tobacco-related disease categories – malignancies, chronic obstructive pulmonary disease, and coronary heart disease – cost India Rs 27,761 crores (approximately 6.5 billion dollars) in 1999 according to the Indian Council of Medical Research (ICMR). More than one in ten deaths from cardiovascular disease (CVD) worldwide in 2000 were caused by smoking (Ezzati et al., 2005). As of yet, the cost of more than 20 life-threatening conditions has not been determined. The direct and indirect costs include the patient's and his family's costs, the cost of the treating institution, the loss of productivity owing to absenteeism, disability, and death as a result of the condition (Tikoo, 2001). South-East Asia's annual growth in adult per capita cigarette consumption (2.8%) is not the only factor that is expected to drive up the death toll, as 55,000 Indian youngsters are added to the 240 million tobacco users, including 45 million women in the country each year (Tikoo, 2001).

Tobacco kills 560 people per hour, or 13,400 per day, or 4.9 million a year. According to a report of the WHO, the intake of tobacco is rising all over the world and is expected to have killed 8.4 million people a year by 2020 unless stringent control measures are enforced. About 1 billion men smoke worldwide (about 35% of men in developed countries and 50% of men in developing countries), Women also enter this list in significant numbers of nearly 250 million women in the world frequent smokers (about 22% of women in developed countries and 9% of women in developing countries) (WHO, World Health Report). If uncontrolled and unregulated, by 2020, tobacco would kill about 8.4 million people worldwide per year. In developing countries, 70% of those deaths will occur, with India and China in the lead. WHO reports that by 2020, 13.3% of all deaths in India will result from diseases related to tobacco (Tikoo, 2001).

Apart from the costs associated with the increased number of deaths and morbidity associated with tobacco consumption, the costs incurred or likely to be incurred by people working in tobacco cultivation and manufacturing as a result of occupational health hazards such as tobacco dust exposure and exposure to hazardous pesticides and chemical fertilisers, which can cause mental impairment, nervous system damage, reproductive defects, and cancer, must be considered. Similarly, the costs of deforestation, soil erosion, and the consequences of tobacco-growing pesticides are yet to be assessed (Tikoo, 2001).

Annual tobacco-related costs will be higher than Rs 27,761 crores (US$ 6.5 billion) every year, which more than covers the market value (Rs 24,000 crores) of all tobacco products in the country (Tikoo, 2001). Approximately 19% of India's tobacco is consumed in cigarette form, while 53% is smoked as beedis. The remaining tobacco is mainly used in smokeless form (Chaudhry, 2000). For every single cigarette sold, 8.5 beedis are sold (Srivastava, 2000). An average cigarette has about 1 g of tobacco while a beedi has about 0.2–0.25 g of tobacco on average. The quantum unit used for chewing is even smaller than a cigarette. Studies, however, show that the tar and nicotine levels in a beedi are equal or higher than those of Indian cigarettes, in turn are higher than their levels in developed countries (Chaudhry, 2000).

The enormous rise and spread of tobacco smoking over the world is both a challenge and an opportunity for the WHO. To solve a problem that crosses borders, cultures, communities, and socioeconomic classes, it is necessary to come up with global solutions. The WHO's message that all tobacco-related deaths may be prevented is a golden chance. It's a great opportunity for the WHO to suggest a first comprehensive response to the "silent epidemic" as the tobacco menace has often been called.

It was the World Health Assembly (WHA), the WHO's supreme governing body, which prepared the ground for multilateral discussions on a framework for curbing the global expansion and spread of tobacco and tobacco products, on 24 May 1999. Research by the Tobacco Control Framework Convention (FCTC), a new legislative instrument that may address issues ranging from tobacco advertising and promotion to agricultural diversification, smuggling, taxation, and subsidies, was overwhelmingly supported by the 191 member states. India, like many other countries, is dealing with a conflict of goals from diverse tobacco-related sectors, according to Chaudhry (2000). For this reason, the Ministry of Health and Family Welfare has taken a number of administrative procedures to reduce tobacco usage. Nevertheless, several industries have rejected or actively sought to increase tobacco usage in light of their mandate in order to oppose particular tobacco control policies.

Indian beedi industry

The beedi industry in India is a highly gender- and class-divided industry since most women do the beedi making along with girls sitting at home, and boys are not involved. Such girls' destiny is symbolically linked to their mothers (Shram Shakti, 1988). These women suffer as a result of their productive job duties being subsumed by the reproductive reality of their everyday household realm. Even in Third World poverty, such an attitude influences the social perception of women's job as secondary. The beedi sector is tailored to the needs of these women, who are primarily thought of as housewives. Tobacco workers' rationale is that their earnings are simply meant to augment their family's income; hence, they are unconcerned about the seasonal nature of their profession (Datar, 1989).

Domestic tasks like cooking, cleaning, and laundry are still carried out by beedi makers. When a housewife or other female members of the household perform domestic duties, they are not counted as labours in the economic sense. The housewife or other female members of the household perform these chores, even though they would have to be compensated for if someone else is employed to do them. Domestic work is underestimated, and as a result, the option to allocate female labour between domestic and financially rewarding employment has not been thoroughly studied.

Tendu leaf

The leaf of the tendu tree is used to make beedis. Karimnagar and Nizamabad are key areas in northern Telangana, having a considerable number of beedi production operations operated by both foreign producers and locals. The forest area of Manthani is a major source of the tendu leaf and is a source for the beedi factories in the district (Nagabhushanam, 1990: 30–32). Because of its simplicity of rolling and extensive availability, tendu leaf is regarded the most suited wrapper for beedis. The use of tendu leaves is mainly based on their agreeable flavour, flexibility, resistance to decay, and capacity to retain fire. Tendu leaves are selected and categorised for beedi making on the basis of size, thickness, texture, and relative thickness of mid rib and lateral veins. Collecting Tendu leaves is a seasonal job that takes place in the months of April and May. Tendu leaf gathering is the main source of nutrition during this lean season because there is little employment available for agricultural labourers. This is a significant vocation for both children and women (Srinivasulu, 1997).

The protocol for collecting and processing tendu leaves has been standardised across the country, and it is followed uniformly. Between February and March, the tendu plants are trimmed, and the mature leaves are taken after around 45 days. The leaves are gathered in bundles of 50–100 leaves and dried for a week in the sun. After sprinkling the dried leaves with water to soften them, they are packed firmly into jute bags and exposed to direct sunshine for two days. The packed and cured bags are kept in storage. To avoid decay and degradation of quality, tendu leaves must be plucked, cured, and stored with care.

The bundles of tendu leaves are subsequently collected by the contractor. The collected tendu leaves are sold to a contractor at his kallam that is managed by a network of people called *kalladars*. The government auctions out the right to buy the leaves to contractors. Contractors compete for more, despite the fact that the auction unit is usually four to five villages. In fact, a few significant contractors control the whole auction process. Through a network of *kalladars*, contractors collect the leaves from the people (V.G., 1984). The tendu is available in 100-leaf bundles. In 1975, the minimum charge for a bundle was 5 paise. Even this was not paid in a timely and proper manner. Previously, contractors were only paid 4 paise each bundle. The impoverished people who had to work so hard to collect tendu leaves had to contribute a certain number of bundles as *vetti* or free labour. In fact the first bundle that is brought to the *kallam* each day is offered in the name of deities like Pochamma and Maisamma (Reddy, Papi, 1990: 180). People in this neighbourhood also suffer as a result of the contractor's small kalladar's mischief and corruption as a collection agent. The *kalladars,* who are given a pitiful wage, resort to a variety of unscrupulous means to supplement their revenue. As a result, in addition to collecting their fair share of *vetti* bundles, *kalladars* frequently reject bundles as a deception tactic. The *kalladars* would pick up the ruined bundles and sell them for profit.

This was the scene of the infamous tendu leaf disputes in the late 1970s. An end to the vetti-extraction technique, an end to the kalladars' inflexible rejection of leaf bundles, and the payment of 5 paise per bundle were all on the table. Afterwards, a campaign was launched to raise the purchase price from 5 to 10 paise. In northern Telangana districts like Karimnagar, Nizamabad, Warangal, and Adilabad, the CPI's mobilisation strategy was a regular feature of the fight for higher piece rates and against the high-handedness of contractors and the petty corruption of the kalladars during leaf collection. A large mass base was established for the CPI (ML) organisations in this region thanks to these efforts and the work of women beedi workers (Balagopal et al., 1982: 1897–1901).

The objectives of the survey

The data for our study was collected through a survey conducted in four Mandals: Armoor, Balkonda, Nizamabad, and Hyderabad. In each Mandal, data was collected from two areas, one urban and one rural, except Hyderabad which was totally urban. Our sample consisted of 665 households. We tried to see that our sample roughly included an urban sample of 40% and a rural component of 60%. Any child working in this industry in the age of 5–14 was considered as a child labour. The areas selected for the study were based on high incidence of family's concentration on beedi making.

The objectives of the survey were to:

- Examine the position of the women and children in the beedi industry.
- Analyse socioeconomic background of the household.
- Evaluate literacy levels of the mother and the child.
- Assess the health statuses of the mother and child.
- Examine the role of the girl child and her contributions to the family.
- Propose corrective actions and policy inputs, and suggest a social action plan.

Materials and methods

To meet our objectives, three questionnaires in the regional languages (*Telugu and Urdu*) and one in the national language, Hindi, were developed. The first questionnaire inquired about the home, the second about the mother, and the third about the child worker. The household questionnaire measured the size of the family, the individuals' occupations, the household's total wages, and beedi-making income. Domestic employment, educational attainments, age of marriage, nutrition and health condition, child-feeding practices, and reproductive history were among the questions posed to the mother. To determine the levels of exploitation, a series of questions were created. The questions were on why the person chose the profession, the working circumstances and nature of the employment, how time was spent during the day, and the risks associated with the job were included. Self-reports of perceived issues caused by beedi manufacturing were used to estimate health hazards. The questions related to the child also assessed the working conditions, reasons for taking up the work, literary status, recreation, domestic work, health status, and ambitions.

Methodology

We can identify the following six stages in our data collection and methodology:

1. First, we collected information on the beedi industry in general from secondary and web sources and got information on the different statistics, polices, and health needs of the beedi workers.
2. Second, we decided on the different Mandals where we would collect our data. We also looked into the profiles of these Mandals and got an idea about their beedi-making activities.
3. In the third stage, we developed a questionnaire and collected data from the women and children working in the beedi industry. Through random sampling, we selected our respondents keeping the geographical location in mind. We also collected case studies and interviewed women whom we thought were exception.
4. Recognising the limitations of a formal questionnaire, interviews and field observations were also employed to give us a lot of insight into the

issue. Participant observation methods were also employed to observe these women working.

5. The data thus collected from the four Mandals was analysed and compared with the help of appropriate statistical tools, such as SPSS to arrive at general and specific findings.
6. Suggestions for follow-up actions and policy formulations were made.

Sample size

To choose the respondents, we first obtained a list of all the households from the village gram panchayats, and if this was not accessible, we conducted rounds of the village or obtained information from the public health facility. We chose a family using the circular systematic random sampling approach after selecting the village. A home was described as a group of individuals who share a kitchen. A child labourer was defined as someone aged 5–14 years old. The location was chosen because of the high prevalence of beedi making among women and children. We used a random selection approach to choose the child worker. If there were 500 houses in a hamlet and we needed to research 100, we chose 500/100 = 5, or the fifth or sixth household. We made sure that if a household had more than four to five kid labourers, we had a fairly representative sample of different age groups in one village. We separated the age ranges into

TABLE 1.1 Sample Size

Town	*Women*	*Girl Children*	*Total Women*	*Total Children*	*Grand* **Total**
1 Armoor					
Pipri	90	85	150	125	275
Armoor town	60	40			
2 Balkonda					
Krishnagar	63	42	150	125	275
Balkonda town	87	83			
3 Nizamabad					
Gaggupalle	40	34	150	125	275
Nizamabad town	110	91			
4 Hyderabad					
Amberpet	49		215	Nil	215
Ramanthpur	76				
Musheerabad	17				
Parsigutta	45				
Malkajgiri	10				
Uppal	18				
Total			**665**	**375**	**1,040**

three categories: pre-adolescents aged 5–12, adolescents aged 13–14, and married child workers. We conducted a reconnaissance of beedi-making locations in Hyderabad and opted to gather samples from six of them.

Our sample consisted of an urban sample of 40% and a rural component of 60%. We had a total sample of 665 women and 375 children, a total of 1,040 sample size. In Armoor, field work was conducted and data collected in Pipri (rural area) and Armoor town (urban area). In Balkonda Mandal, field work was conducted and data collected in Kisanagar (rural area) and Balkonda town (urban area). In Nizamabad Mandal, field work was conducted and data collected in Gaggupalle (rural area) and Nizamabad town (urban area). In Hyderabad, data was collected from six urban areas, namely, Amberpet, Ramanthpur, Musheerabad, Parsigutta, Malkajgiri, and Uppal.

Experiences and limitations of field work

We had some initial difficulty in getting information on the beedi workers and their children. When we visited the factories at first, the managers and contractors at the factory thought that we were government officials and any discussions with us could land them into problems. Hence, we had to first talk to the factory managers and contractors. Knowing the labour laws very well, they kept telling us that they did not employ any children below 14 years. Many a times we could see small children rushing out of the factory, the moment we entered. At home also we got the same response, and it became clear to us that the contractor had asked the beedi workers not to talk to us. Hence, each and every household where we went, we got the same answer that though the women were making beedis, they were doing this alone. None of their children were sitting at home and assisting in the household works. This despite the fact that we could see many young girls sitting at home, but the parents always gave us a different explanation as to why they were not going to school. Though we had spent nearly 15 days in the village, we were making no headway, and finally, we called for a meeting with the village headman, the school teacher, and some senior citizens. Since there were no NGOs working in these areas, our task had become very difficult. We had contacted few trade unions in the beginning, which had their headquarters in Nizamabad city. Since we found them to be following a very strict party ideology and being very political in nature, we decided to go into the field all alone. In Hyderabad, we made contacts through some trade unions, but this also did not bear any fruit. Finally, we could meet a factory owner, and he connected us to some beedi workers, and then we could get many details of their friends working in this area.

In our meeting with the beedi workers, we explained to them the aims and objectives of our investigation. Some of the district officials also helped us in making contacts in the village. We convinced the people that we were not from any police department or government organisation, but from a university with a research agenda. The villagers were convinced with our talk. We were able to establish a rapport with the villagers also by employing three local boys from the village as investigators. The local boys were well versed with the village and knew each and every household. They introduced us to all the parents and child workers, and once we were able to gain their confidence, our work became very easy.

However, throughout our investigation, food, water, and shelter continued to be a problem. From Hyderabad to Nizamabad was a five-to-six-hour journey by bus and often the research team had to walk long distances to villages which were not well connected by bus. In few villages, there was only a single bus service; hence, the team made its headquarters at Nizamabad and Armoor and then travelled to the village every day. In Hyderabad also, we were called for a meeting many times, and then it got postponed as the women were busy with some work or the other and could not find time to talk to us. Finally after making many rounds, we were able to get the interviews.

There was some kind of reluctance on the part of many beedi workers to cooperate with the investigative team due to their feeling that nobody can help them, and it will serve no purpose in answering questions to the team. Prior to us, many agencies had approached them and interviewed them, and there was a general feeling that when there was a chance of getting any benefits from the government or any other organisation, all these were cornered by the well to do beedi workers who had strong union affiliations.

Most of the beedi workers were very busy with the day-to-day household chores and making beedis. They could hardly spare a minute, and we really felt guilty in talking to them and disturbing them. We could have long chats and discussion with the beedi workers when the factory was closed. We had to interview the school-going children in the evening or at night. In the absence of any power connections in the village, most of the investigation was carried out with torch light.

It was very difficult to get the respondents' correct age as the parents were not aware of it. Often we concluded the age by looking at the person and comparing him or her to the other members of the family. Hence, the data on age and weight is only an approximate one and not exact. In a village environment, it was very difficult to get the girl child worker or mother to talk alone. Often there would be 15–20 members surrounding the child workers, and our biggest task was to get the child talking. Children below 7 years were not very articulate and could not give answers to questions like aims, aspirations, and desire for education. Hence, we had to often refer back to the mother or other members of the family. Often many families that we interviewed felt that they would get immediate benefits. There were a number of requests to interview all the households at the later stages. The respondents feared that if we did not interview them, they would be left out of any government benefits. We had a hard time in trying to explain about the concept of a sample and the nature of our study.

Our biggest dilemma was how to deal with the idealistic principles we had and the hard social reality that we saw around us. We knew morally it is unacceptable to have children working. They should be learning, playing, and having a memorable childhood. Child labour has to be banned. But seeing the poverty of our respondents, it seemed that many of the governmental welfare programmes for poverty alleviation and upliftment of the downtrodden had really not made any dent in a large number of households. There was no other way that the households could earn enough. At times it looked very artificial to talk about child labour and a luxury like sending children to school. We could see that many of the children were in school because of the mid-day meal scheme, and this was the only nutrition they were getting nonstop. Removing the children from work would only lead to serious deprivation and starvation for the children had a specific role in the familial economy. It was very clear to us that child labour was largely a product of underdevelopment and absolute poverty where work is necessary for survival. Hence, before any talk on elimination of child labour, there is a need for concerned and concentrated attack on poverty. This issue was not within the scope of our investigation and how were we to deal with this hard hitting reality.

This book has two major sections. Section A consists of six chapters which give an introduction, discuss the beedi industry, globalisation and women's work in the unorganised sectors, the realities of child labour, anti-tobacco history and control, and a discussion about the region. Section B discusses the study.

Section A: The background

Chapter 1: Introduction

This chapter gives an introduction to the beedi industry, and it introduces the beedi industry as one of the largest industries in the informal sector. It is spread throughout India and employs a large number of women and girls, helping the owners make huge profits at low cost, risk, and liabilities. It highlights the project, the objectives in studying this industry, the methodologies, and the experiences and limitation of the field work.

Chapter 2: The beedi industry: structure and organisation

The beedi industry's structure and organisation are examined in this chapter. When it comes to this industry, there is a prevalent practice of using middlemen to distribute products. Workers in agriculture and women in beedi manufacturing were forced to leave their traditional occupations due to the rise of the factory system in the wake of industrialisation. Wives are responsible for supporting their large family because their husbands' jobs are unreliable and earnings are low. "Tendu" is the beedi leaf, which is rolled with tobacco and tied with a cotton thread. Smaller and cheaper than cigarettes, beedis are considered "the poor man's cigarette" by some. Beedi production requires a lot of time and effort on the part of the workers. Many stages are involved in the production of a beedi, all of which are interconnected. The leaves are soaked overnight and left to dry in the sun. After soaking the tendu leaves and drying them, trimming them to size are also an important step. After this, tobacco is filled in the leaves, and both of their ends are folded. An essential part of the beedi-making process is winding the thread earlier from a bundle and then tying it to the beedi. For the most part, the majority of the labour is done by workers who telecommute from their own homes to a *karkhana (work shed)* nearby or do it at home. An individual who owns a factory and serves as its chief employee oversees a network of subsidiaries, collectively referred to as businesses, that operate across a single state or several states. Each branch has a separate geographic area in which it does business. Most branches get their beedis from village workers who roll them, collect them, and then package and label the finished product after they've been gathered.

Over time, beedi making demands learning new skills. As early as the age of 4, some of the households' young daughters are taught to manufacture beedis. Between the ages of 5 and 10, many others are exposed to them. Males do not participate in beedi making since it is considered "women's work". In factories, men and boys are employed to bake, package, and transport products. Beedi making isn't something that women and girls actively seek out, but they appreciate the fact that they have the choice to do so. Due to this job under duress, the feeling of exploitation is heightened. Women from lower castes and lower economic groups, such as OBCs, SCs, and STs, make the majority of the beedi that is made in India. These factors, along with the limitations of the informal manufacturing industry's putting-out approach, contribute to an oppressive atmosphere that is difficult to escape. It is a male-dominated industry where the manufacturer, contractor, and customer are all men, with just the real beedi worker being a woman. Because he provides the raw ingredients, collects the finished product, analyses and grades it against a standard, and then accepts or rejects it, the contractor has tight control over these women.

Chapter 3: Women's work in the unorganised sectors – issues of marginalisation and globalisation

Women's work is examined in this chapter, and how it has changed as a result of globalisation. Men in a given social group have a stronger ability than women in that social group to manipulate institutional rules and resources in order to promote and preserve their own interests, which is how the gender power dynamic is formed. As in any other industry, women contribute significantly to the final product's worth, but their contribution is viewed by all as secondary, unskilled, and often as skill solely of domestic value. Because they work in the unorganised sector and are female, these women suffer a double whammy of oppression. This issue has become more complicated as a result of globalisation.

New class ties have been established between global capital and the global proletariat, as well as between transnational social classes. Women's naturalised assumptions and gendered and racial practices are exploited by global capitalism to develop and profit from women's labour. Naturalised ideas about women must be fostered and maintained in order to secure a cheap female labour pool. A gendered postcolonial perspective on globalisation places women's "invisible" employment in the context of social and economic processes that are critical to globalisation. Feminisation of the workforce is aided by the shift from public to private sector employment and from formal to informal employment. Lower real wages, higher unemployment, fewer commodities, and fewer subsidies are all side effects of structural adjustment policies. This has a disproportionate impact on women's roles as producers, mothers, household managers, and community organisers to say nothing of the harm it does to their personal and professional lives. There has been an increase in transnational production, which relies heavily on the use of low-wage, insecure workers from the developing world as cheap factory workers or subcontracted home helpers, making them easy to sack when necessary. Thus, the global division of labour has become reliant on ideological conceptions of women's work while also producing Third World and immigrant women as a cheap and flexible workforce in the West.

Women's and girls' labours enduring invisibility is an impediment to fully appreciating their economic contribution to the family. In policy-oriented studies of women, two distinct approaches have had an impact on development policy. Assuming that women are economic agents, both methods focus on different aspects of women's economic performance and use different analytical vocabulary. According to the first theory, women are falling behind men in terms of population growth. This perspective acknowledges that traditional economic activity measures undervalue women's unpaid work. Because of progress, the gender pay gap widens, and women are relegated to the lower rungs of the corporate ladder. Women in economic need are the subject of the second approach. This approach focuses on women as participants rather than recipients of development projects for women in need of financial aid. According to this theory, women are more likely to be the breadwinners in low-income households because of their greater ability to earn a living.

Chapter 4: Child work and child labour

Children's labour and child work in India is the focus of this chapter. The modern Third World's socially recognised evil is child labour. Economic development relies heavily on child labour in order to build up wealth, but it also contributes to poverty and deprivation in many parts of the world. In low-income communities in developing countries, it is difficult to run a family on the income of the parents, especially if the latter are daily-rated, piece-rated, or casual or contractual labourers without a stable avenue of long-term employment, and children are often drawn in to help the family's financial situation. The most vulnerable of all labour groups are children. In both the domestic and export markets, their low cost gives employers a potential competitive advantage. Children are always at a disadvantage when it comes to finding a job. Seeing these children's plight always breaks one's heart. Children who are undernourished work long hours for little pay seven days a week. They operate in environments where safety precautions are non-existent and welfare programmes are nil. They operate dangerous cutting and piercing tools in close proximity to furnaces. They work in the most difficult of circumstances: on the street, in small manufacturing units, at home-based manufacturing units, in sweets shops, and the informal service sector to earn a living. Children's poverty, illiteracy, and lack of trade union activity among them, as well as the profit-motive of the employer, apathy of the masses, and inadequate legislation are all factors that contribute to the persistence of child labour.

Chapter 5: Anti-tobacco history and control

Anti-tobacco and control efforts around the world and in India are examined here. When looking at the history of tobacco use, it can be seen as a conflict between the economic benefits of tobacco and the harm that it can cause to people. One of the world's greatest public health challenges is the widespread use of tobacco, which kills more than 8 million people each year. Cigarette smoking became widely popular in the Western world in the early 20th century, and this study examines how this happened. Additionally, it discusses the rise of anti-tobacco sentiment and the ensuing bans. In addition, it explores the relationship between smoking and female health and how a medical consensus has developed over time in favour of smoking cigarettes. Subsequently, the anti-tobacco policies in India are discussed.

Chapter 6: The region: the field

This provides an overview of the area where the research is taking place. Telangana's Nizamabad district is the focus of this investigation. Besides this, it also focuses on Hyderabad city. Telangana, India's 28th state, was created in 2014. By population, it is the 12th most populous and the 11th most expansive state. Telangana was created by the AP State Reorganization Bill, which was passed by the Parliament after decades of struggle for a separate state. The Deccan plateau includes this area, which is largely semi-arid and severely water-stressed. The Deccan is home to nearly half of the world's poor, marginalised semi-arid farmers. In recent decades, changes in agricultural production patterns, technology adoption, urbanisation, industrialisation, and the deterioration of earlier traditional labour relations have led to a dramatic shift in rural occupational structures and job patterns in Indian villages. When Jajmani relations between landlords and specialist service providers broke down, there was less mutual dependency and responsibility, and artisans no longer had to support the landlord in exchange for security and grains. Agricultural labour has been replaced by construction, domestic service, and beedi-making work for women, particularly in rural areas.

Section B: The study

Chapter 7: The beedi worker: socioeconomic profile

This chapter looks into the household, family size, and incomes of the beedi-making women. Our survey was conducted in the three Mandals of Armoor,

Balkonda, and Nizamabad, and the municipal area of Hyderabad. In each Mandal, data was collected from two areas, one urban and one rural, and we had a sample of 40% from the urban areas and 60% from the rural areas. These Mandals' urban areas are also like towns and cannot be compared to a metropolitan like Hyderabad where 100% of our sample was from the urban area. We had a total sample of 1,040, out of which 665 were women and 375 were children. With this data, we analyse through charts and tables the base household size, comparative age of women and men in the family, the educational level of the men and women, occupation of the male members, total monthly household income and indebtedness. We also attempt to look into their awareness about government schemes: lactating mothers and their ambitions for their children.

Chapter 8: Beedi making at home and at the work shed

This chapter looks into the work and labour of beedi making both at home and in the work shed. The survey in the four areas found that most of the families were involved in beedi making from a very long time. The study indicated that beedi making had become their permanent profession. Around 65% of the people in all the four areas have been in this profession for more than 15 years. This had become the sole source of their earnings for their entire lives. We analyse the data related to the family being involved in beedi making and family occupation before beedi making. A very important feature of beedi making in Nizamabad Districts is the work shed, where many of the women and children sit together and make beedis. We found a large number of these work sheds in all the three places of our study. However, our data could not reflect this quite correctly because we wanted to interview the mother and child simultaneously. In these work sheds, the mother would be present at one time and the daughter would be present another. Hence, we had to visit the home of the beedi makers in the evening in order to get both mother and daughter, and they were recorded as working at home. Yet we could interview 41 mothers and daughters working in the work shed. These work sheds were not strictly *karkhanas* or factories but more or less a common space given either by the contractor or the village panchayat to work.

Chapter 9: Invisible labour: the girl child worker

This chapter looks into the contribution made by the girls to beedi making. Our study consisted of 375 children with in the age group of 5–14 years. We did not have any sample of child workers from Hyderabad. Most of the children were going to school here. Some of the issues that are dealt in this chapter include sex of the child beedi workers, actual age of the child worker, educational status of the child workers, current educational status of the child, child workers who dropped out, and child workers who were attending school. It also looks into the monthly contribution of the child and the reasons for not liking beedi making. It additionally also explores recreation and if beedi making improving marriage prospects.

Chapter 10: Beedi making, health, and disease

This chapter explores the awareness about health and disease among the beedi-making women and children and the diseases that they suffer from. When we asked our respondents if beedi making led to any disease or it made no difference, we were shocked to see that majority of them (99.7%) knew that it leads to diseases, and only 0.3% said that it makes no difference. The respondents felt that knowing this reality they continued to be in beedi making because there was no other option open to them since they did not have land or were not educated enough to have some other kind of job. It was interesting to note that when we asked the same question of the child worker also, we got the same response because majority (99.2%) of our child workers said yes and only 0.6% said that it made no difference. We also look into the mother's awareness and child's awareness. Malnourishment was a grave consequence of rolling beedis. There was a lot of burning of the eyes, conjunctivitis, rhinitis, mucous dryness, and bronchitis due to the worker's frequent exposure to tobacco dust. The nature of beedi-making work is monotonous to the point where it becomes mechanical after a few years. There is no place for invention or ingenuity. If a worker wants to make the required number of beedis in a day, she cannot take her gaze away from her task for even a second. These women's eyesight suffers as a result of this, especially as they get older. We learned of a lot of stories about friends and neighbours who were suffering from various health problems. A handful of workers showed us their yellow-coloured nails and hands as proof of skin rashes. Occupational health hazards have never been a focus of legislation or implementation in India, and they are mostly overlooked. Both the mother and the kid worker denied that beedi production was to blame for asthma, bronchitis, tuberculosis, or cancer. They believed that beedi making was to blame for minor maladies (as they called them) like as headaches, giddiness, body aches, joint pains, burning and etching in the eyes, skin peeling, and the development of skin rashes.

Chapter 11: Narratives of vulnerability and exploitation

In this chapter, we present few case studies of the women and the child workers from different villages, so that we are able to move from mere numbers and become a part of the world of these working people.

Chapter 12: Conclusions and way forward

The study's findings are contained in this chapter. It concludes that human rights are gender specific. The women who made beedi were exploited despite the fact that our constitution guarantees equality. Beedi-making females were young and illiterate from landless families based on our study's results. Due to the husband's inability to consistently work and earn a steady income, the women were forced to raise a large number of children. The daughter of the mother frequently skipped school to assist her mother in whatever way she could. The women and children worked 12–13 hours a day on beedi making and related activities such as gathering raw materials, chopping the leaves, soaking and cleaning them, and handing over the finished products to the contractor. Low socioeconomic status and job-related hazards were the root causes of ill health. Education and awareness will lead to increased demands for better working conditions, higher wages, and more welfare measures. The majority of Dalit women and girls aren't involved in beedi making because they want to, but they appreciate the opportunity. This profession, however, is in jeopardy as a result of the government's efforts to control tobacco and public health awareness. Beedi rolling is a physically and emotionally demanding job, but it provides a source of income for those who have no other options, so the women and children continue to do it. However, this source of employment is under threat in many places today.

References

Balagopal, K., and M. Kodandram Reddy, 1982, "Forever 'Disturbed': Peasant Struggle of Sircilla-Vemulawada", *Economic and Political Weekly*, Vol. 17, No. 48, Nov. 27, pp. 1897–1901.

Chaudhry, K., 2000, "Multisectoral and Intersectoral Approach to National Tobacco Control", *Paper commissioned by the World Health Organization on the Occasion of the WHO International Conference on Global Tobacco Control Law: Towards a WHO Framework Convention on Tobacco Control*, 7–9 January, New Delhi, India.

Cook, R., 2022, Ranking of Countries that Produce the Most Tobacco, 26 October, https://beef2live.com/story-ranking-countries-produce-tobacco-263-212893 Accessed, 14th May, 2022.

Datar, C., 1989, *Waging Change, Women Tobacco Nipani Organize*, New Delhi, Kali for Women.

Ezzati, M., S. J. Henley, M. J. Thun and A. D. Lopez, 2005, "Role of Smoking in Global and Regional Cardiovascular Mortality", *PubMed.Gov*, Vol. 112, No. 4, pp. 489–497, https://pubmed.ncbi.nlm.nih.gov/16027251/ Accessed, 10th August, 2020.

Nagabhushanam, G., 1990, *Beedi Kaaluthunna Bhatukulu* (Telugu), T. Bojja (ed), Hyderabad, Hyderabad Book Trust Publication.

John, R. M., R. K. Rao, M. G. Rao, J. Moore, R. S. Deshpande, J. Sengupta, S. Selvaraj, F. J. Chaloupka and P. Jha, 2010, *The Economics of Tobacco and Tobacco Taxation in India*, Paris, France, International Union Against Tuberculosis and Lung Disease.

ILO, 1972, *Employment, Income and Equality: A Strategy for Increasing Productive Employment in Kenya*, Geneva, International Labour Office.

Reddy, P. T., 1990, *Agrarian Unrest, Peasant Struggles and Social Change: A Study in Telangana*, Warangal, Sony Publications.

Satpathy, A., and B. K. Malick, 2020, "When Even Minimum Is Not Enough", *The Statesman*, 11th September, 2020.

Sen, A. K., 1999, "Marlboro, Camel, Rothmans Make Way for Bidis", *Deccan Chronicle*, Monday, 20th September.

Srinivasulu, K., 1997, "Impact of Liberalisation on Beedi Workers", *Economic and Political Weekly*, Vol. 32, No. 11, March 15–21, pp. 515–517.

Srivastava, A., 2000, The Role and Responsibility of Media in Global Tobacco Control. *Paper Commissioned by the World Health Organization on the Occasion of The WHO*

International Conference on Global Tobacco Control Law: Towards a WHO Framework Convention on Tobacco Control, 7–9 January, New Delhi, India.

Shram Shakti, 1988, Report of the National Commission on Self-Employed Women and Women in the Informal Sector, New Delhi.

Towards Equality, 1974, Report on the Committee on the Status of Women, Ministry of Education and Social Welfare, New Delhi, Government of India.

Tikoo, R., 2001, Can Indians Really Afford to Smoke That Cigarette? *Financial Express*, 31 May.

Universal Leaf Tobacco, 2013, UN Trade database, http://www.universalcorp.com/UniversalLeaf Accessed, 16th May, 2022.

VG, 1984, "Tendu Leaf Labourers in Telangana: Working Conditions and Struggles", *Economic and Political Weekly*, Vol. 19, No. 46, November 17, pp. 1941–1943.

WHO, World Health Report, World Health Organization, https://www.who.int/whr/media_centre/factsheet2/en/ Accessed 25th March, 2020.

WHO FCTC, 2003, Framework Convention on Tobacco Control, https://apo.who.int/publications/i/item/9241591013 Accessed 14th May, 2022.

2

THE BEEDI INDUSTRY

Structure and organisation

The beedi industry in India employs over 5 million workers consisting of males, females, and children and spreads over 13 states and 3 union territories. The industry comes under the unorganised sector falling under the small-scale and cottage industries sector. Putting-out system through middlemen is widespread in this industry where most of those engaged are home-based piece-rated workers. The industry has been brought under the purview of various legislations to protect the conditions of workers herein, and welfare measures to provide various facilities to the workers have been introduced by the Indian government at different intervals.

In Nizamabad, the beedi industry employs a considerable number of women and children. The old occupation of weaving did not withstand the factory system as a result of industrialisation, and men gradually migrated into agriculture as labourers and women into beedi making. Participating in beedi production is thus a survival strategy for women in landless families to meet basic necessities and avoid famine in times of heavy unemployment (Bromley, 1982). Because the husband's job was irregular and his earnings were low, the women had to maintain the big families.

Smoking contributes an estimated Rs 11,79,498 crores to the Indian economy and employs an estimated 4.57 crores people according to the latest report from the Indian Industry Chamber Association. To arrive at these conclusions, researchers at the Thought Arbitrage Research Institute (TARI) evaluated the entire historical accumulation of the sector's intrinsic economic value (TARI, 2019).

Excluding a major section of women, and children below ten years of age, the per capita consumption of tobacco is around 1.5 kg per annum which is one-fourth the consumption of salt and one-sixth the per capita consumption of

DOI: 10.4324/9781003317944-3

sugar, which reveals the magnitude of consumption and consequential potentialities for employment in the field. It is quite evident that a meagre percentage of beedis are prepared in the organised sector through direct employees resulting in very big section of the people employment of "home workers".

Structure of beedi production

Beedi is a crude cigarette in which tobacco is rolled in a small beedi leaf ("tendu") and tied with a cotton thread. A beedi is smaller and less expensive than a cigarette; it is considered the poor man's cigarette. Beedi production is very labour intensive. Rewinding the thread, soaking the tendu leaves, trimming them to size, rolling the beedis, and folding the beedi head and tying it with a thread are the primary stages in making a beedi. A factory usually employs a small number of workers, and the majority of the labour is done outside the facility by workers who work from home. The factory owner, who is the primary employment, runs the company through a number of branches, known as firms, that operate inside a state or across many states. Each branch has a distinct geographical jurisdiction within which it operates. A typical branch obtains the beedis rolled by village employees through contractors, gathers them, then packages and labels the finished product. To emphasise the high labour absorption capacity of this occupation, it is vital to understand how the many components of beedi manufacturing support the development and maintenance of the division of labour. Only then can the exploitative relationship between employers and workers and the health hazards resulting from the monotonous nature of work, stress, and tobacco inhaling be put into perspective (Pande, 2001).

Most of the beedi production is done outside of the factory, in the homes of the workers, and the factory employs only a few people. An individual who owns a factory is the company's primary employer, and the company may have multiple locations within or across states. Each branch has a designated area in which it can operate. There are two primary purposes served by a typical branch. Beedis are first procured through contractors, then collected, graded, roasted, labelled, and packed by the branches themselves. To ensure the quality of the final product and to perform all other related tasks, each branch of a company has a manager and a staff.

Beedi workers frequently keep track of how many beedis they've produced in a passbook. Apprenticeship is required before a worker can get a new passbook; this is the period of joint account with another main beedi worker. The mother, sister, or another family member is usually the primary contributor to the joint account. In the joint account, the primary responsibility of the main worker is to supervise and advise the learner, and to point out any errors in her beedi work. Getting a separate passbook takes about five years after a girl or boy begins making beedi on her or his own (Pande, 2003).

The contractor

In the beedi sector, the contractor is extremely crucial. The contractor is the conduit for the factory owner. The factory owner provides large quantities of raw materials, which include leaves, tobacco, and yarn, to the contractor in exchange for a certain number of beedis, and the contractor in turn distributes the raw materials to several workers attached to him to roll a certain number of beedis in their homes. As a result, manufacturers and contractors absolve themselves of duty and save money by passing the savings on to the workers. Beedi makers were paid Rs 45 for 1,000 beedi in 1995, and they worked roughly 25–27 days per month. In the year 2020, these beedi workers were paid Rs 156 per 1,000 beedis, and they work only 15–20 days per month. As a result, these workers' working hours are being cut, and they are not employed throughout the year.

Occasionally, the contractor will provide a work shed or *karkhana,* which is a common workspace provided by the contractor or the village panchayat (local government). Women and children love these work sheds because though these are often dark spaces which do not have much light or ventilation, the workers like to work here for they are not disturbed by home duties and may manufacture a great number of beedis. They are also not bored with their work since while manufacturing beedis, they can sing, converse, and discuss village gossip. These sheds are within walking distance, but they lack toilets, rest areas, lunchtime, medical care, and paid holidays. Drinking water is sometimes offered in the form of a pot. These work sheds are run on a very informal basis, and there are no fixed timings or control on the beedi workers. Women and children come and go as they choose and according to a time that suits them.

Each contractor employs hundreds of home workers who make beedis for him and thousands of beedis are brought in every day. Because counting these by hand would be extremely time-consuming, the employer arranges them in trays built to accommodate thousands of beedis. The beedis are then shipped to factories or enterprises to be cured in an oven at a controlled temperature for 24 hours. It is here that older boys and men are hired. The bundles of beedis are wrapped in thin tissue paper, labelled, and delivered to retail outlets after being removed from the oven. Women who are given huge sheets of paper again frequently label the beedi bundles by cutting thin pieces from the large sheets and adhering them to the beedi bundles.

The low living standards and vulnerability of home-based or factory workers in this industry can be attributed to the poor organisation of this sector. The beedi worker receives a specific amount of beedi leaves in exchange for a certain amount of tobacco. Beedis must be produced in a specific quantity for each specific quantity of tobacco. Only the quantity of thread bundles delivered by the contractors is changeable. There are a number of steps that must be completed before the beedi is ready to be assembled. Because the beedi maker relies solely on the contractor, he or she can weigh as little as they choose (800 g of tendu leaves and 350 g of tobacco are required to roll 1,000 beedis, provided the leaves are not defective). The contractor makes the call on whether or not the beedi is up to the required standard or not. In the event that he is dissatisfied with any of the beedis in the bundle, he can simply discard the entire lot. An employee in this situation loses both her income and the raw material that must be replaced. Consequently, the beedi worker's relationship with the contractor is critical (Pande, 1999).

If employees protest about the poor quality of the leaves delivered, the contractor blames the factory owner and instructs the employee to stop working and wait for better leaves. This is not practicable as it would mean a loss of income and no work for the woman. Thus, workers must continue to work with low-quality materials and lose a significant portion of their income owing to beedis rejection. In fact, there is a booming business of private vendors selling tendu leaves and tobacco dust, and the employees frequently buy from them to make up for the loss and to ensure that they will continue to receive regular labour from the contractor in the future.

"The workers everywhere squat on the floor on ragged mats surrounded by trays containing tobacco and chopped or uncut wrapper leaves, the latter wet in water emitting a distinct odour while the tobacco exhales its characteristic smell", according to a Government of Madras report from 1947. The pungent odour of this concoction penetrates the entire workshop. Men, children, mounds of trash, remains of wrapped leaves and tin trays loaded with tobacco or freshly prepared beedis, and soiled and tattered mats strewn about give a bizarre picture of chaos and clutter. Overall, the working conditions are deplorable. Workers in general, and children in particular, have a haggard aspect with yellowish eyes and haggard cheeks as a result of spending the majority of their lives in such deplorable conditions (Isaac et al., 1998, Government of Madras, 1947). The Madras government established a Court of Enquiry into the working conditions in the beedi, cigar, snuff, tobacco-curing, and tanning industries in 1946. The Court of Enquiry's report pointed out that these industries in South India are well organised. The beedi industry in Madras Province employs approximately 89,500 people, with about 26,600 men and 5,100 women making up the majority of those workers. In addition, it is stated that children were employed in the industry on a universal basis, with two out of every three adults in the workforce being children. Except in Mukkudal, where home workers predominate, the Court of Enquiry found that beedi workers were full-time employees, with beedi making serving as their primary and not a secondary occupation. They were paid less than they should have been, according to their wage structure. The report also discusses how the employers defrauded the gullible purdah women (Madras High Court, 1961). For the most part, nothing has changed except that this environment has now invaded women's homes, which have become their workplace.

Beedi making

Beedi making necessitates the acquisition of skills throughout time. Some of the household's young daughters are taught to make beedis as early as the age of four. Many others are introduced to them when they are between the ages of five and ten. Learning the entire beedi-making process takes around three years. These young people begin by aiding an older with cutting the leaves to give it a proper shape, folding the beedi head, or tying the thread. Assistance with beedi making is only a step on the way to completing the beedi. The speed and skill with which the beedis are rolled is determined by the worker's speed and skill, as well as the amount of aid the ladies may receive at home. Women and girls do not participate in beedi making because they want to, but they are grateful that it is an option. The perception of exploitation is heightened as a result of this employment under duress (Prakasamma, 1993)

The number of beedi leaves required for a given amount of tobacco is predetermined. Beedis must be produced in a specific quantity for each specific quantity of tobacco. All that can be changed is how many thread bundles are delivered by the contractors. In order to make a beedi, you must rewind the thread, cut the leaves, roll the beedi, and then fold the beedi's head. This occupation's high labour absorption capacity can be illustrated by describing the four stages of beedi making in brief. Beedi making facilitates the creation and maintenance of diversion of labour. Children and elderly people can be employed in beedi making, and this provides an opportunity to expose the exploitative relationships between employers and employees, as well as between assistants and main workers. It also helps workers to better understand the health risks associated with repetitive work.

The workers bring the raw materials home and share the work with other members of the family, including children, and at times with neighbours. This is necessary because beedi rolling involves several stages, all of which are time consuming, and it is not possible for one worker alone for a long duration of time to perform all the stages of beedi rolling. The leaves have to be cleaned, washed, and dried. They are then cut according to the size of a particular brand of beedis. Rolling the beedi leaf with tobacco is the main job in the beedi-making process. In order to make a perfect beedi one has to follow three steps after the soaking, drying, and cutting. First, tobacco is to be spilled in the leaf, the head folded and finally tied with the thread. The pinch of tobacco rolled into a beedi must be accurate enough, failing which the beedi may be too small or too big. Such abnormal beedis will not only be rejected by the contractor but the worker will also incur loss because the big beedis consume more tobacco than the required level. In order to rectify the loss, the worker has to buy extra tobacco from the market. While rolling the beedi between the thumb and fore-fingers, enough pressure must be applied to make the top end of the beedi. Second, the top head has to be folded and it has to appear broader than the bottom end. Halfway through the rolling, the beedi bottom is folded in to prevent the tobacco leaking. The beedi is tied when it is fully rolled. Then the beedi head (or top), which is wider than the bottom, is folded in to complete the making process (Pande, 2007).

Many people can be involved in making a beedi. The main worker can stop after putting in tobacco dust, rolling, and tying. The folding of the beedi top can be done by another person. Beedi assistants who are in the learning process are mainly employed in folding the top. The completed beedis are bundled into stacks, each bundle consisting of 16–25 beedis, which are then taken to the contractor. Given the fact that each contractor has hundreds of home workers employed by him, beedis pour in every day in thousands. Since physical counting of the beedis brought in is a laborious task for the employers, they have their own method of counting. Each bundle should fold 12 or 24 beedis. The contractor judges the bundles by stacking them in trays which are designed to hold usually several thousand beedis. The beedis are then sent either to the factory or to another branch from where they are distributed to a different set of home workers for labelling (Pande, 2019:200).

Structure of production

Beedi production takes place in stages, with each stage building on the one before it. A large percentage of beedis are produced outside of the factory by the workers, who usually employ a small number of people. Tobacco, tendu leaves, and yarn are all supplied in large quantities by the factory owner to the middlemen (contractors) in exchange for a predetermined number of beedis. These middlemen in turn distribute the raw materials to different workers who are attached to them, to roll a stipulated number of beedis in their homes. When the rolled beedis are returned to the middlemen, they are then sent to the branch offices which in turn distribute the beedis along with labels to a different set of home workers for labelling. The workers return the labelled beedis to the branch where they are stacked, cured, and booked for dispatch to the principal employers. The workers are given beedis in large quantities for labelling. They are also provided with large sheets of labels which have to be cut into thin strips and pasted on each beedi. The women usually share this work of labelling, as also beedi rolling, with other members of the family or subcontract the work.

The exploitative environment of beedi making

Women from lower castes and low-income communities, such as other backward classes, Scheduled Castes, and Scheduled Tribes, make beedi, and they live in poverty. Societal power structures and the disadvantages of the informal manufacturing system's putting-out system all contribute to the atmosphere of exploitation they foster. The women who make beedis work in a male-dominated industry, where everyone from the producer to the consumer by and large are male. The contractor has tight control over these women, because he provides the raw materials, collects the finished product, evaluates and grades it against a standard, and accepts or rejects it (Prakasamma, 1993). These women work for roughly 14–15 hours a day, performing all domestic activities as well as creating beedis. Because it is a home-based business, children, particularly girls, are easy targets for workers. Many of these girls combine chores and homework with beedi production to work long hours. These young women are frequently denied access to school, entertainment, sports, and relaxation. Because they work in a health-hazardous business, they are constantly exposed to tobacco dust, which is a major health concern. Women and girls suffer not because they use these cigarettes, but because they make them in the absence of any other means of subsistence.

A labour-intensive back-breaking work

While beedi rolling is an extremely labour-intensive, backbreaking, and strenuous occupation, the women and children continue to do it, because this, at least, provides them with a livelihood, in the absence of any other. Thus, while employment training and opportunities for women need to be considerably widened, in the meantime, women will continue to do the beedi rolling. However, in many places, this source of employment itself is under threat.

Despite these efforts, the extent to which welfare programmes need to be implemented and the level of organisation are still lacking (only about 15% of the beedi workers are organised in the unions currently). According to the trade unions, the move from factory-based production to home-based beedi rolling (which is more expensive) began in earnest after the beedi workers' laws were enacted, particularly after 1976. These have negatively impacted the planning process, minimum wage implementation, and dearness allowances. The beedi workers' law's allowance and other regulatory provisions have also been significant difficulty, particularly in home-based jobs. The beedi rolling average real earnings work varies greatly between states (from Rs 25 to 45 for rolling 1,000 beedis) and even between states. The government even began to regulate this industry in earnest after the beedi workers' laws were enacted, particularly after 1976 (Das, 2000).

Beedi workers are not only exploited economically, but they are also subjected to occupational health risks. The nature of the task is so boring that it becomes mechanical after a few years. There is no place for invention or ingenuity. The nature of beedi work is such that if a worker is to manufacture the required number of beedis in a day, she cannot take her gaze away from it for even a second. "As people get older, this takes its toll on their eyesight". There is no bodily movement involved because the beedi worker is seated in the same spot and in the same position for hours, save for the rhythmic movement of the two forearms. This causes back pain, limb pain, headaches, piles, and other symptoms. The inhaling of tobacco vapours, to which beedi workers are regularly exposed, poses a more serious hazard to their health. TB, asthma, allergies, and a persistent cold are all common among beedi workers, according to studies from other parts of India.

Various studies have been conducted on working and living of the workers in the beedi industry. The general conclusions reached by most of these are that labours in general, and home-based piece-rated workers in particular, work under the most explosives conditions typical of the unorganised sector in India. With respect to the impact of labour legislations, available evidence from investigative reports reveals that

1. Employers do not implement the provisions of the various acts applicable to the industry and
2. The state labour departments have been unable to enforce the legislations effectively.

While these are useful pointers, there have hardly been systematic attempts, based on detailed household surveys, to analyse the impact of labour legislations on working conditions in the beedi industry. Furthermore, if laws have generally been ineffective in regulating the conditions of work, the underlying reasons have received hardly any attention in these studies.

Workers problems

The production process and the organisation of the beedi industry are such that there is scope at every stage for exploitation of the workers. This gives rise to a variety of problems. Problems related to wages comprise shortage of raw materials, improper counting of bundles of beedis, incorrect entries in the passbook, irregularity in the work, and payment of bonus to workers. The question of employee benefits such as provident fund, bonus, and paid leaves are inconceivable in the working scenario. Contractual system is malicious, and as demonstrated in a study on women beedi workers in Tamil Nadu, the very existence of contract work originated to avoid stringent labour laws (Gopal, 1999: 12).

Shortage of raw materials

It is understood that to roll 1,000 beedis, 800 g of tendu leaves and 350 g of tobacco are required, provided the leaves are not defective. Since bundles of tendu leaves are usually given to the workers, poor quality or damaged leaves in the bundles will necessarily mean shortage of leaf to roll beedis. Similarly, shortage of tobacco may often occur, due to sudden gust of wind which blows away tobacco from open trays. In either case, the worker is held responsible for the number of beedis short of the quantity specified by the contractor and wages are cut accordingly. For instance, if a worker is short by one bundle, the wage count varies from 50 to 75 paisa, although the average cost of one bundle would be only 30 paise, if they were to buy the raw material on their own. By and large workers usually fall short of leaves and tobacco and prefer to buy raw material to make the loss good rather than incur large wage cuts.

Improper counting of beedi bundles

When stacking bundles in trays for counting, the contractor takes unfair advantage on the pretext that a large number of beedis need to be collected and counted from many workers in a limited time. Usually more bundles are stacked on a tray than it should hold. Naturally, in the final count, there is always a shortage of beedi bundles, but the women worker, though present at the spot, is not permitted to do the stacking and counting herself.

Improper entries in the passbook

In some factories, each home worker is allotted a number and provided with a passbook containing a number of beedis she has turned in and the wages due to her. This book is checked by the inspector of excise. However, wage cuts due to shortage or in other words actual wages paid to each worker are never entered in the passbook. The details of shortage of beedis of each worker are maintained separately by the contractor and wages are cut accordingly. Most of the beedi-making women being illiterate have no means to understand these numbers and work on trust in the contractor. The wage details entered in the book necessarily mean that wage has been paid to the labourers, but it may not really reflect her total payment for the beedis made.

Irregularity of work

The supply of raw material in a number of branches is reported to be sufficient for only four days a week. Furthermore, the quantum of work given to the worker depends on the absolute will of the contractor. During the monsoons, there is no beedi production and often workers find themselves unemployed without any compensation. As a result, these women workers are put to a lot of hardship. These women have to wait endlessly for the trucks to supply the material to the contractor, and often there is no supply of the raw material, and hence, no work on these days.

No payment of bonus

Parliament passed the Bonus Bill on 25 September 1965, and it was renamed the "The Payment of Bonus Act, 1965". Acting to ensure that bonuses are paid to workers in specific establishments on the basis of profits or production or productivity, as well as matters related thereto, was the act's purpose (Chief Labour Commissioner, 1965). However, there is a big different between theory and practice. We spoke to a large number of beedi workers, and they informed us that there is no system in place to compensate them with bonuses. Before the pandemic in 2020, some branches did pay a bonus to their employees. A daily deduction of 20 paisa is made from the salary, and a yearly bonus of 30–40 rupees is given out.

Indebtedness

The shortage of raw materials, seasonality of work, and intermittent lay off force the workers to seek loans at very high rates of interest (40% per month) from local money lenders. The result of this situation is that most of the families are ironically indebted. The villagers spend a lot of money on festivals, celebration of marriages, and deaths, and often borrow money for this purpose.

Pledging of children

The occurrence of any religious or social function means additional expenditure to the worker ranging from Rs 500 to 2,000 or more. Workers often borrow from their employers by pledging their children for want of any other security; the child is forced to work for the employer for a very low wage (Rs 150) and for long hours of work (10–12 hours per day) till employer justifies the abnormally low wage paid to the child as payment towards interest or the loan but not towards the principal. The child is bonded to the employer till the principal is repaid.

Non-recognition by unions and the state labour departments

Apparently, the local unions have not been concerned with the problem of women workers because most of them are not members of any union. Union leaders agree that since their husbands are already members of their unions, women workers are entitled to the benefit of union membership. Such an argument unfortunately ignores the existence of women workers who are otherwise destitute or with husbands not necessarily employed in the beedi industry.

The state labour department appears to be so helpless to identify women workers because of their sheer number and the absence of any records with the employer. As a consequence, the women workers do not get any identification, which would entitle them to medical benefits from the beedi workers welfare fund dispensary.

Miscellaneous problems

With one or two helpers, the raw materials are weighed by the contractor who provides the materials. The contractor employs these ancillary workers based on the number of beedi workers in a branch. Neither the contractor nor the main employer has any contact with the beedi workers. Because of this, village leaders approach the contractor if any company employee's behaviour towards workers is unacceptable.

For the sake of the beedi workers, the nature of their relationship with their checker, who may or may not be an accountant, is critical. One or two beedis in a few bundles are checked at random; if any one or two of those beedis are found to be poorly made, the entire bundle is sometimes destroyed, and a worker could end up losing 30–40% of their beedis. In such a scenario, the worker not only forfeits their salary, but they also lose the raw materials they used to make the beedis that were destroyed.

The raw material weigher is the second most important person. As long as the worker isn't happy with their pay, he can manipulate their wages by making them smaller. As a result, workers are forced to purchase raw materials from the open market at a price that is often higher than their wages for producing a certain number of beedis. Another way to short-change workers is by giving them bent or broken beedi leaves, which are usually found in a bundle's centre. It is only if the weigher is in a good mood or the worker has a well-connected family then she is successful in having the damaged leaves replaced. Every beedi worker would get a piece of the damaged leaves if they were all supplied. There would be no substitute for anyone. According to the contractor's instructions, the employees are to provide the following explanation: "We have no control over the situation because that is how the factory delivered the leaves to us. If you refuse to accept this, you may be asked to stop working until we receive adequate vacation time". As a matter of fact, the beedi worker has no choice but to accept whatever the beedi contractor offers because there is no other work available.

The beedi workers must maintain good relations with other employees, especially the beedi checker and weigher, in order to minimise the number of beedis rejected, the shortfall in beedi leaves and tobacco, and damaged beedi leaves. This is where there is a lot of room for profiteering. An unmarried beedi worker can achieve this goal by utilising her "feminine" traits.

Post-independence legislations

Various acts have been passed by the government to regulate the working conditions in the beedi industry.

Minimum Wages Act, 1948

The Minimum Wages Act of 1948 states that any minimum rate of wages set or revised by the appropriate government in regard to scheduled employments under Section 3 may include either of the following: (1) a basic rate of wages and a special allowance at a rate to be adjusted, at such intervals and in such a manner as the appropriate government may direct, to accord as nearly as possible with the variation in the cost-of-living index number applicable to such workers; or (2) in all-inclusive rate allowing of the basic rate, the cost of living allowance and the cash value of the concessions, if any.

Beedi and Cigar Workers (Conditions of Employment) Act, 1966

The Beedi and Cigar Workers (Conditions of Employment) Act, 1966 was enacted by the Government of India for regulating the working conditions in the beedi industry. Prior to the enactment of the Act, beedi units were registered under the Factories Act, 1948. In view of the limitations regarding the size of the units under the Factories Act, many beedi units employing a small number of workers did not come into the purview of this Act. However, under the Beedi and Cigar Workers (Conditions of Employment) Act, 1966, this limitation of the size of the beedi units has been renewed. This Act came into force in July, 1966. It provides measures for safeguarding the health and welfare of the workers, regulations of hours of work, wages for overtime, restriction of employment of children and women, and provision for leave and holidays. This Act does not differentiate between home and shed workers and treats them on par for extension of various benefits. This Act set out to protect workers' health and welfare by regulating working hours, providing overtime, and allowing time off for vacations, but it has been mostly ignored due to a lack of oversight. This Act expressly specifies that no kid under the age of 14 shall be permitted to work in any establishment where any manufacturing process related to the production of beedi or cigars is carried out.

Beedi employees' working and housing situations are being improved through welfare programmes. The Beedi and Cigar Workers (Conditions of Employment) Act, 1966 has a limited coverage as it prescribes some measures to improve the working conditions of the beedi and cigar workers in industrial premises only, such as cleanliness, first aid, ventilation, canteen, working hours, and weekly holidays. The Act does not provide for labour welfare such as medical, educational, and recreational facilities. The Act's definition of "establishment" has been so defined by the employer that it ignores the existence of the home workers. As the women workers' names are found nowhere in the records of either the subcontractor or the principal employer, neither of them feels responsible for their welfare.

The Beedi Workers Welfare Fund Act, 1976

The Beedi Workers Welfare Fund Act, 1976 provides for certain welfare facilities for the beedi workers.

These include improvements in public health and sanitation, disease prevention, and the provision and improvement of medical facilities, as few examples. Others include ensuring that everyone has access to clean water and sanitation, ensuring that schools have adequate resources, and ensuring that social conditions are conducive to learning, to grant loans or subsidies to a state government, a local authority, or an employer in aid of any central-government-approved scheme for welfare of persons engaged in beedi establishments (The Beedi Welfare Act, 1976).

According to an International Labour Organization (ILO) report in 1992, 5,78,800 tonnes (7.0% of the worlds manufactured tobacco) was produced in India making it the third-largest world tobacco-growing country. In 1992, India produced about 7,67,436 million manufactured cigarettes and beedis accounting for 13.5% of the world's total (WHO, Geneva, 1997: 415). However, a very little amount of this reaches the worker, and they often live in poverty. Our study has clearly shown that these workers live in poverty. The contractors, who supply the materials for the manufacture of beedis in homes, rarely pay more than the equivalent of half the statutory minimum wage, since this is almost impossible to enforce. The Beedi Workers Cess Act (1976) and the Beedi Workers Welfare Fund Act (1976) provide for housing loans, mobile medical units, and children's scholarships, although nothing has been done due to the contract system (Beedi Workers Welfare Cess Act, 1976). There are multiple layers of exploitation in this system, which is open-ended. The profit margin is dispersed among a lot of intermediaries in this system, and as a result, the basic minimum and reasonable comforts and services are denied.

Policy issues for beedi workers

In today's globalised society, the beedi industry remains one of the few industries which still employs such a large number of workers. With India's prevailing unemployment problem, unless the workers were given alternative means of employment in order to sustain themselves, it would indeed be a disadvantage to all those employed in the beedi industry if the industry were to close down. The advantage of the beedi industry is that it provides an income, however meagre it may be, to lakhs of people engaged in this industry (Hirji, 2000).

Employment in the tobacco industry, and beedi rolling in particular, is an example of an important dilemma. On the one hand, the workers in question are extremely vulnerable, and a multi-faceted effort is needed to improve their working conditions and levels of income security. At the same time, the occupation itself may be under threat, particular if anti-tobacco feeling continues to grow within the country and tobacco control becomes more important (Sudarshan et al., 1999).

Better counting of home-based workers is thus the first strategy that needs to be implemented in order to empower workers. Recognising the home-based workers, in particular the women and girls, as "workers" needs to be the first step, because without such an identity, it would be difficult to influence resource allocations in their favour, even where legislation already exists. A related aspect is the assumption that women in home-based work do not face difficulties in combining productive and reproductive work burdens, so that welfare legislation is designed without sensitivity to the need for support structures relating to child care, care of the elderly, etc. Second, workers in this occupation have often just one acquired skill (beedi rolling) and lack the resources to access any other work. Low levels of literacy, poor health status, and absence of entitlements to credit, land, or other resource all combine to make transitions to new occupations virtually impossible. In the absence of perceived alternatives, vulnerability is transmitted to the next generation, with children, specifically girls, being introduced to beedi work at a very young age. Another strategy to strengthen the position of beedi workers, in particular the women and girls, would therefore be to increase their access to different types of resources, including the access to education and health. The assumption behind this strategy is that such increased access will empower them and will lead them to demand their rights as also to seek out better opportunities. Often caught in a situation of extreme dependence, a third approach to the problem is to organise the workers, so that they at least demand the rights they are already entitled to within the existing framework of legislation and production organisation (Sudarshan et al., 1999).

If tobacco control becomes more important, the issue that may be most relevant, in the light of expected policy changes (which are desirable from a health point of view), is not how best to strengthen beedi workers as beedi workers, but how best to help them in a transition away from this work. The point to note here is that one of the reasons why beedi work is so popular among women, particularly in some communities, is that it meets some of the compulsions of patriarchal norms of seclusion. Engaging in the effort to develop new sources of livelihood for this large group requires a direct confrontation with the manner in which gender roles have traditionally constructed in India. Creating new livelihoods for women beedi workers (assuming that policy directions relating to tobacco will be as expected) will not be easy, because apart from the standard requirements of raising productivity and skills, perceptions of "appropriate behaviour" also have to change. It provides an opportunity for concerted actions not just towards the generation of new livelihood but also for a new articulation of gender roles in this society (Sudarshan et al., 1999).

The ILO is investigating alternative employment prospects for beedi workers and attempting to establish self-help groups in order to get the beedi workers to consider alternatives on their own and to lead them through practical exercises. It is necessary to develop a market for the substitute goods. Beekeeping for the purpose of producing honey is one solution that the ILO is testing. Another suggestion is to have beedi workers cultivate herbs for use in cosmetics. Instead of using plastic, beedi employees might make bags from natural resources. According to the ILO, meaningful alternative employment should ideally have a central market but a decentralised production process. However, there is always a chance that finding other work would merely move the issue to a different demographic. Those who had been jobless before will be keen to take up the beedi work.

References

Bromley, R., 1982, "Working in the Streets: Survival Strategy, Necessity or Unavoidable Evil?", in A. Gilbert, J. Hardoy and R. Ramirez (eds), *Urbanisation in Contemporary Latin America*, New York, John Wiley, pp. 59–77.

Das, S. K., 2000, DG, "Labour Welfare, Ministry of Labour", *Report Prepared for ILO*, October 2000.

Hirji, Z., 2000, "Toil and Trouble, The Beedi Workers of Jelligude", *Lifeline*, Vol. 3, March 2000, pp. 11–12.

Isaac, T., T. M. Richard, W. D. Franke, and P. Raghavan. 1998, Government of Madras report, 1947, *Democracy at Work in an Indian Cooperative: The Story of Kerala Dinesh*

Beedi. Ithaca (NY), Cornell University Press. R Ayyar, Bench: Rajagopalan, R Ayyar. https://indiankanoon.org/doc/68600/ Accessed 12th October, 2018.

Madras High Court, 1961, Abdur Rahim vs State of Madras (Secretary, on 21 January, 1960) IILLJ 213 Madras, Author: 29th March, 2020.

Pande, R., 2019, "Globalisation and Women's work in the Beedi Industry", *Studia Historiae Oeconomicae, The Journal of Adam Mickiewicz University*, Vol. 37, No. 1, pp. 191–221. DOI: 10.2478/sho-2019-0010

Pande, R., 2007, "Women's Work in the Beedi Industry in India", in R. Pande, S. Nalini and R. Mahalingam (eds), *Women in Nation Building—A Multidimensional Perspective.* Hyderabad: Panchajanya Publications, pp. 7–34.

Pande, R., 2003, "Girl Child Rights and Labour Exploitation in the Beedi Industry", *Indian Journal of Human Rights,* Vol. 7, No. 1 and 2, January–December, pp. 52–73.

Pande, R., 2001, "Health Issues of Women and Children – A Study of the Beedi Industry", *Women's Link,* Vol. VII, No. 2, pp. 8–16.

Pande, R., 1999, "Structural Violence and Women's Health – Work in the Beedi Industry in India", *Violence and Health, Proceedings of W.H.O. Global Symposium, Japan,* pp. 192–205.

Prakasamma, M. K., 1993, *Women's Employment as EMPOWERMENT AND Exploitation: The Case of Beedi Making Women,* Mimeographed Paper, Research Paper No. 80, Takemi Program. Boston: Harvard School of Public Health.

Sudarshan, R., and R. Kaur, 1999, "The Tobacco Industry and Women's Employment: Old Concerns and New Imperatives", *The Indian Journal of Labour Economics,* Vol. 42, No. 4, pp. 675–685.

TARI, 2019, Thought Arbitrage Research Institute (TARI) on behalf of the Assocham, quoted in, *The Economic Times*, June 5th.

The Beedi Workers Welfare Cess Act, 1976 Act No. 56 of 1976 [7th April, 1976], https://legislative.gov.in/sites/default/files/A1976-56.pdf Accessed 15th July, 2022.

The Beedi Workers Welfare Fund Act, 1976 (Act No. 62 of 1976) [10th April, 1976], http://labour.telangana.gov.in/content/ActsRules/TheBeediWorkersWelfareFundAct1976.pdf Accessed 15th July, 2022.

WHO Geneva, 1997, Tobacco or Health – A Global Status Report.

3

WOMEN'S WORK IN THE UNORGANISED SECTOR

Issues of exploitation and globalisation

Modern economies are a complex web of different types of employments. Different industries help the economy survive and thrive and give employment to a large number of people worldwide. A global trend which one can observe in developed and developing world is the increasing number of women at the workplace. However, more women are found in the unorganised or informal sector than the organised or formal sector. This productive activity, which is predominantly the domain of women, tends to be overlooked in economic statistics and by lawmakers and planners. Because the majority of these women work in the unorganised or informal sector at home, their employment becomes inconspicuous, leaving them vulnerable to exploitation and abuse. There are some sectors which are dominated by women, such as cleaning, care, and domestic work are predominantly done by women, and involve work that is traditionally regarded as "women's work". In the domestic context, much of this labour is likewise done by women and is unpaid. Although part of this job has been outsourced as a result of the surge in female employment, it continues to be performed by women and remains underestimated both monetarily and socially.

Two billion people over the age of 15 in the world are employed in the unorganised sector of the economy, which accounts for 61.2% of all jobs. Men (63% of the workforce) are more likely than women (58.1%) to be employed in the informal sector (ILO, 2018). The percentage of women in informal employment in India is slightly higher than that of men, despite the fact that the numbers are lower. The International Labour Organization (ILO, 2018) report states that the global informalisation of the economy is on the rise. That informality rises in direct proportion to progress in the socioeconomic arena and education level. The level of education is a key factor affecting the level of informality. Globally, when the level of education increases, the level of informality decreases, the

DOI: 10.4324/9781003317944-4

report says. People who have completed secondary and tertiary education are less likely to be in informal employment compared to workers who have either no education or completed primary education.

Many industries employ people under both categories as unorganised and organised based on the type of employment they offer. While the organised, formal employment provides security of work, better income, and stability to the employee, the unorganised, informal sector has the opposite effect. It provides only temporary employment, no job security, less income, and no other kind of perquisites are offered. The main difference is that of skill. The workers in formal sector are well-skilled, educated, and trained, while in the informal sector, they are unskilled, generally low in educational levels, and untrained for the jobs. Hence, there is a dualistic approach to these sectors.

Hart's (1973) and the ILO's (1972) works form the foundation of the dualist approach. The formal and informal sectors of the economy are posited in these works. Because of the low barriers to entry, reliance on local resources, family ownership, small-scale operations, labour intensiveness, adapted technologies, and skills acquired outside of the formal education system, the informal economy is characterised by competitive markets and unregulated markets. As a rule, the formal sector is more difficult to enter, relying heavily on foreign resources, having large-scale operations, requiring large amounts of capital, and employing expatriates. The formal sector is also protected by tariffs, quotas, and trade licenses. When it comes to the theory of dualism, Maloney (1999) claims that unskilled workers can find employment in both the formal and informal sectors. Because of labour protection taxes, jobs in the private sector may be unattractive.

The working population is not uniform either (in terms of education, social status). Due to the contract system of hiring workers and job outsourcing, there is a growing trend towards the establishment of informal jobs today, even in formal settings. As a result, there are four categories of employment that are feasible in different sectors: formal employment in the formal sector, informal employment in the formal sector, and formal employment in the informal sector. However, it cannot be denied that informal work predominates in developing countries' economy, where it is a defining and traditional aspect of labour markets (Parker et al., 2017).

Invisibility of women's work in informal settings

Women continue to be disproportionately employed in "invisible" sectors of the informal economy, such as domestic work, piece-rated labour, housekeeping, and support roles in small family businesses, where they receive employment status with low to no pay, limited access to social security to protect them from harm, and little organisational ability to ensure compliance with global labour and human rights standards (Carr and Chen, 2002). Women often have more challenging starting conditions and a larger range of restrictions during their employment than male informal workers. Being self-employed or operating small or micro-businesses increases their likelihood of encountering social constraints on the kinds of activities they can engage in, which makes it more challenging for them to access other facilities and enabling characteristics like bank financing and government programmes. Additionally, they struggle more with bureaucracy and patriarchal officialdom. In addition to being more prone to experience patriarchal restrictions in both their personal and professional lives, women are also more likely than men to experience harassment at work, both in formal and informal contexts, and to have lower educational aspirations (Ghosh, 2021: 4).

Women here may view their work in terms of the survival of their families or their own financial well-being. Their roles as workers, mothers, wives, and members of their community don't necessarily fall neatly into one or the other category. Furthermore, they frequently agree with the general public's view that their work lacks value. In order to foster a sense of collective identity among their members, organisations employ a variety of self-perception narratives and practices. Claim making is based on the processes of identity formation. As a result of their upbringing, women are often reluctant to embrace a work-based identity because they see their paid work as a means of fulfilling their domestic duties (Kabeer et al., 2013: 252).

The opacity of women's and girls' labour continues to be a barrier to understanding their home economic function. With regards to approaches to policy-oriented research that have influenced development policy with regards to women, there have been two kinds of approach. Despite the fact that both approaches begin with the assumption that women are economic actors, they focus on distinct aspects of women's economic performance and employ different analytical vocabulary. The first viewpoint contends that as growth progresses, women lose ground to men (Irene et al., 1976). This viewpoint stresses women's reproductive roles and asserts that the less the economic system is monetised, the more significant women's reproductive roles become. This view admits that conventional measure of economic activity underestimates women's unpaid work. With development women are relegated to traditional sector and income gap between the sexes increases. The other approach, focusing on women as participants rather than recipients of development projects, focuses on women in economic need. It is founded on the assumption that, in lowest income households, the ratio of women to men is greater and is linked to women's economic activity in these household. As a result, this approach highlights the importance of focusing on the productivity and income of women in low-income households in order to foster balanced economic growth (Buvinic et al., 1983). Here individual and household surveys are used to measure women's contributions and economic value is imputed depending on the time spent at home in the production process. But it is very difficult to find out in these time use surveys as to which household activities can be termed productive and which can be termed as leisure.

There is an interdependence between the process of production and consumption, and it is with the combination of the two that many families survive. In the labour market, the women sell their capacity to work or their labour power to the employer, and this generates a wage or salary. In the homes and in the consumer market, these earnings of the unpaid labour at home are used to produce the means of subsistence. Each day the means of subsistence are prepared and consumed, and the capacity to work again is produced (Luxton and Corman, 2001: 29). Women's unpaid domestic work is an essential part of the output of the working population, not a private service for their families (Hamilton and Barrett, 1986). While wage work assumes the exchange of labour power, domestic labour entails the creation of labour as a good to be sold on the market (Sercombe, 1986). However, women's unpaid domestic work and home-based productive jobs are frequently disregarded and undervalued (Singh et al., 1987). This is ironic because, oftentimes, the income provided by a home-based business is crucial for family survival, especially for those who are less fortunate. Data collection systems, policy makers, and administrators frequently ignore this sector because it is mostly an unorganised one that belongs to the small-scale and cottage industry group.

Capitalism benefits by keeping these divisions and the labour divisions and the paid and unpaid work. The women and girls under this system can be exploited. Capitalist systems move from domestic production system to large-scale production. With the decentralising production and the existing hierarchy in them, capitalism does away with labour organising against exploitation. By employing women, it is able to get huge benefits at very little capital investment. Under this structure, men's employment is mainly focused in a small number of industries (especially services, where access to jobs is easier but salaries are often lower and job security minimal). Women are concentrated at the lower levels of those sectors. Women make up a larger portion of workers in "informal" and other precarious occupations, which appear to be outside the purview of labour law and inspection and are therefore more prone to be exploited. In wealthy countries, between 65% and 90% of all are part-time employees (ILO, 1995).

In light of their underprivileged status, the issues that women face in the unorganised sector demand special attention. Both socially productive and reproductive labours take up a significant percentage of their time. This is referred to as the "double load of work", which separates women from males. Wages, job security, and opportunities for advancement in the business are all affected by gender division in the workplace. The total image paints a picture of growing disadvantage for women workers, particularly those in rural areas and those belonging to Scheduled Castes and Tribes (Rameshwari Pandya and Sarika Patel, 2021).

There are strong correlations between informality and growth, and informality, poverty, and inequality. There is a reality that can be seen today, and this is that much of the informal economy is now intertwined with the formal economy and contributes to the entire economy, and that assisting the working poor in the informal economy is a vital approach to reducing poverty and inequality. Supporting working poor women in the informal economy is an important road to reducing women's poverty and gender inequality. There is a growing realisation that women tend to be concentrated in the more insecure kinds of informal employment (Chen et al., 2004).

Many observers believed that the informal sector was marginal or peripheral, unrelated to the formal sector or contemporary capitalist development, and that it would vanish once the country had achieved sufficient levels of economic growth or modern industrial development. Others claimed that industrial development in developing countries might follow a different path than in rich countries, including the expansion of informal economic activity. By the 1980s, the informal sector discussion had broadened to cover changes in mature capitalist economies as well. Production was increasingly being reorganised into small-scale, decentralised, and more flexible economic units in both North America and Europe. Mass production was being replaced by "flexible specialisation" or, in certain cases, sweatshop manufacture (Piore and Sabel, 1984). These changes were (and continue to be) linked to the informalisation of labour relations. Standard jobs were being transformed into non-standard or atypical jobs with low hourly earnings and limited benefits, or piece-rated jobs with no benefits; manufacturing was being outsourced to small-scale informal units and industrial outworkers. The informal economy had become a permanent, but subordinate and dependent, part of capitalist development as a result of this process (Portes et al., 1989).

According to some academics, the economy's informal sector is separate from and unrelated to the official operations that give the poor a means of subsistence and operate as a safety net during times of crisis. They observe an imbalance between the skill sets of individuals and the design of contemporary economic prospects (Sethuraman, 1976; Tokman, 1978). Others believe that the informal economy is made up of small businesses (micro-enterprises) and workers who enable big capitalist companies to compete by reducing their labour and input costs. In particular, formal firms' efforts to lower labour costs and boost competitiveness, as well as formal firms' responses to organised labour's power, state economic regulation (particularly taxes and social legislation), international competition, and the industrialisation process, drive informality. This is because of the nature of capitalism and capitalist growth (Castells and Portes, 1989). According to theory, the informal sector consists of "lucky" microentrepreneurs who work without formal registration in order to avoid the costs and save time and effort, and who need property rights to transform their assets into legally recognised assets. As a result, the self-employed operate according to their own informal extra-legal norms (de Soto, 2000).

In the short, medium, and most likely long terms, informal employment will continue to exist. For the vast majority of the workforce and population in the developing countries, it serves as their primary source of employment and income. Informal workers typically make less money and suffer greater risks than formal workers, are less likely to benefit from economic opportunities and legal safeguards, and are less able to exercise their economic rights and collective voice (ILO, 2002). It is important to acknowledge that the informal sector makes up a sizable portion of the global labour and economy. In order to fully utilise them in economic planning and legal frameworks, both informal businesses and the workers must be recognised for their contributions. A variety of interventions need to be taken into consideration and put into practice in order to solve the issues related to the informal economy; there cannot be just one policy intervention. Additionally, these interventions must be specialised and targeted to address the unique challenges, requirements, and risks of various categories of informal workers, including those who are self-employed as well as those who are employed on a wage; those who work for high-end as opposed to low-end informal enterprises; those who avoid regulations; and those for whom current laws and regulations are inapplicable or inappropriate (Chen, 2012: 20).

Regarding how to deal with the problems of exploitation in the informal sector, there has been a lot of discussion. These include organisations, representation, and conversation along with local economic development, growth and productivity, the regulatory environment and labour standards, entrepreneurship, skills, and social security and protection. If gender-sensitive programmes are implemented in conjunction with initiatives to address other areas simultaneously, social and economic exclusions, including gendered disparities, have a better chance of being transformed. To improve low-income, women's employability and skills, it is important to take into account the gendered structure of the care economy as well as gendered power dynamics at the domestic, communal, local, national, and international levels. Women's lack of access to money and property rights must be addressed in order for the promotion of women's entrepreneurship to be successful. Low-income women's access to microcredit will be constrained unless adequate training is provided to combat illiteracy, better infrastructure and social services are developed, and assistance is given to lessen caregiving obligations (Sylvia Chant et al., 2008).

Women in the unorganised sector in India

An intense debate has taken place in India about what constitutes work, and what should be counted as productive or economically meaningful in the country's national statistics. A patriarchal view of what constitutes "work", and what can be considered productive or economically significant, must be taken into account when analysing this debate. Before the 1981 census, work was defined as participation in any economically productive activity, and family's consumption was ruled out. By the 1991 census definition, all economic activities, whether physical or mental, is considered work. In addition, the census counted activities such as cultivating food for personal consumption and doing unpaid work for family businesses (Sankaran, 2006). Even so, the unpaid domestic work performed by women that may not amount to "work" as defined above is not included in this definition (Patel et al., 2017: 594). Another reality is that most of these works are done by women in the unorganised sector.

Workers who do not have a written contract, paid leave, health benefits, or social security are referred to as informal workers. From 2011–2012 to 2017–2018, a gradual formalisation of the workforce can be seen in Table 3.1. The unorganised sector employs 83% of the workforce, while the organised sector employs just 17%. Informal workers (those without a written contract, paid leave, or other benefits) account for 92.4% of all workers. Additionally, there are 9.8% non-unionised employees in the organised sector indicating the extent of outsourcing. Most likely, these are subcontractors. In 2017–2018, employment in the unorganised sector rose by 3.6 percentage points, while employment in the formal sector rose by a meagre 0.9%. There has been a rise in the percentage of people working in the formal sector. The government's efforts to provide social security for workers in the unorganised sector are also evident in this.

The unorganised sector in India is very big and persistent sector. It is dominant in India in terms of contribution to employment. According to National Commission for Enterprises in Unorganised Sectors (NCEUS) in 2004–2005, unorganised sector workers were 86% (NCEUS, 2007) Almost all workers in the agriculture and forestry areas fall within the informal sector. About 98.7% of workers in fisheries also fall within this category. Similarly, workers in construction, transport, hotel industry, storage, real estate, and private households belong to this sector. The informal economy accounts for more than 90% of the population and about 50% of the national product. Informal economic practices concentrate a high proportion of socially and economically underprivileged groups of society. A majority of India's population is working in the unorganised or informal sector (*Report on Jobs in the Informal Sector and Informal Job Conditions* (2013–2014)). The share of unorganised sector is highest in agriculture as the holdings are small and fragmented. This is followed by trade, construction, real estate, professional services, and other services

Women contribute significantly to the value addition of the final product in every form of activity, whether it is agriculture or allied activities, fishing, weaving, garment making, or construction, and yet their work is seen as secondary, unskilled, and often as a skill only of domestic value by all. Many of these women labour at home or in home farms, where they are burdened with two jobs and subject to exploitation. Both urban and rural settings are used to stage these

TABLE 3.1 Distribution of Total Employment

2011–2012				*2017–2018*		
Worker	**Unorganised**	**Organised**	**Total**	**Unorganised**	**Organised**	**Total**
Formal	**82.0**	**9.8**	**92.4**	**85.5**	**5.2**	**90.7**
Informal	**0.4**	**7.2**	**7.6**	**1.3**	**7.9**	**9.3**
Total	83.0	17.0	100.0	86.8	13.2	100.0

Source: Computed from NSS 68th unit level data on employment unemployment, 2011–2012 and Periodic Labour Force Survey, 2017–2018.

productions. The ease of entry, reliance on indigenous sources, family ownership of businesses, small scale of operation, labour-intensive and adapted technology, skills gained outside of the official school system, and the unregulated and competitive market characterise these activities (Kalpagam, 1994). Deprivation and discrimination are frequent among all employees in the informal sectors, despite the fact that they are not a homogeneous group in terms of caste, class, or economic activity. They face a dearth of employment opportunities, low and discriminatory salaries, and exploitative working conditions, all of which lead to casualisation. They don't have access to new technologies, skills, or knowledge, and they don't have social security (Shramshakti, 1988). Long and unpredictable working hours, workforce dispersion and atomisation, and the absence of any sort of workers organisation characterise these women who labour in the informal sector. Because women often combine this labour with their unpaid domestic duties, most of this work is underestimated and classed as "subsidiary activities". Since there are no overhead costs or the need to invest in tools or machinery, there are no trade unions to deal with, and there is a lack of legislation outlining workers' rights or requiring welfare measures, minimum salaries, or social security benefits, businesses have a significant advantage. Because the salaries are so low, every member of the family is expected to help with some component of production, resulting in widespread child labour in many home-based businesses (Pande, 1999). The agricultural development plan and specific programmes intended to improve the situation have failed to take the high number of women working in the informal economy into consideration, and as a result, these workers are largely invisible. According to the Delhi-based International Expert Group on Informal Sector Statistics, the idea and measurement of jobs in the informal sector need to be supplemented by a description and measurement of informal employment (CSO/India 2001) (Tables 3.2 and 3.3).

India's government highlighted a serious issue in its 2015/2016 Economic Survey, in very plain terms. This was the difficulty of producing "stable employment" in India, which could also be viewed as a challenge of creating more formal sector jobs (The India Economic Survey, 2015/2016). The formal sector is made up of registered companies paying taxes and obeying labour laws. It is also known as "ordered" business. It offers the work that is nice in the sense that it is well-paid and connected to benefits such as holidays, sick leave, and social security such as health insurance and pension schemes. However, many do not get jobs in India's formal market. It employs only about 10% of the workforce of the country. In the financial year 2011/2012, only 48 millions of India's 472 million economically active citizens worked in the formal sector.

The rest of the population, particularly women, rely on the informal economy for a living. May women from lower income families and living in poverty belonging to lower castes, with limited resources and education, have only to fall back upon the informal sector as housemaids, domestic staff, construction workers, agriculture, dairy farming, and garment manufacturing. These groups are most exploited and vulnerable in Indian society for they are generally underpaid

TABLE 3.2 Share of Formal-Informal Employment across Organised and Unorganised Sector

	Organised		*Unorganised*		*Total*	
	2011–2012	2004–2005	2011–2012	2004–2005	2011–2012	2004–2005
Formal	45.4	52.0	0.4	0.3	8.1	7.3
Informal	54.6	48.0	99.6	99.7	91.9	92.7
Total	17.3	13.0	82.7	87.0	100.0	100.0

Source: Economic Survey, 2015–2016. Table 15, Quoted by Niti Aayog.

TABLE 3.3 Percentage Distribution of Women across Socio-Religious Groups in 2017–2018

	Schedule Tribe	*Schedule Caste*	*Muslim*	*Others*	*Total*
Informal Employment	87.1	90.4	95.1	85.7	92.1
Formal Employment	13.0	9.6	4.9	14.3	17.9

Source: Computed from the Periodic Labour force Survey (2017–2018) unit level data.

and lack formal employment opportunities. Due to economic restructuring, there have been significant changes in economies all over the world. As part of the Structural Adjustment Policy, India introduced the New Economic Policy in 1991. This was a reaction to globalisation and liberalisation forces at work all across the world. The primary themes were competition and export production, and the eventual outcome was economic liberalisation and deregulation. This presents India with fresh issues, as structural change is never gender-neutral.

Third World women, members of underrepresented groups, and immigrants in the West have evolved into flexible worldwide categories of employees with low wages and precarious job conditions who are simple to fire when necessary. Due to this, subaltern women are now required for transnational production as low-wage factory employees or as contracted housewives. Due to the production of cheap and flexible workers in the West in the shape of Third World and immigrant women, the global division of labour has grown to depend on sexist notions regarding women's employment. Due to the unevenness of global integration and the reinforcement of existing inequalities, nation governments' capacity to promote human development has been severely damaged. As the social sector has shrunk, women's burdens have grown. These reorganisations mostly affect the poor and marginalised, particularly subaltern women in the developing world's unorganised and informal sectors. Also, according to publicly available figures, the number of women working unorganised informal sectors has increased, while the number of women working organised sectors has decreased.

These employers can be stated to be in informal employment.

- Self-employment: workers employed in their own informal sector enterprises.
- Owners themselves who fulfil the role of both proprietor and worker.
- Family members who contribute to the business.
- Members of informal producers cooperatives.
- Employees in formal sectors holding informal jobs.
- Paid domestic workers employed in households.
- Own account workers engaged in the production of goods exclusively for their own household use (Tripathi, 2018: 262).

Home-based workers can be divided into two kinds. The distinction is critical in comprehending the difficulties these workers face: home-based individuals who work for themselves accept all of the risks that come with being self-employed. All raw materials, supplies, and equipment are purchased by them and they are also responsible for paying for utilities and transportation. For the most part, they sell their final products to local customers and marketplaces, but they do occasionally sell to international markets. Unpaid family members may be employed by the majority of people, but this is a rare occurrence. Individuals or businesses hire subcontracted home-based workers (also known as homeworkers) by going through a middleman. As a rule, they are given raw materials and paid for each item produced. In most cases, they do not sell finished products. These costs include everything from the office to the equipment to the supplies to the utilities (Sarika Patel and Rameshwari Pandya, 2021: 597).

Although it has major market share, the unorganised sector is considered secondary and less important sector because of certain characteristics such as the size of enterprises is very small, income of workers is low, and there is no stability or job security, and employment is subject to volatility. In this sector, the availability of jobs is subject to other factors like capital availability, raw material access, market factors, and unskilled workforce. Since no particular skill is required to do the odd jobs that form part of industries in unorganised sectors, it is difficult to find a foothold. The workers are also easily replaceable. No other perquisites or assurances like pension in old age, compensation in case of accident or any other calamity are assured. If they don't work, they don't earn. These issues make the sector undesirable and secondary to the formal sector which provides better security to its employees.

In 2004, the Government of India established the NCEUS (National Commission for Enterprises in the Unorganised Sector). According to it, the unorganised sector includes all privately owned, proprietary or partnership-based, and employing fewer than ten people, unincorporated businesses that are engaged in the sale and production of products and services. NCEUS has been making efforts to ensure decent work in the unorganised sector, and accordingly it has recommended two comprehensive legislations for unorganised agriculture and non-agriculture workers. These legislations include all conditions of work along with social security. The draft of the Bill has recommended several measures for improving the condition of the workers.

- An eight-hour working day with at least a minimum of an hour break.
- Every week one rest day.
- A minimum wage for all wage workers and home workers.
- A penal interest on delayed wage payment.
- No payment of fines from the wages.
- Right to organise.
- No discrimination, with regards to sex, caste, religion, etc.
- Compensation for accidents and provision of safety equipment at the workplace.
- Protection from sexual harassment, provision for childcare, and basic amenities at workplace.

The "Unorganized Workers Social Security Act, 2008" addressed some of these issues. This act has potential to cover other areas of concern listed here as well.

Gender inequality, class, and caste nexus in the unorganised sector

As discussed, the unorganised sector in India provides the majority of employment. The sector is also clearly more inclined towards employing the women workforce than men. According to scholars' women here are overworked, their work is unrecognised and not properly valued monetarily. They are also often displaced by men. These days technology is also impacting negatively. In addition, high incidences of physical and sexual exploitation have become a common factor. Women in all regions either work for low wages or are unpaid family members, according to the ILO report released on the 8 March. According to the ILO, there is a "surprisingly considerable gender inequality" in terms of salaries, job stability, and so on (ILO, 2007). They work as wage earners, piece-rated workers, casual labour, and paid family labour. The main categories in urban areas include domestic labours, rag pickers, coolies, vendors, construction labours, and garment workers. These women face several problems due to lack of education, insufficient skill or knowledge, and no proper training. There is a lot of exploitation of female workers here due to the insecure jobs and lack of sustainability. They do not have any unions and hence cannot exert any pressure. The wage payment here is very irregular, and there is wage discrimination. This is a very seasonal employment, and the work conditions are bad leading to the rise of a large number of health issues.

Another important fact is that a significant percentage of the jobs in this sector are undertaken by women belonging to lower caste and class. Traditionally, women in India have not been work oriented. They prefer or are compelled to stay at home and undertake domestic responsibilities. But for economically lower status women, economic compulsions make them take up these jobs. Because of economic and caste-related issues, they exhibit certain characteristics like illiteracy, lack of skills, and taking up seasonal nature of employment. Class, caste, tribe, and communal divisions, as well as gender disparities, are all indicators of inequality. The thick, long-lasting paint used to depict the class, caste, and gender divides overlaps greatly, which is the final point. The most vulnerable people face the triple burden of being landless, belonging to a socially marginalised group, and being female.

Informal work takes place in both urban and rural settings. They can be found in a wide range of activities, such as casual, part-time, irregular, and often home-based. They're hidden away in the shadows of urban underclasses or out in the sticks of rural poverty. As a rule, they are self-employed people. A lot of people are in direct competition with each other/in the workplace, in the marketplace, or in the space they occupy to sell their goods and services. These women, many of whom live at the intersections between various forms of inequality, face an even greater challenge in establishing a common identity and interests. Their working conditions don't exactly promote self-awareness of their position as employees, let alone social acceptance of their work status (Kabeer et al., 2013: 250). Because of the ease of entry, reliance on indigenous resources, family ownership of firms, small scale of operation, labour demanding and adapted technology, skills learned outside of the official school system, and the unregulated and competitive market, women choose these activities (Kalpagam, 1994). As a result, workers in the household production sector who operate directly under their own account or under some type of putting-out system would be included in this sector. It would also cover women working in petty jobs and all other forms of informal labour in both rural and urban areas, as well as small workshops and factories. While the unorganised sector is not a homogeneous society in terms of caste, class, or economic activity, all employees face deprivation and prejudice. They face a shortage of job possibilities, low and unequal pay, and exploitative working conditions, all of which lead to casualisation. They lack social security, are exposed to workplace health risks, and do not have access to contemporary technology, skills, or knowledge (Shramshakti, 1988).

The women who work at home have long and erratic working hours, fragmentation, and atomisation of workforce. There is an absence of any form of workers organisation in this area. Because women often combine this labour with their unpaid domestic duties, most of this work is underestimated and classed as "subsidiary activities". Employers benefit substantially from a home-based piece-rated system because there is no need to invest in tools or machinery or overhead costs. There are some legislation establishing workers' rights and demanding welfare measures, minimum salaries, or social security benefits, but this is hardly having any impact. Because the salaries are so low here, every family member is expected to help with some component of manufacturing, resulting in widespread child labour in many home-based businesses (Pande, 2008).

A study by Hill indicates that there is a positive and developmental relationship between a worker's identity, or psychological integrity, and her actual capacity to engage in the political economy for constructive change, using empirical data collected among Self Employed Women's Association members. The findings show that membership-based organisations can promote the social foundations of recognition and respect that are critical to identity and agency, as well as provide workers with real opportunities to develop non-exploitative economic institutions that provide better wages and social security. However, by uniting informal workers for collective action, current power and wealth distributions, as well as gender privilege, are challenged. As a result, there is social friction and, on occasion, violence. This type of conflict is inevitable in the development process, yet it is frequently overlooked (Hill, 2010).

The invisibility of women's and girl's work

The invisibility of women's and girl's work continues to be an obstacle in understanding their economic role in the household and in society. One reason for this is the elusive definition of `work' given by economists and census commissioners. Another reason for the non-recognition of women's economic contribution has been neglect of the household economy and the unorganised sector in which women play an over whelming role. Gopal contends that the portrayal of the women working from home as "housewives" and the task of working from home which includes performing domestic chores, taking care of children, and beedi making indicates that women put long arduous hours in fulfilling targets but have no idea how their employers have arrived at the arbitrary amount that they receive at payment. Thus, "women's subordinate status as workers is built in the production process" (Gopal, 1999: 12).

We take up few sectors in the unorganised sectors to look into women's work here.

The agricultural sector

The majority of India's labour, both male and female, is employed in the agriculture sector. The fast expansion of public irrigation systems during the First and Second Five Year Plans resulted in a period of strong agricultural productivity and output growth from the early 1950s to the mid-1960s. The second phase of agricultural transition and economic development began in the early 1970s and was characterised by a new policy of intensive and selective development, programmes to assist farmers in increasing their income, and a shift in emphasis from major private irrigation projects to minor public irrigation projects. The larger farmers benefited from this new programme because they received loans, high yielding seed types, energy and water subsidies, special incentives at heavily reduced rates, and other benefits. While numerous initiatives were put into place to aid small farmers, the growth cycle was constrained and many facets of society skipped over it. This has resulted in widespread migration with female migrants more than double the number of male and rural migrants to rural migration, accounting for more than 70% of domestic migration and women dominated (Kasturi, 1990: 5). Consequently, the benefits of agricultural production did not benefit those who needed them most.

Despite this, Indian agriculture has advanced quickly since independence. The annual production of food grains increased from 51 million tons in the early 1950s to 206 million tons around the end of the 20th century. It has helped people become food self-sufficient and prevent food shortages. However, the agricultural expansion pattern has left behind uneven development across regions and crops, diverse farming communities, a low level of productivity, and the deterioration of natural resources in some areas (National Agricultural Policy, 1998). This has had an impact on women too.

Women as farmers: essential but invisible

Indian women make a major and essential contribution to agriculture that is essential to both agricultural output and the women's households. The nature and structure of the agricultural economy, with its distinctive aspects of land relations, labour usage, and the role and functions of the credit system, must be taken into consideration in any assessment of the role and issue of women in Indian agriculture (Towards Equality, 1974).

Although almost all rural women are involved in agriculture to some degree, the kind and degree of their involvement varies widely and is highly influenced by the financial situation, caste, and ethnicity of their household. According to the gender ideology, a woman's position and that of the household rise the more her employment permits her to stay "inside" the domestic sphere. All Indian women perform domestic work, but as their household's financial situation deteriorates, they are forced to combine it with other sorts of work, increasing their exposure to the "outside" (Gender and Poverty Report, 1991: 11). In India, a significant portion of adult women are employed as farmers. However, the mistaken notion that "farmers are males" and "women are only housewives" still dominates agricultural policy.

A shift from cultivator to labour status

In agriculture, we come across two categories of women.

- Cultivators are women, who work on farms, held by themselves in ownership or lease. These are self-employed women.
- Labourers are those women who do not own any land and work in another person's land and have no supervision and direction in cultivation. These women work for wages in money, kind, or share in produce. They have no right or lease or contract on the land on which they work.

The distribution of female agricultural employees varies significantly between states. The population of Scheduled Castes and Scheduled Tribes who live in poverty has significantly greater rates of female participation. In Orissa, West Bengal, Gujarat, and Madhya Pradesh, the percentage is between 30% and 40%, although it is only approximately 17% throughout all of India's Schedule Tribes. Between 1961 and 1981, the proportion of women in the combined Scheduled Caste and Scheduled Tribe climbed from 44% to 47%. In spite of making up only roughly a quarter of India's rural population, Schedule Caste and Tribal women work as over half of all female agricultural labourers (Gender and poverty Report, 1991: 23). These figures are only going up. A startling 84% of rural Indian women rely on agriculture for their livelihood. Women make up 47% of agricultural labourers and 33% of farmers, making up more over half of the industry (Rao, 2006).

If we look at the statistics, they show us a dramatic shift from cultivators to labour status. Increasingly there have been more and more women now coming under the status of an agricultural labour. The Census of India points out that in 1981, the percentage of women cultivators was 33.09, and in 1991, it was 34.22%, and in 2011, it was 55%. In comparison, the percentage of labourers was 46.34 in 1981 and it increased to 43.93% in 1991 it was 24% (Census of India). This number continues to increase with the passage of time, and now after the pandemic, more women are getting involved in agriculture, once they returned to their homes in rural areas. Hence, one can see a shift in the status of women from cultivator to agricultural labourers.

The decline of women cultivators can be attributed to increasing pauperisation leading to loss of land or inadequate growth of productive employment opportunities on family farm leading to withdrawal of women from active cultivation (Towards equality, 1974). The increase in agricultural labourers is the greatest indicator of increasing poverty and reduction in the level of employment and not of improving rights and opportunities for economic participation (Mies, 1987: 125). The increased commercialisation of agriculture and magnetisation of economy have resulted in the transformation of agriculture labour into wage employment. In order to survive, these farmers in the absence of sustainable agriculture have no choice but to encroach on forestlands and other fragile environmental areas. Peasant farming systems of which women are an integral part are based on local resource management and are now under pressure from the mounting competition for natural resource like forests, fisheries, and biomass. Through trade, technologies and market forces control over resources shifts from local to national to international agencies. Women's loss of control over production process has been associated with an increase in the burden of work and increased dependence on wage labour and women have to fall back upon survival production (Mies, 1987: 5). Globalisation has increased the number of displaced farmers, as more land is now being used for large-scale commercial export led production of cash crop.

Long-term agreements between those with land rights and landless labourers have mostly been supplanted by cultivators hiring agricultural labourers on a day-to-day basis. Individuals are employed rather than entire families to work for a landlord. Agricultural work is seasonal, with lengthy periods of underemployment throughout the year. There are no advantages for these women because the bulk of them work in the subsistence sector and have no surplus that can be sold. The relationship between women and the market gains greater relevance as a result of the increased emphasis on market forces brought about by globalisation and the reform package.

Economic Survey 2017–2018 says there is "feminisation" of agriculture sector with the rural to urban migration by men, with rising numbers of women in multiple roles as farmers, entrepreneurs, and labourers. Globally, empirical evidence exists that women have a key role to play in maintaining food security and sustaining local agro-biodiversity. It is the woman in rural areas who through integrated management use the diverse natural resources to meet the daily needs of the home. This needs woman farmers to have increased access to resources such as land, water, credit, technology, and training which warrants critical analysis in India context. Moreover, women farmers' entitlements would be crucial to increasing productivity in agriculture. We need to discuss women's unequal access to resources like land, credit, water, seeds, and markets (Economic Survey, 2017–2018: 20).

In order to increase agricultural productivity, gender-specific techniques are essential given that women predominate at all production phases, including pre-harvest, post-harvest processing, packing, and marketing. In order to boost the productivity of small farms, a "inclusive transformative agricultural strategy" should work to increase gender-specific activity, include women as active actors in rural transformation, and involve both men and women with gender expertise in the extension services.

Women doubly burdened: working longer and harder than men

Women put in more time and effort than males do, whether it's in shifting cultivation, subsistence and low-input agriculture, or high external input agriculture. In many states, women actually outnumber men. In terms of gender ratio, the States of Andhra Pradesh, Tamil Nadu, and Gujarat have more female than male labourers, whereas Maharashtra and Rajasthan have more female than male cultivators. Women are involved in pre-sowing and sowing, which includes preparation of land, puddling of land, repairing bunds and channels, maintenance of agricultural tools and implements, preparation of compost and farm yard manure, seed selection, seed treatment before sowing, preparation of nursery beds, transplanting, thinning, weeding, scaring of birds, using plant protective measures, and harvesting and post-harvesting activities. The participation of women varies from carrying out actual farm operations the field to supervision, management, and decision-making in different agricultural operations. Women join men in chopping up lumps of earth in fields. At sowing time, they walk besides men driving ploughs, pouring grains into sowing funnels that supply seeds to the furrows. They crouch besides men weeding rice and vegetables crops and work with men to harvest grains with hand sickles, handling home sheaves in headloads (Pande, 2006: 71). Another study found that the burden of the domestic and other chores was literally "back breaking" for women, i.e., they suffered spinal injuries due to constant bending (Shatrugna et al., 1990). In Orissa, Tamil Nadu, West Bengal, Kashmir and Kerala, women do the work of transplanting, weeding, harvesting, and threshing the paddy but usually do not plough the fields or are involved in marketing of the crop (Shramshakti, 1988: 10). In northeastern states like Manipur, Meghalaya, and Nagaland, women even control marketing of agricultural products to a little extend.

The type and extent of participation by farmwomen in farm operations varies from state to state. In the tribal economy of Orissa, shifting cultivation (Bogodo) women spend 105.4 days per year on agricultural operations compared to men who spend 59 days per year on agricultural work (Fernandes and Menon, 1987). In the Indian Himalayas, a pair of bullock works for 1,064 hours, a man for 1,212 hours and women for 3,485 hours in a year on a 1-hectare farm. In the hill agriculture of Himachal Pradesh, women do 37% of sowing work, 59% in intercultural (weeding), 66% of harvesting, 59% of thrashing, and 69% of tending farm animal (Bhati and Singh, 1987: 10). Through their work, knowledge, and skill, both categories of women (cultivators and labourers) make crucial contribution to the production process as well as to household income.

Whatever the culturally ideal role of men and women in society may be, massive economic and social upheavals are taking place now that are fast and significantly altering household formations and patterns of obligations. A total of 35% of homes below the poverty line are headed by women (Omvedt, 1981). This finding casts doubt on the notion that farming is a primarily male occupation and that it is the ideal poor rural home. Women's earnings make up a significant portion of the income in poor households, even if there is a male earner. Women therefore spend a larger percentage of their income on basic family maintenance than do males. Better child nutrition and health were more strongly correlated with rising women's income. It also improves a woman's sense of security, which in turn boosts the security of children in families struggling with poverty (Saradamoni, 1987: 5). In contrast to men, women have a more important role in food production and consumption, which has implications for family well-being.

The distribution and availability of high-quality seed is essential for Indian agriculture to multiply, which will speed up food production. Providing high-quality seeds at reasonable prices is getting more difficult as multinational corporations enter the seed distribution and production industries, along with the resulting implications of patenting under the WTO regime. Any influence women may have had on traditional occupations has been removed by the government's growth-oriented programmes. The marketisation of the economy has increased inequities between regions and the burden placed on women as a result of the loss in the state's interventionist role in the economy. Women who work in agriculture are more marginalised and reduced to poverty despite already bearing the brunt of class and gender inequality (Pande, 2000: 411).

It has been noted that women as producers stand to gain from trade liberalisation in agricultural production and exports only if they belong to the category of surplus farmers and not the category of subsistence production. Women as consumers stand to benefit under protectionism if the price of domestic products is higher than those on the world markets (Mehta, 1999: 67). The majority of people live in subsistence economies; hence, globalisation discourages the weaker members of society. Today's shifting market dynamics have caused unforeseen economic challenges for weaker countries, and this is especially true for impoverished women who face a double disadvantage as members of an underprivileged class and a marginalised gender. Vulnerable women in the household now face a variety of paradoxical situations thanks to modernisation and mechanisation. In an increasingly cash-based economy, it has become expensive for these households to convert cash into grain and dry feed. Poor landless farmworkers are more excluded in the absence of other employment possibilities and other necessary forms of support, and the number of women living in poverty has increased (Tanwar, 1999: 130). A single harvester, for example, combines harvests of about 100 acres of crop in three days. Only farmers with smallholdings now find it more viable to get the crop harvested by these machines against cash payments, due to its effective and speedy operation. From the farmers "point of view, the job is completed easily, saving time and swift completion of harvest operations and shielding the farmer from grain because he is now making cash payments". Sadly, as a result of this, a large number of farm labour families who have been happy with earlier grain during the year have been made surplus, now in most cases, and those few who manage to find jobs have to struggle hard to turn their cash into grains, which is typically quite costly as time goes by. That means hard work but less earning (Tanwar, 1999: 131).

Growing rice and wheat grain yields by methods like dwarfing, monocultures, and multicopying have been the focus of the so-called green revolution. For an Indian woman farmer, rice serves as both a meal and a supply of straw for thatch and cattle feed. High producing cultivars have increased the amount of work for women. By degrading biological sources of food, fodder, fertiliser, fuel, and fibre, the elimination of biological variety undercuts the numerous contributions made by women to agriculture (Shiva, 1991). Women's influence over seeds and genetic resources may be lost as a result of the abandonment of local varieties and indigenous crop development techniques (Towards equality, 1974). In a similar vein, women have extremely limited access to finance. They lack the necessary collateral for agricultural loans (land title and cattle).

Though in the field of irrigation, a transition can be seen as well. Traditionally irrigation was focused on water collection, and water was transferred to the fields from the small ponds via the manually operated bucket method, and women were very involved here. The advent of diesel pumps enabled irrigation, to become a male monopoly. This however has not reduced the workload for women. Many women's access to resources like energy is increasingly decreasing, although there is a growing need for food and employment. Women are the most important biomass consumers and users. Multiplying the work of women is due to the growing scarcity of biomass (Jigging, 1986: 14).

Women's traditional land rights were diminished with the commercialisation process. Land reform programmes as well as the propensity to break up communal land holding particularly tribal and customary tenure ideas have resulted in the transfer of exclusive land rights to males as household heads. The definition of "head of the family", which is used as the basis for land redistribution, has traditionally neglected both the nature of the female-headed households and the married women's claim to a shared share of land. With the process of commercialisation, women's traditional land rights were eroded.

Women and the livestock industry

Sustainable agricultural development and food security in low-income and food-deficient countries can only be achieved if the efficiency of animal agriculture is improved. Despite the growing demand for animal products and services, the importance of animals in food and agricultural development programmes is widely underestimated, especially in developing countries. The identification, testing under local conditions, and promotion of appropriate technologies utilising local and affordable resources are prerequisites for the long-term development of animal agriculture. It's imperative that policies, infrastructure, and support services are put in place to help small-scale farmers take advantage of these technologies. Short-term benefits and long-term sustainability can be gained by integrating livestock and agriculture. The livestock industry has a wide range of capabilities and is adaptable enough to deal with shifts in the overall economy. These animals can use local resources to produce valuable goods and services because they have been bred for particular environments and environments with different climatic conditions

Besides agriculture, in major parts of the country tending to animals is mostly women's occupation. The largest cattle and buffalo population in the world, accounting for about one-sixth of the world's cattle and half the world's buffaloes, is found in India. Reliable data on employment in dairying is difficult to obtain, since most of this work is performed in the non-market sector, usually intermittently in combination with many other farming tasks and it is missed by Census. There are 15 million men and 75 million women who are engaged in dairying (Thakur and Chander, 2006). Women in dairy industry perform the tasks like milking, collecting and processing of dung, and preparation of cooking fuel by mixing dung cakes with twigs and crop residues. The major credit for India's position as the highest milk producer and subsequent increase in per capita availability of milk has to be given to illiterate rural women dairy farmers (Patel, 1993).

Women in rural areas play an important role in animal husbandry, participating in activities such as feeding, breeding, management, and healthcare. The majority of women's time is spent caring for and managing dairy animals. Women contribute to the success of the dairy business by being major stakeholders in its growth. In livestock farming, they account for 71% of the workforce (Kaur et al., 2017:1051). Women's share in activities of animal husbandry is scattered across all the caste groups. They play significant role in activities like milking cattle, fodder cutting, preparing feed for calves, taking animals for grazing, collection of dung, preparation and storage of dung cakes, storage of hay, storage and marketing of milk, *ghee* (*refined* butter), and other dairy products. Besides dairying women also actively participate and play an important role in running successfully other enterprises like poultry, piggery, goatary, duckery, quail rearing, sheep rearing, rabbit rearing, fisheries, sericulture, and mushroom cultivation. The indigenous dairy sector has relied heavily on women's wisdom.

Dairy as managed by women in rural India embodies practices and logic rather different from those contained in the dairy science imparted at institutions of formal education since the latter is essentially an import from Europe and North America. Therefore, with dairy development, trade in dairy product shifts out of the household, and the income is no longer under female control. Increase in sale of milk may mean less consumption in the household. It means more work for women who are engaged in the task of care and feeding of livestock with less control over resources. A very ambitious programme in India at alleviating rural poverty is an operation flood. Funded by the host of international agencies, this is India's dairy development project aimed at benefiting India's landless and small peasants. A large number of women especially from among medium and lower farmers are drawn into it. For them dairying involves an intensification of the work process accompanies by little or no changes in the statue or access to milk for consumption (Mitra, 1987: 127). In fact, with more and more commercialisation, the consumption of milk in dairy-producing households is declining. This has an adverse impact on women who already suffer from cultural constraints and follow the protocol of eating in the end when little is left.

The downward mobility of women

As there is no means of livelihood throughout the year and drought seasons, the families have no other option but to migrate in search of other employment. In an Odde caste study of women agricultural workers from the Salem district of Tamil Nadu, D. Padmavathi and Vijayalakshmi Rammohan showed how agricultural mechanisation and inflation contributed to the pauperisation of women agricultural workers who are forced to migrate and, together with difficulties in obtaining work, changing places and changing the environment experienced an increase in the number of women agricultural workers (Padmavati et al., 1999: 151). This specific caste community was forced to migrate to the cities in search of jobs due to modernisation and technological transition. Until migration, they sold their lands to the major farmers since they couldn't cope because of changes in the economy. The "pull" factor for these migrants to Tirupati in

Andhra Pradesh was quarry mining, which due to liberalisation and privatisation generated new labour demands in the unorganised market. Earlier quarrying was considered the task of people, but since the 1980s, the increasing liberalisation and privatisation of the quarry economy has made all this possible due to the subcontracting of stone cutting and rock dynamiting on the quarries. The contractors at the quarry now recruit workers by paying them lower salaries. In a day these women work for more than 15 hours and yet do not have job permanence, accommodation, or earn any benefits. Employment in the quarries often poses significant health hazards. Globalisation has only exacerbated the problem by moving women further down the job ladder.

The textile and garment industry

The emerging social distortions, exclusions, and marginalisation are also becoming a feature in another allied activity, the textile industry and the garment industry, which gives work to a number of people in seasons when the agrarian activity is dull or to worker who migrate to urban areas looking for work. As one of India's oldest industries (dating back centuries), the textile industry is a vital one. Hand-spun and hand-woven textiles are on one end of the spectrum, while capital-intensive complex mills are on the other. The decentralised power looms/hosiery and knitting industry dominates the textiles industry in the United States. Other industries in the country have little to do with textiles because of the industry's reliance on agriculture (for raw materials like cotton) and the country's long history and traditions surrounding textiles. India's textile sector has the capacity to create a wide range of products appropriate for a variety of market segments, both domestically and internationally. Though large-scale factories using capital-intensive production methods and small workshops using power looms dominate the textile industry, now increasingly home production is also carried out by the handloom weaver's families using manually operated looms. Here most of the unpaid family labour is done by women and children, who do most of the preparatory work (Savara, 1986).

Around 4.5 crore people are involved in the textile business, with 35.22 lakh of them working on handlooms. The guidelines for the New Economic Policy of 1991 for small-scale industrial sector have legitimised the subcontracting operation of big business houses and foreign firms by permitting them to have ownership stakes. With gradual focus on investment and export, the handloom weaving industry is losing importance as compared to the power loom weaving. The conditions of the marginalised and dependent weavers are becoming more pathetic. The worst hit are the women for whom weaving has always been a traditional source of livelihood.

Multinationals in their efforts to maintain and increase profits have tried to relocate the industry to areas where labour costs are cheap. They have also utilised the most vulnerable sections of the workforce such as immigrants and women. The nature of relocation of the clothing industry to India has not taken the form of factories set up by multinationals, instead local clothing manufacturing companies have formed links with international buying houses or manufacturing companies. This maintains the dependence of Indian companies on foreign buyers while foreign capital is not utilised (Rao, 1987: 51). In this process of global reorganisation, the most important links are these home-based workers. Furthermore, in the modern age of emulative competition and the age of globalisation and privatisation, the handloom sector is facing many more hurdles. Since globalisation and reform package place a great emphasis on market forces, the relationship of women with market and the state assumes great importance. Globalisation has further precipitated and aggravated the already marginalised conditions of this vulnerable section of society especially the women.

Piece-rated work: the garment industry

One can see a similar kind of trend in the garment industry too. This industry has grown fast due to a shift in urban consumer's tastes from custom-tailored garments to ready-made garments and introduction of exports. The ready-made garment industry thrives because it offers the consumers ready to wear clothes at a price cheaper than the actual cost he or she would incur if they had to buy the material from the market and get it stitched from a tailor. Women do various kind of work such as cutwork, embroidery crochet, tracing pattern on to dresses stitching various types of hooks and buttons, and supply to the garment industry. In this industry, the production process is organised either in a piece system or the assembly group system. While the former is adopted in the non-factory system in the factory system, the assembly group system is adopted. In this while every worker stitches one part, the consecutive parts are stitched serially and one can see the garment taking shape along the assembly line (Kalpagam, 1994: 159). A major portion of the garment industry work is carried out in small work places and subcontracting. Here the distinction between the organised sectors has often become blurred, the factory exists side by side with the putting-out system, and the housewife in the home is also linked indirectly to the world market. This process of capitalist development has led to increasing polarisation, and the people living below poverty line have increased. Here the small and medium economic units are pitted against the big and large.

In the garment industry, production is split up into several processes, and each process is carried at a different location. Exporters subcontract the work and the contractor makes use of the putting-out system, which draws out a large number of women. The industry has a low capital base and many entrepreneurs enter and leave the field. Most of these jobs are low-skilled and low-paying, and since labour legislations are easily flouted poor working conditions, lack of facilities is the norm. The women have no control over the production process, and since the contractor increases his profit by squeezing the price of labour, women are the worst hit. Inspire of this, women accept home-based work as a last means of earning a livelihood. Many of these women come from destitute homes and are forced to do so because to the insecurity of their male family members' work or unemployment (Rao, 1987: 57). The employer takes advantage of this situation. The large reservoir of suitable women easily available in resettlement colonies maintains and often tends to lower the already low piece rates. The women here work under great pressure. Contractors often demand the completion of work within few hours. Some contractors want the piece back on the same day because they felt that the workers' homes were filthy and the garments would be soiled. If any piece was lost or ruined beyond repair, the worker is made to pay part of the damages and her chances of getting work in future also becomes dim. Women did a multiplicity of tasks like cutwork, embroidery, crochet, tracing, button stitching, and this along with house work kept them busy the whole day. In spite of this, women's perception about their work and themselves were shaped by the nature of production, which was characterised by low wages and uncertainty and the predominant social values which are rooted in the family. Women have internalised their family's view that their work is only marginal.

Occupational health hazards

Another important feature of some of the work that women do in the informal sector is the occupational health hazard. Occupational hazards are risks to one's health and well-being that are linked to specific jobs. While steps are taken to mitigate hazards, the nature of the profession means that they will always exist in the workplace. Falls from height are an occupational hazard for a telephone lineperson, for example, because members of telephone crews must operate at heights to complete their jobs. Recognising occupational hazards is the first step towards developing workplace risk reduction initiatives to keep workers as safe and healthy as feasible. Workplace dangers can result in disease, injury, or death. Physical dangers, such as falls and exposure to heavy machinery, might be combined with psychological risks, such as stress. Chemical, biological, and radioactive agents, as well as other occupational dangers, are a worry. Special training is frequently provided to persons who work in jobs that have a recognised occupational safety concern so that they are aware of the hazard.

The production of beedis is one of the most significant occupational health hazards. Significant risks to one's health are posed by beedi rolling. According to the ILO, beedi workers are more likely to suffer from conditions like worsening of tuberculosis, asthma, anaemia, giddiness, postural and visual problems, as well as gynaecological troubles. Tobacco that has not been burned enter primarily through the cutaneous and nasopharyngeal pathways. Beedi rollers are susceptible to fungal diseases, peptic ulcers, haemorrhoids, and diarrhoea, according to a review that was conducted in 1995 by Ranjitsingh and Padmalatha. These researchers found that beedi rollers were affected by respiratory disorders, skin diseases, gastrointestinal illness, gynaecological problems, and lumbo-sacral pain. In addition, beedi roller users have reported experiencing numbness in the fingers, shortness of breath, and stomach symptoms including cramps and gas (Dikshit and

Kanhere, 2000; Rajasekhar and Muley, 2001). Postural difficulties, eye troubles, and a burning sensation in the throat are common complaints voiced by women who are beedi rollers, according to Das and Pande (2000), Kuruvila et al. (2002), and Mittal et al. (2008). According to Bhisey et al. (2006), the workers in the tobacco factory were at an increased risk of developing chronic bronchitis as a result of their ongoing exposure to the dust from tobacco. Researchers Ratna and Kaur (1999) and Aghi and Gopal (2001) found that women who are beedi rollers experienced induration of the hands and difficulties during pregnancy. Although a number of occupational health issues have been identified for the women who work in the beedi-rolling industry, there is a paucity of knowledge on the impact of tobacco dust on a variety of blood parameters for beedi rollers.

A variety of research on the occupational health issues of beedi rollers have been conducted in various locations. Mohandas (1980) conducted a thorough investigation into the socioeconomic realities of Kerala's beedi rollers. He found a high rate of occupational ailments as a result of cigarette exposure and postural difficulties as a result of the monotonous labour. In another study, the four districts of Tamil Nadu accounted for respiratory, gastrointestinal, and osteological issues among beedi rollers (Nakkeeran et al., 2010). Joshi et al. (2013) conducted an epidemiological investigation of occupational health hazards among beedi workers in Amarchinta, Andhra Pradesh, and discovered that about 90% of the workers experienced pain in various body areas, with shoulder discomfort, back pain, and neck pain being the most common. In Ajmer, Prakash and Vyas (2013) investigated the link between occupational tobacco exposure and health concerns among female beedi rollers. They concluded that toxic nitrosamines included in tobacco dust are easily absorbed by bodily tissues, causing cough, dyspnoea, ocular, and dermatological problems. Mittal et al. went on to address the ocular symptoms of beedi rollers (2008). Umadevi et al. (2003) conducted research on the cytogenetic effects of tobacco dust exposure in workers and found that in the exposed group, there was an increase in the frequency of chromosomal abbreviations. Similar conclusions were reached by Mahimkar Bhisey (1995). Bagwe and Bhisey (1995) reported an increase in mutagenic load among employees in the beedi business. Kuruvilla et al. (2002) looked into beedi rollers' occupational dermatoses. The presence of callosities and nail alterations has been linked to the amount of work done. According to Bagwe and Bhisey (1991) and Swami et al. (1995), beedi rollers are exposed to unburnt tobacco, mainly through the cutaneous and nasopharyngeal routes. Most of the beedi makers just brush aside these health concerns as nothing serious and a day-to-day occurrence in their daily lives (Pande, 1999).

Move from organised to unorganised employment and feminisation of poverty

Today in India, more and more women are entering the labour force as compared to the men, and most of them are in the unorganised sector. As more men lose their jobs and are forced into part-time work with no guaranteed income, women begin to hunt for alternative sources of money in order to maintain a minimum standard of living. Because the income is insufficient, a big number of girls are dragged into it as well. Girl child labour must be understood in the context of the larger social matrix, as well as the interconnectedness of the larger social and planetary processes. Since 1981, the rate of female employment has risen, despite a significant reduction in male employment. This is almost certainly a compensation mechanism designed to keep the family economy afloat (UNICEF, 1989: 66–67). The shift from formal to informal employment, as well as from public to private sector employment, favours feminisation of work at the edges, but always in more insecure and low-paying conditions. Structural adjustment policies result in lower real earnings, more unemployment, decreased availability, and reduced subsidies for fundamental commodities and services. This has a greater influence on women and has negative consequences for their roles as producers, mothers, household managers, and community organisers. It lowers their salaries, lowers their level of living, and increases the amount of unpaid labour they must do (Ghosh, 2002). Unemployed and underemployed people are too poor to be unemployed for long periods of time. They don't have much of a choice except to accept any casual work, wage labour on a day-to-day basis, regardless of the pay. A huge number of women working in unorganised sectors suffer from frequent unemployment and mostly remain in abysmal poverty (Jayadevan, 1996: 763).

Globalisation and women

Transnational corporations and financial institutions are frequently pitted against the dwindling nation state in discussions of economic globalisation. Globalisation then becomes something that excludes certain groups and individuals from involvement in the market, but they remain dependent and impacted by decision made in other locations both in their own nation and overseas irrespective of where they are in the economy. Globalisation has established new class ties between global capital and the global proletariat, as well as transnational social classes (Robinson and Harris, 2000). The transnational bourgeois are able to recreate the system and exert their authority through supranational institutions such as the International Monetary Fund (IMF) and the World Bank (WB).

The development of global capitalism relies on gendered and racialised practices, which in turn profit from women's labour. Global capitalism also capitalises on the naturalised assumption about women. It is necessary to generate and maintain naturalised ideas about women in order to obtain and keep a cheap supply of female labour. The establishment, consolidation, and ongoing maintenance of world order, in addition to the normalisation of women's work and the employment of women, are all dependent on a well-functioning international division of labour. It is essential to have a solid understanding of the gendered politics of capitalism as well as the mechanisms behind the creation of vulnerable and exploitable positions for women. Homework, part-time outsourcing, patriarchal sweat shops, flexibilisation, informalisation, and casualisation of work are examples of new terms of employment that have been created as a result of new forms of transnational production, the power of global capital, and the requirements of the WB and the IMF. Feminisation of the labour force is another new term of employment that has been created. New developments in these fields include the idea of de-unionisation, "ad hoc" and "just-in-time" labour supply, an increase in the exploitation of immigrant workers, longer working days, and new racial and gendered hierarchies. During the post-reform period, the quality of rural employment, particularly among women, appears to have deteriorated significantly. There is sufficient evidence to conclude that the rate of casualisation and informalisation of work has risen in recent years. Casualisation is not evenly distributed throughout all levels of schooling and activities in both rural and urban locations. It is observed to be higher among illiterate women than men, especially in rural areas (Biradar et al., 2001: 550).

Despite the fact that the global system is reliant on these workers in a variety of ways, the prevalent concept of globalisation does not consider specific jobs to be a part of the global system. The majority of these tasks are carried out by women in Third World countries and by immigrants living in Western nations. A gendered postcolonial perspective on globalisation places women's "invisible" employment (such as the production of beedi) within social and economic processes that are significant to globalisation. One example of this is the production of beedi (Pande, 2019: 194). Castells contends that the emergence of the network society has significantly worsened the working and living conditions of the global working class as a whole as a direct result of the adverse effects on those conditions. The growing marginalisation of Third World countries that are lagging behind in terms of economic development is one symptom of this issue (Castells, 1996). The concept of a network society is intricately intertwined with the interpretation of the social implications of globalisation as well as the function of electronic communication technologies in contemporary society. The proliferation of information technology has brought about changes not only in the quantity but also in the quality and gendered aspects of job characteristics. Those segments in society, who cannot keep up with the technological pace, will be excluded or lose their status as workers, which will lead to increased polarisation between countries and within countries. Groups within countries, which are traditionally marginalised and excluded from education and information, like women in India, who work in informal industries like agriculture, dairying, textile and garment making, and beedi industry, will continue to get exploited in an increasingly globalised market. The shift from formal to informal employment, as well as from the public to private sector, encourages feminisation of the workforce. Structural adjustment policies result in lower real earnings, more unemployment, decreased availability, and reduced subsidies for fundamental commodities and services. This has a considerably greater influence on women and has negative consequences for their roles as producers, mothers, household managers, and community organisers.

Most developing-world economies began restructuring in the 1990s in the direction of free market and liberalisation, with the overarching goal of establishing outward-looking, internationally competitive economy, notwithstanding unfavourable social effects. The ideology and the guiding dialogues in the global world is the movement towards capitalism. The free play of markets, liberalisation, privatisation, and competition have become the key words in the path towards globalisation. This is followed by the withdrawal of the state from more and more welfare-oriented activities. However, the responses of different countries have varied substantially with reference to the length of adjustment period, intensity of adjustment, and the component of the adjustment package. Since there was already a disparity existing in the world, the reduction in the social sectors undermined the quality of human resources, thereby jeopardising the countries prospects for achieving sustained economic development in the future.

Although there has been a significant disconnect between the official statements of intent and the actual situation on the ground, India has made efforts to carry out the New Structural Adjustment programme. The fundamental structure of Indian society has not been altered as a result of the new economic programmes, and in many cases, these programmes have actually contributed to a worsening of existing inequality. As an essential component of the Structural Adjustment Policy, India had adopted the New Economic Policy in 1991, following the debt crisis, at the urging of the WB and the IMF. This was done as part of the Structural Adjustment Policy. The policies of structural adjustment and stabilisation were both included in the measures that were finally approved. It was hoped that by doing so, India would be able to reduce its deficits in foreign exchange, increase its level of overseas investment, and improve its overall balance of payments. To help mitigate the effects of the crisis, the WB provided sizeable loans. The internationalisation of business and commerce was included in this deal as well. Prior to this, India's human development was characterised by low levels of attainment as well as sharp regional and gender disparities. In spite of the many different five-year plans, the amount of money allocated to this sector has decreased. The growth of the country's human resources suffered as a direct result of all of this. In 1993, it was realised that India was lagging behind many of the other Asian countries in terms of human development indicators such as life expectancy, literacy, school enrolment, and medical care. India was one of the most populous countries in Asia at the time (Government of India, 1993).

During the 1990s, economic globalisation helped informalise the workforce in many sectors and countries (Standing, 1999). Although globalisation can create new jobs and open new markets, many of the jobs are not "healthy" jobs, and many of the new markets are inaccessible to poor or small-scale producers. This is because formal companies prefer to employ all but a few core staff under informal contracts, or outsource products and services to other firms and countries in response to global competition (Rodrik, 1997). Moreover, informal companies and small producers frequently lack business awareness and expertise to compete for export markets with formal firms, and instead face domestic market competition from imported products.

Globalisation rhetoric aims to eradicate backwardness through a worldwide exchange of knowledge and expertise to create a genuinely cosmopolitan society. There is an implicit assumption that in this programme, shared solidarity and respect for social justice are necessarily taken care of. Such problems are held in place in real action as the global system is focused on unequal power relations. Globalisation enables the ghettoisation of and the poor in the poorer nations. When trade does, globalisation tends to expand options but only for those with capital and market access. They are widely influenced by the global cycle due to the current gap between women and men's access to information, expertise, roles and concerns, and power over resources.

The new growth-oriented policies have stripped women of any power over conventional jobs and denied them better job opportunities. Women have been the hardest affected in the transition from welfare to economic growth, since a significant number of them are in the informal sector. Over the years, the socioeconomic conditions are worsening, and women are slowly losing power over the means of production over which they have a traditional right because of the introduction of modern technology. Women tend to bear the brunt of inequality of gender and class, experiencing growing marginalisation and pauperisation. Globalisation has only broadened the gender gap and accelerated poverty feminisation.

Not only for rich countries, but also for emerging ones, the concept of informal employment is crucial. The increased "informalisation" of work can be traced in part to the economy's globalisation process. Today's businesses use mixed-mode labour arrangements, in which some workers follow labour standards while others use non-standard, atypical, alternative, irregular, insecure, or other sorts of labour or various forms of subcontracting. In the ILO report "Decent Work and the Informal Economy", which was prepared for debate by the International Labour Conference at its 90th Session in June 2002, a conceptual framework for defining informal employment was offered (Hussmanns, 2001).

Statistics show a drop in the number of women working in organised industries and a rise in unorganised sectors. Women's participation in the unorganised sector climbed from 94% in 1971 to 96% in 1991. Despite their enormous numbers, women in this country continue to be overlooked in economic statistics and by legislators and planners. Women contribute significantly to the value addition of the final product in every form of activity, be it agriculture and related activities, fishing, weaving, or construction, and yet their work is seen by all as secondary, unskilled, and sometimes as a skill primarily of domestic worth. A considerable proportion of these women work at home, putting them under a double weight of labour and making them vulnerable to abuse. Even when women work in a factory-like environment, there is a risk of de-skilling as a result of men's greater access to skill acquisition, skill training, and skill upgradation. Women in this country are exploited on two levels: for their job in the unorganised sector and for their gender. This problem has become even more complicated as a result of globalisation.

Migrants from rural areas with poor background in schooling, training, and skills are a significant proportion of the workforce engaged in the urban unorganised market, and are working in low-paid, semi-skilled, or unskilled employment. In most businesses, the efficiency and earning levels are poor and often do not provide full-time jobs for those engaged. The working climate is not favourable for the employees; working hours are long and most of the conditions of good jobs (e.g., paid leave, pension, bonus, medical assistance and health insurance, maternity leave benefits, and injury coverage) are almost non-existent. The past patterns and all the data available indicate that the bulk of potential job growth will come from the unorganised market. Ensuring that employment in this sector comprises workers with secure working conditions, fair and increasing wages and a measure of income and social security would be a significant challenge. Moreover, an important task to accomplish in the immediate future would be to increase the proportion of coordinated sector jobs.

Legislative measures related to the unorganised sectors

The government realised the pivotal role performed by unorganised sector in the economy. Therefore, many legislations and schemes are initiated by the government for the benefit of unorganised workers and for providing security and better working conditions for these women. Two acts in particular have been formulated. *Unorganized Workers' Social Security Act, 2008,* and *Domestic Workers' Welfare & Social Security Act, 2010.* The *Unorganized Workers' Social Security Act, 2008,* provides for the constitution of National Social Security Board at central level. The Board is responsible for implementation of social security schemes like life and disability cover, health and maternity benefits, and old age protection. Similarly, the second act is specifically for domestic workers. Here the domestic worker need to be registered with the Board. The fee is paid by the employer. The benefits include fixing of minimum wage, working hours, weekly holidays, interval for rest, and overtime wages. However, these laws have not been effective. The problems of the women concerned continue with the same intensity (The Unorganised Workers' Social Security Act, 2008). This act also talks about the various social security schemes for unorganised sectors, namely, Indira Gandhi National Old Age Pension Scheme, National Family Benefit Scheme, Janani Suraksha Yojana, Handloom Weavers' Comprehensive Welfare Scheme, Handicraft Artisans' Comprehensive Welfare Scheme, Pension to Master Craft Persons, National Scheme for Welfare of Fishermen and Training and Extension, Janshree Bima Yojana, Aam Admi Bima Yojana, and Rashtriya Swasthya Bima Yojana (The *Unorganised Workers' Social Security Act,* 2008, See sections 2(i) and (3)).

The Domestic Workers' Welfare & Social Security Act, 2010, describes a domestic worker as a person working for in cash or in kind, in any household holding "or similar establishments" through any agency or directly, either temporarily or contractually or permanently, part-time or full-time, in order to do the household or related work. It establishes a domestic workers welfare fund (*The Domestic Workers' Welfare & Social Security Act*, 2010). It establishes a Central Advisory Committee, State Advisory Committee and District Boards, and the registration of the domestic workers for the benefit of this scheme. Yet in the lack of any monitoring mechanism, this is not implemented with much seriousness.

The unorganised sector in India is in an abysmal condition. It is largely unregulated, though it contributes to the economy in a major way. The case of women is even worse. A woman in unorganised sector is underpaid, untrained, lacks security, and is subject to exploitation. None of this however deters her from working as she is economically and sometimes socially deprived and her family compulsions force her to continue working under these conditions. The attention of government as we can see is inadequate and does not address her concerns concretely. The acts passed so far has been largely ineffective. The organisations like NCEUS and ILO along with others have done serious studies about these women. Further such studies are required to understand the existing conditions of these women and how the present government and society can help alleviate their problems.

Globalisation and the beedi worker

According to the findings of a number of studies, the proportion of women entering the labour force is growing at a faster rate than that of men, with the vast majority of these women finding employment in the informal sector. As more men lose their jobs and are forced into part-time work with no guaranteed income, women are beginning to look for alternative sources of income in order to maintain a minimum standard of living. This is because more men are losing their jobs than ever before. The vast majority of people who work in casual jobs don't have consistent employment and are forced to make do with meagre incomes (Jayadevan, 1996: 763). A significant number of young women are forced to participate in the practice as a result of the insufficient income. The exploitation of young girls as labourers needs to be understood in the context of the larger social matrix, as well as the interconnectedness of the larger social and planetary processes. Since 1981, the number of employed women has increased, while the number of employed men has significantly decreased. This is almost certainly a form of compensation that was devised so that the family's economy could continue to function normally (UNICEF, 1986: 66–67). All of this has an effect on women and their roles as producers, mothers, household managers, and community organisers, with negative consequences such as lower salaries, a lower standard of living, and a higher load of unpaid labour. Women also bear a disproportionate share of the responsibility for caring for their children (Ghosh, 1999).

The transition from formal to informal employment, as well as the transition from public to private sector employment, promotes the feminisation of work at the margins, but always in conditions that are more precarious and pay less. Policies of structural adjustment lead to lower real earnings, an increase in unemployment, a decrease in availability of fundamental commodities and services, and reduced subsidies for these goods and services. In such a setting, employing children to work becomes a necessary means of subsistence. People who are unemployed or underemployed are too financially strapped to remain unemployed for extended periods of time. They don't really have much of a choice other than to take whatever casual or wage work is offered to them on a day-to-day basis, regardless of the rate of pay.

References

Aghi, M. B., and M. Gopal, 2001, "Exploiting Women and Children–India's Beedi Industry", *Lifeline*, Vol. 6, pp. 8–10.

Bagwe, A. N., R. A. Govekar, and R. B. Bhisey, 1992, "Toxic Effects of Exposure to Tobacco Among Beedi Rollers", *Toxicology Letters*, Vol. 22, No. 6, pp. 1205–1205.

Bhati, J. B., and D. V. Singh, 1987, "Women's Contribution to Agricultural Economy in Hill Regions of North West India", *Economic and Political Weekly*, Vol. 22, No. 17, April 25, New Delhi, pp. ws7–ws11.

Bhisey, R. A., and A. N. Bagwe, 1995, "Occupational Exposure to Unburnt Beedi Tobacco Elevates Mutagenic Burden Among Tobacco Processors", *Carcinogenesis*, Vol. 16, No. 5, pp. 1095–1099.

Biradar, R. R., and S. T. Bagalkoti, 2001, "Changing Facets of Employment in Rural India: Emerging Issues and Challenges", *Indian Journal of Agricultural Economics*, Vol. 56, No. 3, July–September, pp. 538–552.

Buvinic, M., M. A. Lycette, and W. P. McGreevey, 1983, *Women and Poverty in the Third World*, London, John Hopkins Press.

Carr, M., and M. Chen, 2002, *Globalization and the Informal Economy: How Global Trade and Investment Impact on the Working Poor*, Working Paper on the Informal Economy Working No. 1 Integration, Geneva, International Labour Office.

Castells, M., 1996, *The Rise of the Network Society*, New York, Blackwell.

Castells, M., and A. Portes, 1989, "World Underneath: The Origins, Dynamics, and Effects of the Informal Economy", in A. Portes, M. Castells & L. A. Benton (eds), *The Informal Economy: Studies in Advanced and Less Advanced Developed Countries*. Baltimore (MD), John Hopkins University Press, pp. 11–37.

Census of India, series 1, paper 2 of 1992 as quoted in *Women and Men in India 1996–97*. Central Statistical Organization, Department of Statistics, Ministry of Planning and Program Implementation, Government of India. Different Census Data.

Chant, S., and C. Pedwell, 2008, Women, Gender and the Informal Economy: An Assessment of ILO Research and Suggested Ways Forward, Discussion Papers Are Preliminary Documents Circulated to Stimulate Debate and Obtain Comments, International Labour Organization.

Chen, M., J. Vanek, and M. Carr, 2004, *Mainstreaming Informal Employment and Gender in Poverty Reduction: A Handbook for Policymakers and Other Stakeholders*, London, Commonwealth Secretariat.

Chen, M. A., 2012, *The Informal Economy: Definitions, Theories and Policies*. Manchester, Cambridge, United Kingdom: Women in Informal Employment: Globalizing and Organizing (WIEGO).

CSO/India, 2001, Central Statistical Organisation/India: Expert Group on Informal Sector Statistics (Delhi Group), Report of the Fifth Meeting, New Delhi, 19–21 September.

Das, S. K., and R. A. Pande, 2000, "Better Deal for Beedi Workers", *Occupational Environment Health*, Vol. 109, No. 3, pp. 23–25.

de Soto, H., 2000, *The Mystery of Capital: Why Capitalism Triumphs in the West and Fails Everywhere Else*, New York, Basic Books.

Dikshit, R. P., and S. Kanhere, 2000, "Tobacco Habits and Risk of Lung, Oropharyngeal and Oral Cavity Cancer: A Population Based Case-control Study in Bhopal, India", *International Journal of Epidemiology*, Vol. 29, No. 8, pp. 609–614.

Economic Survey 2017–18, Ministry of Finance, New Delhi, Press Information Bureau, Government of India. https://timesofindia.indiatimes.com/realtime/Economic_Survey_2017_18.pdf Accessed 14th September, 2020.

Economic Survey 2015–16, Ministry of Finance, New Delhi, Government of India.

Fernandes, W., and G. Menon, 1987, *Tribal Women and Forest Economy*, New Delhi, Indian Social Institute.

Gender and Poverty in India, 1991, Washington (DC), A World Bank Country Study.

Ghosh, J. (ed), 2021, *Informal Women Workers in the Global South: Policies and Practices for the Formalisation of Women's Employment in Developing Economies*, New York, Routledge: Taylor & Francis Group.

Ghosh, J., 2002, "Globalization, Export-Oriented Employment for Women and Social Policy: A Case Study of India", *Social Scientist*, Vol. 30, No. 11/12 (November–December), pp. 17–60.

Gopal, M., 1999, "Disempowered Despite Wage Work: Women Workers in Beedi Industry", *Economic and Political Weekly*, Vol. 34, No. 16/17, pp. WS12–WS20.

Government of India, 1993, *Economic Reforms: Two Years After and the Tasks Ahead*. New Delhi: Ministry of Finance.

Hamilton, R., and M. Barrett (eds), 1986, *The Politics of Diversity: Feminism, Marxism and Nationalism*, London, Versa.

Hart, K., 1973, "Informal Income Opportunities and Urban Employment in Ghana", *Journal of Modern African Studies*, Vol. 11, No. 1, pp. 61–89. DOI: 10.1017/S0022278X00008089.

Human Development Report, 1999, New York, Oxford University Press.

Hussmanns, Ralf, 2001, *Defining and Measuring Informal Employment*, Bureau of Statistics. Geneva, Switzerland: International Labour Office, https://www.ilo.org/public/english/bureau/stat/download/papers/meas.pdf Accessed 25th March, 2020.

ILO, 2018, *Women and Men in the Informal Economy: A Statistical Picture*, 3rd ed. Geneva: International Labour Office. https://www.ilo.org/wcmsp5/groups/public/---dgreports/---dcomm/documents/publication/wcms_626831.pdf Accessed 6th June, 2022.

ILO, 2007, *ABC of Women Workers' Rights and Gender Equality*, 2nd edition, Geneva, International Labour Office.

ILO, 2002, *Women and Men in the Informal Economy: A Statistical Picture*, Geneva, ILO. Written by Marty Chen and Joann Vanek using multi-country data analyzed by Jacques Charmes and country studies by Debbie Budlender, Peter Buwembo, Nozipho Shabala, Jeemol Unni, Marge Guerrero, Rodrigo Negrete, Françoise Carré, and Joaquin Herranz, Jr. Geneva, ILO.

ILO, 1995, *Women Work More, But Are Still Paid Less*, ILO/95/22, Press release | 25 August 1995, https://www.ilo.org/global/about-the-ilo/newsroom/news/WCMS_008091/lang--en/index.htm Accessed 26th March, 2020.

ILO, 1972, *Employment, Incomes and Equality: A Strategy for Increasing Productive Employment in Kenya*, Geneva, International Labour Organization (ILO).

Irene, T., and M. B. Bramsen, 1976, *Women and World Development*, Washington (DC), Overseas Development Council.

Jayadevan, C. M., 1996, "Casualisation of Work-force in India: An Analysis of Spatial Variations", *The Indian Journal of Labour Economics*, Vol. 39, No. 4, pp. 763–784.

Jigging, J., 1986, "Gender Related Impacts and the Work of the International Agricultural Center", *Consultative Group on International Agricultural Research (CGIAR)*, The World Bank, No. 17, pp. 2–21. https://cgspace.cgiar.org/bitstream/handle/10947/582/study17.pdf Accessed 4th June, 2022.

Joshi, K., A M. Robins, P. Venu, and K. Mallikarjunaih, 2013, "An Epidemiological Study of Occupational Health Hazards Among Bidi Workers of Amarchinta, Andhra Pradesh", *Journal of Academic and Industrial Research*, Vol. 1, No. 9, pp. 561–564.

Kabeer, N., K. Milward, and R. Sudarshan, 2013, *Gender & Development*, Vol. 21, No. 2, pp. 249–263. DOI:10.1080/13552074.2013.802145

Kalpagam, U., 1994, *Labour and Gender, Survival in Urban India*, New Delhi, Sage Publications.

Kasturi, L., 1990, "Poverty, Migration and Women's Status", in Vina Majumdar (ed.), *Women Workers in India*, New Delhi, Chanakya Publications.

Kaur, S., H. K. Verma, J. Singh, S. K. Dash, and S. K. Kansal, 2017, "Knowledge Level of Women Dairy Farmers about Various Farming Practices in Border Area of Punjab", *Journal of Animal Research*, Vol. 7, No. 6, pp. 1051–1059.

Kumar Nakkeeran, S., and Bharathi, S., 2010, "A Study on Occupational Health Hazards Among Women Beedi Rollers in Tamilnadu, India", *International Journal of Current Research,* Vol. 11, No. 1 (5 December 2010), pp. 117–122.

Kuruvila, M., S. Mukhi, P. Kumar, G. Rao, K. S. Sridhar, and M. S. Kotian, 2002, "Occupational Dermatoses in Beedi Rollers", *Indian Journal Dermatol Venereol Leprol*, Vol. 68, pp. 10–12.

Luxton, M., and J. Corman, 2001, *Getting by in Hard Times: Gendered Labour at Home and on the Job.* Toronto, Canada, University of Toronto Press.

Mahimkar, M. B., and R. A. Bhisey, 1995, "Occupational Exposure to Bidi Tobacco Increases Chromosomal Aberrations in Tobacco Processors", *Mutation Research,* Vol. 334, pp. 39–144.

Maloney, W. F., 1999, "Does Informality Imply Segmentation in Urban Labour Markets? Evidence from Sectoral Transitions in Mexico", *World Bank Economic Review*, Vol. 13, No. 2, pp. 275–302. https://www.jstor.org/stable/3990099 Accessed 2nd June, 2022.

Mehta, A. K., 1999, "Globalization and the Third World", in R. M. Sethi (ed.), *Globalization, Culture and Women's Development*, New Delhi, Rawat Publications, pp. 55–76.

Mies, M., 1987, *India Women in Subsistence and Agricultural Labour*, New Delhi, Vistar Publications.

Mitra, M., 1987, "Women's Work: Gains Analysis of Women's Labour in Daily Production", in A. M. Singh and A. Kelles-Viitanen (eds), *Invisible Hands, Women in Home Based Production*, New Delhi, Sage Publication, pp. 109–143.

Mittal, S., M. Apoorva, and R. Rengappa, 2008, "Ocular Manifestations in Beedi Industry Workers", *Indian Journal of Opthalmology*, Vol. 56, pp. 319–322.

Mohandas, M., 1980, "Beedi Workers in Kerala: Conditions of Life and Work", *Economic and Political Weekly*, Vol. 15, No. 36, pp. 1517–1523.

National Agriculture Policy, 1998, Confederation of Indian Industry, Agro-Tech, Chandigarh.

NCEUS, 2007, *Report on Conditions of Work and Promotion of Livelihoods in the Unorganised Sector.* New Delhi: National Commission for Enterprises in the Unorganised Sector, https://msme.gov.in/sites/default/files/Condition_of_workers_sep_2007.pdf Accessed 13th September, 2020.

NSSO, 2014, 2011–12 Unit Level Data, 68th Round, Employment Unemployment Survey, National Sample Survey Office—Ministry of Statistics and Programme Implementation (MOSPI), New Delhi, Government of India (GOI).

NSO, 2019, 2017–2018 Unit Level Data, Periodic Labour Force Survey, National Statistical Office, NSSO Ministry of Statistics and Program Implementation, New Delhi, Government of India.

NSSO, 2019, 2017–2018 Unit Level Data, Periodic Labour Force Survey, NSSO Ministry of Statistics and Program Implementation, New Delhi, Government of India.

Omvedt, G., 1981, Effects *of Agricultural Development in the Status of Women*, Maharashtra.

Padmavathi, D., and V. L. Ramamohan, 1999, "Technological Dichotomy: The Story of Women Quarry Workers", in R. M. Sethi (ed.), *Globalization, Culture and Women's Development*, New Delhi, Rawat Publications, pp. 146–163.

Pande, R., 2019, "Globalisation and Women's Work in the Beedi Industry", *Studia Historiae Oeconomicae, The Journal of Adam Mickiewicz University*, Vol. 37, No. 1, pp. 191–221.

Pande, R., 2008, Women and Children Workers in the Old City of Hyderabad, India, *Intersections: Gender and Sexuality in Asia and the Pacific: Women Workers and Traders and the Globalisation Agenda in the Asian Context,* Guest editor Barbara Hartley, No. 17, June.

Pande, R., 2007, "Role of Women in Indian Agriculture—A Historical Perspective", in A. Sahida and L. K. Sami (ed.), *Indian Women in Development Perspective*, New Delhi, Anmol Publication, Pvt. Ltd., pp. 66–96.

Pande, R., 2006, "Gender Concerns in Rural Settlement-looking at Sustainable Agriculture", *Journal of Development Alternatives and Area study*, San Antonio, Texas, USA, Vol. 25, No. 3, September, pp. 63–86.

Pande, R., 2001, "The Social costs of Globalization : Restructuring Developing World Economies", *Journal of Asian Women's Studies*, Vol. 10, December, Kitakyushu Forum, Japan, pp. 1–14.

Pande, R., 2000, "Globalization and Women in the Agricultural Sector", *International Feminist Journal of Politics,* Vol. 2, No. 3, London: Rutledge, pp. 409–412.

Pande, R., 1999, "Structural Violence and Women's Health-work in the Beedi Industry in India", *Violence and Health, Global Symposium, Japan, Proceedings of W.H.O*, pp. 192–205.

Parker, J., J. Arrowsmith, and A. Boyd, 2017, "Papua New Guinea: Work and Care in a Subsistence Economy", in M. Baird, M. Ford, and E. Hill (eds), *Women, Work and Care in the Asia-Pacific*, Sydney, Routledge, pp. 245–259.

Patel, R. K., 1993, "Present Status and Promise of Dairying in India", *Indian Dairyman*, Vol. 45, No. 7, pp. 276–308.

Piore, M. and C. Sabel, 1984, *The Second Industrial Divide*, New York, Basic Books.

Portes, A., M. Castells, and L. A. Benton (eds.), 1989. *The Informal Economy: Studies in Advanced and Less Developed Countries*, Baltimore (MD), John Hopkins University Press.

Ranjitsingh, A. J. A., and C. Padmalatha, 1995, "Occupational Illness of Beedi Rollers in South India", *Environment Economics,* Vol. 13, No. 4, pp. 875–887.

Rao, E. K., 2006, "Role of Women in Agriculture: A Micro Level Study", *Journal of Global Economy*, Mumbai, India: Research Centre for Social Sciences, Vol. 2, No. 2, pp. 107–118, June.

Rao, R., and S. Hussain, 1987, "Invisible Hands: Women in Home Based Production in the Garments Export Industry in Delhi", in A. M. Singh and A. Kelles-Viitanen (eds), *Invisible Hands, Women in Home Based Production*, New Delhi, Sage Publication, pp. 51–67.

Report on Jobs in the Informal Sector and Informal Job Conditions (2013–2014), Volume IV, Government of India, Ministry of Labour & Employment, Labour Bureau Chandigarh.

Robinson, W. I., and J. Harris, 2000, "Towards a Global Ruling Class? Globalization and the Transnational Capitalist Class", *Science & Society*, Vol. 64, No. 1 (Spring), pp. 11–54.

Rodrik, D., 1997, *Has Globalization Gone Too Far*? Washington (DC), Institute for International Economics.

Saradamoni, K., 1987, "Labor, Land and Rice Production: Women's Involvement in Three States", *Economic and Political Weekly*, Vol. 17, No. 52, pp. ws2–ws6.

Savara, M., 1986, *Changing Trends in Women's Employment—A Case Study of the Textile in Bombay*, Bombay, Himalayan Publishing House.

Seccombe, Wally, 1992, *A Millennium of Family Change: Feudalism to Capitalism in Northern Europe*, London, Versao.

Sethuraman, S. V., 1976, "The Urban Informal Sector: Concept, Measurement and Policy", *International Labour Review*, Vol. 114, No. 1, p. 69.

Shatrugna, V., N. Soundarajan, P. Sundaraiah, and L. Raman, 1990, "Backpain, the Feminine Affliction", *Economic and Political Weekly*, Vol. 25, No. 17, WS2–WS6. http://www.jstor.org/stable/4396219.

Shiva, V., 1991, *The Violence of the Green Revolution: Ecological Degradation and Political Conflict in Punjab*, New Delhi, Zed Books.

Shram Shakti, 1988, *Report of the National Commission on Self-Employed Women and Women in the Informal Sector*, New Delhi.

Singh, A. M., and A. Kelles Viitanen (eds), 1987, *Invisible Hands, Women in Home Based Production*, New Delhi, Sage Publication.

Standing, G., 1999, *Global Labour Flexibility: Seeking Distributive Justice*, New York, St. Martin's Press.

Swami, S., A. N. Suryakar, and R. V. Katkam, 1995, "Absorption of Nicotine Induces Oxidative Stress among Beedi Workers", *Toxicology Letters*, Vol. 18, No. 2, pp. 259–265.

Tanwar, R., 1999, "Women and Falling Incomes: The Impact of Cash Economy in Rural India", in R. M. Sethi (ed.), *Globalization, Culture and Women's Development*, New Delhi, Rawat Publications, pp. 129–145.

Thakur, D., and M. Chandar, 2006, "Gender Based Differential Access to Information among Livestock Owners and Its Impact on House Hold Milk Production in Kangra District of Himachal Pradesh", *Indian Journal of Dairy Science*, Vol. 59, No. 6, pp. 401–404.

The Domestic Workers' Welfare & Social Security Act, 2010, http://bslsa.bih.nic.in/PDF/acts16/domestic_worker_welfare_and_social_security_act_2010.pdf Accessed 25th March, 2020.

The India Economic Survey, 2015/2016, https://www.thehinducentre.com/resources/article8285564.ece Accessed 13th September, 2020.

The Unorganised Workers' Social Security Act, 2008, Act No. 33 of December 30th, 2008, http://legislative.gov.in/sites/default/files/A2008-33.pdf Accessed 20th January, 2020.

Tokman, V., 1978, "An Exploration into the Nature of the Informal-Formal Sector Relationship" in Saha, D., Decent Work for the Street Vendors in Mumbai, India—A Distant vision, *World Development*, Vol. 14, No. 2, pp. 229–250.

Towards Equality, 1974, Report on the Status of Women, New Delhi, Government of India.

Tripathi, R., 2018, "Unorganised Sector in India", *International Journal of Academic Research and Development*, Vol. 3, No. 1, pp. 261–266.

Umadevi, B., M. Swarna, P. Padmavathi, A. Jyothi, and P. P. Reddy, 2003, "Cytogenetic Effects in Workers Occupationally Exposed to Tobacco Dust", *Genetic Toxicology and Environmental Mutagenesis*, Vol. 535, No. 2, pp. 147–154.

UNICEF, 1989, *The Invisible Adjustment – Poor Women and the Economic Crisis*, Santiago, UNICEF.

4

CHILD WORK AND CHILD LABOUR

The World Day against Child Labor was established in 2002 by the International Labour Organization (ILO), to draw attention to the global scope of child labour and the actions and efforts required to eradicate it. More than a million people from around the world participate in the annual World Day on 12 June in an effort to highlight the plight of child labourers as well as the steps that can be taken to improve their lives. When they decided to adopt the Sustainable Development Goals (SDGs) in 2015, the leaders of the world reaffirmed their commitment to putting an end to the use of child labour. The goal on decent work and economic growth (SDG 8) also provides for the complete elimination of any and all forms of child labour. This goal is part of the target 8.7, and it entails taking immediate and effective steps to eradicate forced labour, put an end to modern slavery and human trafficking, secure the prohibition and elimination of the worst forms of child labour, including the recruitment and use of child soldiers, and, by the year 2025, put an end to all forms of child labour.

The use of children as labourers in today's Third World is a socially accepted but morally reprehensible practice. While the process of economic development results in child labour becoming an important source of capital accumulation, it is also an integral part of developing countries that are associated with poverty and deprivation. Developing countries are characterised by poverty and deprivation. It is difficult to maintain a family on the income of the parents in communities that belong to lower income groups in developing countries. This is especially true if the parents are daily-rated, piece-rated, casual, or contractual labourers without any stable avenue of durable employment. In situations like these, the income of the working child, which was initially considered to be of low value, takes on a much greater significance. Child labour in the beedi industry is a very common sight because the women here are from lower incomes and find it difficult to make ends meet unless the children also contribute in making the beedis.

DOI: 10.4324/9781003317944-5

Child labour refers to children who are growing up too soon, working long hours for low pay in conditions that are harmful to their health and development, being separated from their families, and being deprived of meaningful education and training opportunities that would allow them to have a better future. According to the ILO's 2016 Globe Report on Child Labour, there are over 265 million working children in the world, accounting for nearly 17% of the global child population (ILO, 2013).

Though India has seen a drastic reduction in child labourers in the last two decades, yet child labour continues to be a reality. According to a Campaign Against Child Labour (CAC) study, India has 1,26,66,377 child labourers of which UP has 19,27,997 child labourers (Save the children, 2016). The five states that employ the most children in India include: Bihar, Uttar Pradesh, Rajasthan, Madhya Pradesh, and Maharashtra. Here, more over half of India's total child labour population is employed. Uttar Pradesh is India's largest child labour hotspot, accounting for over 20% of the country's child labourers.

Throughout human history, child labour has occurred in various ways in every civilisation. Children have always participated in, and continue to participate in, those economic activities that are necessary for the community to which they belong to survive, to a greater or lesser amount throughout every type of human history (Mendelievich, 1979). Child labour is not a new phenomenon in our times, according to a report by the Government of India's Committee on Child Labour from 1979. It has existed in some form or another throughout history. Parents and other family members used to enlist the aid of children in their daily routines and household chores. It also gives them the opportunity to learn a trade, which will eventually provide them with a source of income (Report, Committee on Child Labour, 1979).

Children are the most readily exploited lot all labour groups. Their low cost gives to the employers a potential competitive advantage, both in the domestic and export market. Children face a permanent disadvantage in the labour market. The drift to urban areas in the early stages of industrialisation is usually associated with high unemployment which forces many families and their children to search out a living in marginal and usual forms of employment.

In the context of child labour, the terms work, labour, and child need to be understood. The terms "work" and "labour" have been used interchangeably and synonymously, although some critic see a semantic difference that has existed throughout. Differentiating work and labour is determined by a particular social context, the quality of the various interactions and dynamics present in the production process. Those elements that make labour and work apparently synonymous are:

- Both work and labour are organised human responses to design ways of securing resources and satisfying human needs for subsistence.

- The process involves an exchange between human beings and the "natural" world.
- Both work and labour require human effort – an exercise of body and mind (UNICEF, 1986).

Distinguishing child labour and child work

The difference between work and labour can be found by conducting a comprehensive analysis of the setting in which these processes are carried out, paying close attention to both the nature of the connections that are present and the conditions under which they are carried out. The term "work" has been replaced by "labour" due to significant shifts in sociopolitical structures, scientific understanding, and technological advancements that have occurred throughout history. The contrast between the child who is working and the child who is labouring can be better understood with the help of the distinction between the concepts of work and labour. Many children would enjoy having the opportunity to work, provided that it is structured and phased appropriately. Work that a child does that does not interfere with their ability to participate in other activities important to their development, such as leisure, play, or education, is not considered child labour. Children benefit both physically and mentally from the kind of work that is being done here. However, the most extreme forms of child labour, such as children working in slave-like conditions in factories and mines, using dangerous chemicals in pesticide-soaked fields, being imprisoned in homes as domestic servants, working as prostitutes, or serving in guerrilla armies, need to be questioned and reexamined. These forms of child labour have to be addressed head-on. Thus, when it poses a risk to the children's health or development, work performed by children is considered to be child labour. Concern should be directed towards child labour, and not work done by children, in this context (UNICEF, 1986).

Additionally, the following circumstances are outlined in the report by UNICEF as conditions under which child labour can be considered exploitative. This includes starting a full-time job at an excessively young age when one is still young. This historically took place in Europe during the early stages of industrialisation, when children as young as nine, eight, or even five years old began working in factories. Children are forced into labour on a regular basis in a great number of developing countries. When children are forced to work for long periods of time and are unable to attend school, or even when they do have access to schooling but are unable to make the most of it due to exhaustion or a lack of time, this is another form of child labour that can be considered exploitative. There are some instances in which children work for 12–16 hours per day.

Sometimes work resulting in excessive physical, social, and psychological strains upon the child as in the case of sexual exploitation in prostitution and pornography, work in sweatshops, as well as such dangerous work as military service and mining is also exploitative. The work and life of a child in the streets is unhealthy and dangerous. Often children are paid inadequate remuneration for working outside of the family as in the case of child workers in carpet weaving who are paid a pittance is also exploitative. Too much responsibility too early as in the domestic situation where children under ten years may have to look after young brothers and sisters for a whole day, thereby preventing school attendance. Work hinders a child's psychological and social development, such as the tedious and repetitive labour associated with industries such as handicrafts. Work lowers a child's self-esteem, such as bonded labour and prostitution, and in a less severe situation, negative perceptions of street children (UNICEF, 1986).

As a result, child labour is defined as the employment of children in lucrative occupations or as a meaningful contribution to the family's revenue. It is both an economic and a social blight since it puts people's health at risk and denies them the opportunity to grow physically and mentally. Child labour is described as both an "economic practice" and a "social evil", according to Sri. V.V. Giri, who served as President of India previously. First, it should be considered an economic practice. Second, it should be considered a social evil. In the first instance, it referred to situations in which children were used in productive occupations with the intention of contributing more money to their families. Regarding the second context, when analysing the characteristics and dimensions of social evil and when discussing the issue of child labour, it is necessary to take into account the nature of the work that the children are doing, the risks to which they are exposed, and the opportunities for growth that they have been denied (Giri, in Mehat and Jaswal, 1996: 13).

In every country either to a greater or lesser extent, in every type of society children have taken part in domestic economic and in other economic activities which are necessary for the family as well as the group to which they belong and to survive. However, child labour is a social as well as an economic problem which deprives children of harmonious physical and mental development. This term not only applies to children working in industries, but also to them who are working in different activities in unorganised, and non-industrial sector as well.

We are all aware the concept of childhood was historicised by Philippe Aries classic, "Centuries of childhood", using the sources like pictures, school attendance sheet, dolls, and miscellaneous writings. Aries' analyses dress, games, art, sexual behaviour, educational policies, social and economic activities, all within the context of family and childhood. To him children are in some way distinguished from adults and that entails more specific ideas about childhood's distinctiveness from adulthood. Attitudes towards children began to change in the 16th and 17th centuries under the impact of a rapidly changing socio-cultural environment, which required that children be educated/trained for protracted periods and under protected conditions (Aries, 1962). According to Aries, "there was no place for childhood in the medieval world" (Jenkes, 1982: 31). In medieval times in the 16th and 17th centuries, the child or infant of the upper strata dressed in special dress and thereby distinguished from adults. By the 18th century, everything to do with children's health and education had become established as a concern worthy of serious attention. Today, childhood in industrialised countries is problematic, protracted ill-designed, and the centre of vehement claims and counter-claims concerning "what is best for the child". This modern conception of childhood sustained and invented by adults has two features. First, a rigid age hierarchy separates children from adults. The institutionalisation of children is marked by special dress, games, and language and literature. Second, there is a myth of childhood innocence where the child must be both happy and separated from the corrupt adult world. This becomes expressed in the child-centred family, which is determined materially if in no other way, to make these the best years of life (Fyfe, 1989: 3).

Shulamith, however, has challenged Aries' view on the absence of childhood in the European Middle Ages. She points out the presence of the idea of childhood in medieval Europe and how the medieval notion of childhood was different from modern notion of childhood. She has taken example from both noble and peasant class to trace out their condition during childhood. Parents were concerned about their children but for a limited period of time (Shahar, 1990). Even Linda A. Pollock challenges the method of Aries' interpretation of medieval paintings regarding the idea of childhood during that time. She argues that Aries deduces from paintings that adults became increasingly aware of children through the centuries. There are difficulties with his interpretation. And she questions the notion as to how far can painters representing reality. She states that there must have been technical improvements through the centuries and painters learnt how to paint in three dimensions and also how to depict such things as the proportions of a child's body. The different types of childhood portrayed in paintings through the centuries may have more to do with changes in art rather than changes in the way children were seen (Pollock, 1983: 46–47). Aries's greatest contribution, however, is his insistence on the historicity of childhood: that childhood was not an essential condition, a constant across time, but something that changed – or, if childhood itself, bound by biologically and psychologically determined phases of development, is constant, then the understanding of it differed, as did the way it was experienced by both adults and children. He also was the one who first put forward the preposition that childhood is a modern Western invention.

These adult modes and prescriptions have been codified into international standards expressed in declarations and covenants. These date back to the early part of this century and express a productive view of childhood. In such instruments, the child cannot by definition be a worker in the formal economy, but requires a protracted period of socialisation in which schooling becomes the acceptable, form of "work" for the child.

The process of purchase and use the child labour is systematically differentiated from the labour power of the adult working for the capitalist enterprise. The reason for this is that the child remuneration is much lower than that of the adults. There is a difference in the labour process too for the children are seen as trainers, apprentices, helpers, mates, casual, or temporary labourers subject to the authority of the adult worker as well as the owner of the enterprise (Elson, 1982).

According to the ILO, 152 million children – 64 million girls and 88 million boys – are involved in child labour around the world, accounting for about one-tenth of all children. Nearly half of all children working – 73 million youngsters in total – are doing dangerous employment that jeopardises their health, safety, and moral development. There are 218 million children in employment, which includes both child labour and allowed kinds of employment for youngsters of legal working age (ILO, 2017: 11). Besides this there are many children who work in the homes and also attend school simultaneously and hence are not reported as economically active. According to Prof. Bondhiba, who was asked to produce the first report on child labour for the United Nations, nearly 90% of working children are found in the developing world (Bondhiba, 1982: 3). Bondhiba estimated that 145 million children worked worldwide but admitted that it is an approximate estimate. He states that in Nepal, there has been a steady rise over the last 30 years in the protection of children aged between 10 and 14 years engaged in work: from 28% in 1952–1954 to 50% in 1971, and to 58% in 1981 (Bondhiba, 1982: 3).

Even if the majority of working children are still found in rural regions, expanding urbanisation is the cause of growing concern on a global scale because it is linked to employment that is done outside of the setting of the family. The success of early measures to fight child labour and of later interventions supporting a successful transition to respectable work depends on taking gender issues into consideration. Due to issues including early marriage, the pressures of domestic duties within their own homes, and traditional roles, girl children have particular challenges in exercising their rights to education and protection from child labour. This emphasises the imperative need for all-encompassing educational initiatives, such as girl-friendly schools that are sensitive to and supportive of the particular educational problems faced by young girls. Additionally, it advocates for focused interventions to address the various cultural, social, and economic issues that make female children particularly susceptible to certain forms of child labour, such as domestic work and commercial sexual exploitation. In many areas, female kids face less employment choices and more challenges getting into quality jobs. In comparison to their male counterparts, they are frequently restricted to a smaller variety of employment options. Because of societal and familial expectations that force young women to leave their jobs after getting married or having their first child, their career paths may be severely constrained. The disadvantageous status of young women in the labour market highlights the necessity for ongoing efforts to ensure equitable opportunities and treatment of young men and women in both school and the workforce (ILO, 2015: 64).

Child labour in India

In India, nearly 80% of children under the age of 14 who are involved in child labour live in rural areas. Most of these children are employed in agriculture and related occupations, according to the 2011 Census. This is as per the global trend, which shows that this sector accounts for 71% of all child labour. According to the 2011 Census, 61.7% children aged 5–14 worked as agricultural labourers and farmers in India. This number was definitely less than the 77.5% shown in the 2001 Census. The total number of child labourers was projected to be around 1.3 crores (marginal and main workers combined) (Rawat, 2019). In the Indian context, there are various reasons for the existence of child labour. To many, the child's earnings are a much-needed supplement to the total family income (Bromley et al., 1979: 52). In many families where death and accident has incapacitated the family members, the child earnings are the mainstay for the family's survival. It is also assumed that by learning a trade, a child achieves proficiency at an early age. From the employer's perspective, child employment is cost efficient as maximum output is obtained at minimum input. This they try to hide under the guise of the need for nimble fingers of the children. According to these employers, many industries like the carpet and weaving industries in Kashmir and Assam would collapse in the absence of the availability of nimble fingers of little children. The same is said about beedi Industry in India. Those who argue that the employment of children increases the earnings of the family and keeps the children off the streets only reflect the callousness of a free enterprise system where the earnings of family and the conservation human resources are not the responsibility of an individual employer.

In point of fact, from a social and economic point of view, child labour may very well be a workable alternative for all of the children who are forced to work under horrible conditions at this time. This is because child labour can be a source of income. It is of the utmost importance to provide work environments that are not exploitative to children and which support the growth of children. This is of paramount importance in the effort to alleviate the difficulties that face children and their relatives. The alternate strategy is based on the distinction that was made earlier between work and labour. The employment of children and the extraction of their productivity for the purpose of economic benefit by another party is known as child labour. This practice has a negative impact on the mental and physical development of the child.

A significant number of these children find work in businesses such as carpeting, beedi, matches, fireworks, glass, and jewellery. Other prominent industries that make use of child labour include the diamond polishing business in Surat and the precious stone industry in Moradabad in India. In addition to these children, children make up a significant component of the workforce in urban domestic service positions. Additionally, children are employed in the sales industry as vendors, shoe shine boys, and newspaper vendors. They also contribute to the labour force in other industries, including as building and construction, coolies, tea gardens, transportation, stone and quarry operations, and other industries. In addition to this, they help with the care of animals, engage in fishing, and labour on plantations, where they assist with planting, weeding, and harvesting.

The vast majority of these children find employment, contrary to popular belief, in the unorganised labour market rather than the organised labour market. The predicament that these children are in consistently boggles the mind. Small children who are very malnourished are forced to work for a pittance around the clock, seven days a week. They labour in environments where the need of safety precautions is minimised and welfare arrangements are never made. They operate in close proximity to furnaces and engage in potentially hazardous activities such as operating a variety of cutting and piercing equipment. They typically do not have access to even the most fundamental amenities, such as toilets, medical assistance, or clean drinking water. Child labour puts children in danger of major health problems and prevents them from reaching their full physical and mental potential. It also robs them of their childhoods.

It is fair to emphasise here that one of the goals of the 1986 Child Labor Prohibition and Regulation Act was to safeguard youngsters from dangerous and exploratory jobs. The statutory definition of child labour differs across several acts with diverse goals; thus, this act aims to achieve uniformity in the definition of the child in the associated legislation (The Child Labour, Prohibition and Regulation Act, 1986). The ILO conference report from Amsterdam in 1984, in which virtually all nations participated, bears witness to the wider realisation and acceptance of child abuse as a global problem of frightening proportions. Children working in "Dhabas", (small eateries), begging on the streets, and picking up trash or rags in the streets are all mentioned in this report. Long-term domestic workers who work alongside their parents or employers in industries including carpet and handloom weaving, printing presses, and carpentry face several physical and emotional risks due to their exposure to poor ventilation and filthy working conditions. As a result, their physical and mental development is hindered, which also has an impact on their eyesight. This eventually causes dilatation, headaches, joint discomfort, chronic diseases like tuberculosis. Some of the young workers in the chemical industry also suffer from skin conditions and pick up undesirable behaviours including stealing, stumbling, smoking, and drinking, among others (ILO, 1984: 8).

Due to the social changes they experience, the issue is particularly severe in developing nations. In developing nations, the nature of children's labour has undergone fundamental changes as a result of industrialisation and urbanisation. India exhibits the distinctive characteristics of child labour as a developing nation. Rural and urban places have different varieties of it. Farm work, which makes up 70% of the labour force in rural areas' agricultural sector, is one type of child labour there (Rai, 1986). For example, child labour can be seen in the match and fire industry of Sivakasi in Tamil Nadu, the glass industry of

Firozabad in Uttar Pradesh, the lock industry of Aligarh in Uttar Pradesh, the carpet industry of Jammu and Kashmir and Uttar Pradesh, the beedi industry of Andhra Pradesh and Madhya Pradesh, the pottery industry of Khurja in Uttar Pradesh, the coir industry of Kerala, the zari industry of Banaras, and the brick kiln industry of West Bengal (Rai, 1986: 9).

The effects of child labour on the child

Any unfavourable effect that work has on children is an inevitable consequence of the actual circumstances surrounding their job. Employing children is primarily justified from the perspective of the business owner from the point of view of maximising profits; this justifies the lower costs associated with employing youngsters. On the other hand, child labour is not completely devoid of any redeeming qualities; this is because there are some aspects that are shared by both the labour process and the working process. However, the potential drawbacks of employing children far outweigh any potential benefits of doing so. The effects of child labour on children vary widely depending on a number of factors including the kid's age, gender, geographic region, and the sort of work being performed by the child.

Studies show that in urban areas, children are exploited more and undergo greater privations than their counterparts in the rural sectors (Mendelievich, 1979: 25). With increasing mechanisation of agricultural methods, many farmhands are displaced and forced to move with their families to nearby cities in search of a better life; this phenomenon augments the number of children in the urban labour force. Generally, it is found that the child employed in a family undertaking, whether in agriculture or industry, is exploited less than the wage earning child. This is because – in terms of operating independently, serving and earning a wage, hours of work, kind of work, and so on, there is a difference between the self-employed child and wage-earning child in service for an employer. Children who are self-employed experience a greater degree of freedom than those children who labour for an employer. They are, however, only relatively free, for they are constantly sought after and harassed by financial depends like family. For instance, self-employed children have regular income patterns. Since most of these children are engaged in some form of street trading, their incomes are dependent on several factors: location of their trade, season of the year, time of the month, the demand for the goods on sale, the purchasing power at the disposal of the buyer, percentage of the projects that the children allowed to retain if they are working for a third party, and various other related factors.

Because the employer makes decisions on employment conditions on an arbitrary and unilateral basis, the manner in which the children are treated and the conditions under which they labour are typically depending on the whims and fancies of the employer. In many instances, there is not even a formal contract of work that protects the protection of the child; the employer employs and fires at will. This is a problem because official employment contracts are supposed to safeguard employees. Children are employed anywhere from six to seven days a week in a variety of industries, and those working in the domestic service industry have virtually no breaks other than the time they spend sleeping at night (Menon, 1979).

The degree of disparity between various forms of compensation is shockingly high. Since the income of the family is regarded as a unitary entity, it is quite common for children who work for family businesses to not receive any compensation for the costs they incur as a result of their labour. This is also the case when families are employed by third parties; the children take part in the employment, but the family receives the total earnings, and the children are deprived of enjoying what may only be a token of the fruit of their labours as a result of this arrangement. The following passage does the best of describing the actual working conditions those children were subjected to.

> Long hours of labour, late-night shifts, constant standing or sitting, or usage of a single set of muscles, and a focus on the finer neuromuscular coordinators are all factors that can cause nerve strain. Unsuitable occupations that put the developing child at risk for certain deformities and diseases include being confined indoors in noisy factories and dusty trades; carrying heavy loads under the arm or lifting heavy weights; pressure of speed in the performance of simple mechanical acts; contact with industrial poisons; and exposure to inclement weather.
>
> *(Encyclopedia of Social Sciences, Vol. III, 197: 412–424)*

Child labour in the unorganised sectors

Most of the child labour is found in the unorganised sector or the informal sector, including restaurants, tailor shops domestic services, street vending, car parks, garbage collecting, building construction, machine tools, and repair shops all under dehumanising employment conditions. The milieu of these children outside their job environments contribute to the variety of factors that influence their growth and development. Their housing conditions call for considerable improvement. They often live in decrepit, squalid conditions, with no sanitary installation. The conditions are also far more pronounced in the urban centres. It is not unusual for nine to ten members huddling together in one room. In general, the walls also made of beaten tin sheets and the roof of thatched palm leaves. One only has to speculate on the quality of human relationships under such cramped circumstances. In many instances, the father is usually unemployed or if employed, only seasonally so. Many fathers are also alcoholics and gamblers. The mother may or may not be employed, and there are several children in the house including toddlers and infants, who demanded her undivided attention. The house is also a refuge for the many relatives who come from the rural areas in search of a better life. All the family members' earnings combined is still insufficient to ensure three square meals a day for all. Invertible, the child's growth and development is bound to be affected by such an environment.

The nature of the urban working children is very complex particularly in India for these urban working children are found in unorganised manufacturing sector and in "marginal occupations on the street". Unfortunately both these areas have been constantly neglected by the social scientists and other researches interested in this problem. In fact, many aspects of the problem of urban working children in India have not been explored and therefore not known. However, while analysing the nature of the problem of urban child labour in India, different kinds of childhood works may be kept in mind, such as domestic work, non-domestic work, non-monetary work, bonded labour, wage labour, marginal economic activities, schooling, recreation and leisure, and productive activities (Rodyers and Standings, 1981).

Out of the above activities, children in urban areas of India are mostly found performing domestic wage labour and other productive and income generation activities. The problem of child-wage labour in the unorganised urban industrial sector and in the service sector is also immense. Children work in the most adverse working conditions is subjected to physical and mental torture and is super-exploited. However, child-wage labour in urban India can be analysed in term of the following: family or individual bases, mode of payment, time-rated or piece-rated work within a training component or regular or casual, legal or illegal work, and work compatible with schooling.

Nature and magnitude of the problem

Before going into the magnitude of the problem of urban working children in India, it is pertinent to glance over the problems of poverty and expansion of the slum sector (i.e., the urban ghetto) because the problem of working children is positively correlated with these problems. The actual magnitude of the problem of child labour, particularly urban working children (which includes street children) is not known. Several factors explain this fact. First, the varying nature of work done by urban children is partly responsible for this since work of a large section of urban children – such as street children, children engaged in part-time and other casual occupations – cannot be documented, at least exhaustively.

Second, the definition of child labour varies from investigator to investigator, and this creates a practical problem while collecting data on child labour. Moreover, the definitions of "employment" and "unemployment" vary between researchers, thereby sometimes underestimating the actual figure on child labour. Third, some part of the problem of child labour such as the psychological stress and future benefits foregone by them cannot be quantifiable, or represented throughout quantitative data. Thus, whatever data on the phenomenon of child labour are available in India, they are just guess estimates.

Child labour is more in unorganised sector with in the age group of 5–14 years. The unorganised sector includes tea shops, vendors, small hostels and restaurants, construction work, stone breaking, brick kiln, handicrafts, slate industry, cottage, spinning and weaving, road-side motor garages, and beedi making. Though a large number of children are employed in these set ups, it is difficult to measure the extent of problem because so far accurate statistics are not made. The identification and classification of this phenomenon is problematic because of its informal character. Even though the data is collected by various agencies such as voluntary organisations, it does not reflect the ground reality of the problem. The state is to see that the tender-aged children are not abused, and the children are given opportunities and facilities to develop their personalities in a healthy manner with protection against exploitation and child abuse. In spite of the fact that the state has been working very hard over the past seven decades to plan welfare programmes, pass legislation, and take administrative action, the majority of children in India continue to be in a state of anxiety and unrest. The employment of children is governed by a number of pieces of legislation, including the Employment of Children Act of 1938, the Employment of Children (Prohibition and Regulation Act of 1986, the Factories Act of 1948, the Mines Act of 1952, the Plantation Act of 1951, and the Shops and Commercial Establishment Acts of various states. These pieces of legislation make up the scope of child labour legislation, which regulates the employment of children. However, these have not been successful in gaining any ground so far.

The Child Labour Act was revised in 2016 to classify children over 14 years of age and up to 18 years of age as "adolescents". The amendment allowed the employment of teenage kids in non-hazardous industries. The United Nations said the move would disadvantage tribal and lower caste children after the amendments were passed in the Rajya Sabha. UNICEF said that among tribal and lower caste groups, child labour rates are highest at almost 7% and 4%, respectively. The amendments would adversely affect oppressed and disadvantaged communities.

Reasons for increasing incidence of child labour in India

There are various reasons as to why there is an increase in the child labour in India. The process of restructuring the economy in favour of the informal manufacturing and service sectors is important. Besides this, the uneven nature of the growth of the Indian economy (i.e. – simultaneous expansion of the urban industrial sector and under development of the vast agricultural sector) has accentuated the process of rural-urban migration. With the low labour absorption capacity of the urban industrial sector, the high rate of rural-urban migration has built up a large pool of poverty-ridden "mass of people" and "marginalised" labour in urban India, which in turn has produced a future generation of prospective citizens caught in "vicious circle" of poverty, deprive of their childhood. These children are found working in the most adverse circumstances: on the streets in the small manufacturing units, in households, in home-based manufacturing units, in sweets shops, in the informal service sector, to make ends meet. It can be stated that poverty, ignorance, illiteracy of parents, lack of any trade union activity among children and the profit motive of the employer, the general apathy of the masses, inadequate legislation, and their defective implementation are the reasons for the continuation of child labour.

In spite of the fact that the state has taken action over the past seven decades by way of planning welfare programmes, passing legislation, and taking administrative action, the vast majority of Indian children are still forced to work, and their lives continue to be fraught with anxiety and unrest. The employment of children is governed by a number of pieces of legislation, including the Employment of Children Act of 1938, the Employment of Children Prohibition and Regulation Act of 1986, the Factories Act of 1948, the Mines Act of 1952, the Plantation Act of 1951, and the Shops and Commercial Establishment Acts of various states. These pieces of legislation make up the scope of child labour legislation, which regulates the employment of children. However, these have not been successful in gaining any ground so far. In 2016, the Child Labor Act was updated to include a provision that defines "adolescents" as children who are between the ages of 14 and 18. The amendments would have a negative impact on communities that are already oppressed and disadvantaged.

Strategies for elimination of child labour

Policy makers and social scientists have historically advocated for either the complete elimination of child labour or an improvement in the working conditions of children who are employed in labour-intensive industries. The realities on the ground have frequently resulted in the awkward combination of two different approaches, one emphasising the amelioration of the conditions of child labour and the other emphasising the abolition of child labour. However, as of late, UNICEF has taken the position that the eradication of child labour is not something that can be negotiated, and that the end of child labour must occur even before the end of poverty. This comes at a time when a country like India is being forced to accept structural adjustment, which weakens its position and especially the positions of its poor, particularly women. The process of structural adjustment must be given a more humanistic appearance. Education is regarded by UNICEF as the most effective strategy for preventing and putting an end to the practice of child labour. However, UNICEF also discusses other possible solutions, including the generation of income, the payment of minimum wages, the empowerment of women, the enforcement of laws, and the convergence of social services on families that have been identified as having children who work.

References

Aries, P., 1962, *Centuries of Childhood: A Social History of Family Life*, trans. R. Baldick, New York, Random House.

Bondhiba, 1982, as quoted in Ale Fyfe, 1989, *Child Labour*, Cambridge, Cambridge University Press.
Bromley, R. and C. Gerry (ed.), 1979, *Casual Work and Poverty in Third World Cities*, New York, Chichester, John Wiley.
Census, 2011, Census data, Office of the Registrar General & Census Commissioner, India Ministry of Home Affairs, Government of India, https://censusindia.gov.in/2011census/B-series/B-Series-01.html
Elson, D., 1982, "Differentiation of Children's Labour in the Capitalist Labour Market", *Development and Change, Wiley Online Library,* International Institute of Social Studies, The Hague. https://doi.org/10.1111/j.1467-7660.1982.tb00132.x
Encyclopaedia of Social Sciences, 1979, Ministry of Labour Report on Child Labour, p. 3.
Fyfe, A., 1989, *Child Labour*, Cambridge, Cambridge University Press.
Giri, V. V., 1996, as quoted in P. L. Mehta, S. S. Jaswal, *Child Labour and The Law*, New Delhi, Deep and Deep Publications.
ILO, 2017, *Global Estimates of Child Labour: Results and Trends, 2012–2016*, Geneva, International Labour Office.
ILO, 2015, *World Report on Child Labour, Paving the Way to Decent Work for Young People*, Geneva, International Labour Office.
ILO, 2013, ILO-IPEC, *Yacouba Diallo, Alex Etienne and Farhad Mehran, Global Child Labour Trends 2008 to 2012. ILO International Programme on the Elimination of Child Labour (IPEC).* Geneva, International Labour Office.
ILO, 1984, International Labour Organisation, *Towards an Action Programme on Child Labour,* Technical Commission.
Jenkes, C., 1982, *The Sociology of Childhood*, London, Batsford.
Mendelievich, E., 1979, "Child Labour at Work", *International labour Review,* Vol. 118, No. 5, September–October. Geneva, International Labour Organization, pp. 557–568.
Menon, S., 1979, "'Sivakasi'—The Little Japan of India", *The Time of India*, New Delhi, 7th October.
Pollock, L. A., 1983, *Forgotten Children: Parent-Child Relations from 1500 to 1900,* Cambridge, Cambridge University Press.
Rai, U., 1986, "Controversy Hounds Child Labour", *The Times of India*, August 9th.
Rawat, M., 2019, "Child Labour in India: Violators Go Scot-free as Only 25% Cases Reach Conviction", *India Today*, 12th June.
Report. Committee on Child labour, 1979, New Delhi, Government of India.
Rodyers, G., and G. Standings, 1981, "Economic Roles of Children in Low Income Countries", *International Labour Review,* Vol. 120, I, January–February.
Save the Children, 2016, *Statistics of Child Labour in India State Wise*, https://www.savethechildren.in/education-for-all/?utm_source=Website&utm_medium=popup&utm_campaign=education_popup&utm_term=education&utm_content=website_popup_education Accessed 13th June, 2022.
Shahar, S., 1990, *Childhood in the Middle Ages,* London, Routledge.
The Child Labour (Prohibition and Regulation) Act, 1986, https://labour.gov.in/sites/default/files/act_3.pdf Accessed 27th March, 2020.
UNICEF, 1986, *The Report on Child Labour*, United Nations Organisation.

5

ANTI-TOBACCO HISTORY AND CONTROL

The beedi-making women live in a world where her livelihood is often at risk due to the consciousness related to health and the anti-tobacco stirs that have become a normal part of her day-to-day world. As the world becomes more conscious on health-related issues, it is this woman's livelihood that is at the cross roads. However, this crisis is not a new one and has a long history. There is a general understanding that smoking harms a person and leads to many diseases for the lungs get affected, and it impacts the overall health of a person who smokes.

Tobacco use is responsible for the deaths of more than 8 million people around the world each year, making it one of the most significant threats to public health in the history of the world. It is estimated that heavy cigarette use is responsible for approximately 7 million of these deaths, while passive smoking by non-smokers is responsible for approximately 1.2 million of these deaths. If you don't smoke at a healthy level, it doesn't matter what kind of tobacco you use; it will still make you sick. The use of tobacco in the form of cigarettes is by far the most common practice anywhere in the world. Tobacco is found in a wide variety of products, such as cigarettes, cigarillos, roll-your-own tobacco, pipe tobacco, beedis, and kreteks. In addition, water pipe tobacco, a variety of smokeless tobacco products, and cigars are also available. The use of tobacco in a water pipe is also hazardous to one's health, just like the use of cigarettes. Despite this, consumers continue to be unaware of the dangers that using a waterpipe to smoke tobacco can pose to their health. The use of smokeless tobacco can lead to severe addiction and is harmful to one's health. The use of smokeless tobacco increases the risk of developing cancers of the head, neck, chest, oesophagus, and oral cavity (including cancers of the mouth, tongue, lips, and gums), as well as a variety of dental conditions. Smokeless tobacco also produces a large number of cancer-causing contaminants.

DOI: 10.4324/9781003317944-6

History of tobacco in 19th and 20th centuries

Native peoples from Mesoamerica and South America are credited with making the initial discovery of tobacco, which was subsequently brought to Europe and the rest of the world. Tobacco had already been used for a significant amount of time in the Americas by the time European settlers arrived. These settlers brought the practice to Europe, where it eventually became widespread. In the past, indigenous communities in the eastern part of North America would bring tobacco wrapped in sackcloth as a readily accepted form of trade. They would also smoke tobacco during ceremonial pipe rituals, which could be for religious purposes or to sign legal documents (Heckewelder, 1881: 149).

Prior to 20th century, tobacco was primarily used for chewing, pipe smoking, inhaling (as snuff), and cigar smoking. The cigarette was an invention which appeared in the early 19th century at some point. During the 1840s, the word "cigarette" first appeared in English language (Apperson, 1916). The drug quickly caught on among tobacco consumers for reasons including cost and ease of use. The number of people smoking cigarettes in the United States increased to such a degree that, in 1864, the federal government decided to begin taxing cigarettes (Tennant, 1950). However, the production of cigarettes did not become a significant part of the tobacco industry until after the invention of the cigarette machine. In the late 19th century, the mechanisation of the production of cigarettes, along with that of a variety of other products (including cooked cereals, photographic film, matches, flour, and canned food items such as soup) led to a revolution in marketing. This was also the case with the production of a number of other products, such as matches. Industries that developed "continuous cycle" production were able to increase their unit output without an accompanying increase in their production costs (Chandler, 1977: 249). In contrast to these other industries, the tobacco business was suddenly able to produce almost an infinite quantity of product at a lower cost per additional unit.

Cigarette smoking in America developed steadily in the early part of the 20th century, following the invention of automated cigarette-rolling machines and an unparalleled increase in advertisement and promotion (Proctor, 2011). Unlike many other social phenomena, tobacco use has produced a tapestry of themes, motives, and social forces, woven together with a sophistication that has begun to catch the social historians' imagination (Brandt, 1990; Tate, 1999). Tobacco has cultural, social, and political reverberations and is closely tied to the representations and attitudes of the group. The long history of tobacco use can be viewed as the dispute between tobacco as an economic benefit agent and tobacco as an agent of human damage. Upon the introduction of tobacco by American Indians to the European colonists, tobacco was exported from the colonies to Europe, where it soon became a commonly used consumer good. Nevertheless, just as quickly tobacco use was controversial, tobacco use has been criminalised in many northern European countries (Best, 1979). Part of the criticism in England and elsewhere was that selling gold for tobacco to Spain – the finest tobacco came from the colonies of Spain – was dangerous to the state economy. Yet with Virginia's English conquest and increasing need for more state revenue in England and elsewhere in Europe, governments turned around their policies, despite continuing moral opposition to tobacco use. King James I himself put aside his previous objections and found ways for the tobacco trade to support the crown (Morgan, 1975).

Cigarette smoking's growing prevalence coincided with the years of 19th-century conservative health reform. Anti-tobaccoism was a standard feature of various personal health writings which held any "stimulant" to be unhealthy (Nissenbaum, 1980). Some of such belief in well-being is linked to a religious orientation. The prophetess who founded the Seventh-day Adventists, Ellen Gould Harmon White, spoke out strongly against tobacco. In 1848, she taught the moral obligation to abstain from cigarettes, tea, and coffee for a healthy living. She criticised such items because of the squandering money on them and their health risks. However, it was not until 1855 that tobacco abstention among the Adventists became a larger theme. The demonstration was an important part of the anti-tobacco crusading network of the time. In addition to the religious theme, the hygiene movement, which labelled a disease as "tobaccoism, " considered tobacco a poison (Burnham, 1989: 6), and called cigarettes "coffin nails" (Tate, 1999: 24), had significant influence. The American Anti-Tobacco Society, founded in 1849, discovered that tobacco was causing ailments ranging from madness to cancer. Cigarettes were also considered drugs during this period, as they seemed to have addictive properties (Tate, 1999). This litany of physiological ills linked to tobacco use, however did not reflect the social influence.

The National Woman's Christian Temperance Union (WCTU) is credited with being the first organisation to call for the prohibition of smoking (Tate, 1999). Frances Willard, a friend of Harvey Kellogg who was further influenced by the death of her brother from smoking-related illnesses, pushed for the WCTU to make plans as early as 1875 to educate members of its youth branch, the Juvenile Program, on the dangers of cigarettes as well as the dangers of alcohol. Frances Willard was further motivated by the fact that her brother had died from smoking-related illnesses (Tyrrell, 1991). The WCTU established the Tobacco Addiction Overthrow Department in 1883. In 1885, this department was renamed the Narcotics Department (Lander, 1885; Tate, 1999). The cigarette drive had developed into a consistent component of the WCTU's operations. Research presented at their annual meetings documented the achievements of individual states and communities in the war against smoking. In the year 1884, the superintendent of the Department of Overthrow of Tobacco Habit acknowledged the difficulty of the task that lay ahead of her. She stated, "With a spittoon in the pulpit and the clear trail of the drug in countless churches, with its enclosures bearing the seal of respectability, its fortifications, so long impregnable, must yield gradually and unwittingly to the strongest opposing forces" (WCTU, 1884, St. Louis, Missouri convention, V). She made the observation that tobacco use was a costly habit for people, one that costs "more than the expense of all [their] ministers of the gospel" or the cost of educating their children; that it caused sickness, "particularly the loss of sight, paralysis, prostration, and scores of illnesses previously attributed to other sources"; and that it "lowered the level of morality" (WCTU, 1884, V). The WCTU's efforts have not been carried out in isolation. Several prominent businesses and individuals were outspoken in their opposition to the use of tobacco products, even going so far as to lend their support to Gaston's unsuccessful proposal for the 20th Constitutional amendment, which would have prohibited the manufacture and shipment of tobacco products (Junod, 1997). Henry Ford was against the habit of smoking cigarettes, so he asked Thomas Edison to conduct research on the dangers (Brandt, 1990).

The American soldier became a major tool against the tobacco-prohibition movement. Since the Civil War cigarettes were popular among the armed forces. By 1918, during the First World War, tobacco was part of the everyday ration of the army (Dillow, 1981). Soldiers used tobacco for relaxation at the tedium and anxiety levels typical of the occupation. When the popularity of the cigarette increased, there was concern about its health implications as well. Significant work of the day tried to link tobacco with a variety of conditions (Burnham, 1989), but found little new ground (Tate, 1999), although sobering findings were frequently lost in the midst of overblown charges. With the end of Prohibition (1933) and the fall of the temperance movement, advertising was characterised in the 1930s and 1940s by advertisements that often contained clear health statements. In 1930, Lucky Strike, an American tobacco manufacturer, released an ad that stated that "20,679 doctors say 'LUCKIES are less painful'" to the throat. To get this figure, the company's marketing agency had sent Lucky Strike cigarette cartons to doctors and a letter asking if they felt Lucky Strikes was "less painful to sensitive and tender throats than other cigarettes, " though "a decent number of people" had already said they were (Lucky Strike, 1930). Camel had another advertisement that "They don't get your wind" (Camel, 1935). In 1937, the Philip Morris Company made it one step forward with a Saturday Evening Post ad saying doctors had performed a study showing "when smokers transferred to Philip Morris, every case of irritation cleared up fully and certainly improved". What was not reported was that Philip Morris had supported those doctors (Philip Morris, 1937). For this reason the R.J. The Reynolds Tobacco Company formed a Division of Medical Affairs and marketed it in medical journals. Reynolds started paying for research, and then quoted it as Philip Morris in his ads. Reynolds initiated an ad campaign in 1946 with the slogan, "More doctors smoke camels than any other cigarette". They had demanded this "test" by offering a free Camel cigarette carton to doctors and then asking what brand they smoked. 1946 Ads of cigarettes initiated by R.J. Business Reynolds Tobacco (Stanford Research).

Women and cigarettes

The cigarette's primary distinguishing characteristic is its mildness. This feature, combined with its cheap unit cost, made the cigarette particularly appealing to boys and women. Before the cigarette became popular, it was likely that adolescent males first tried smoking cigars, which was very powerful. Cigarette had clearly triumphed cigars for they used a milder type of tobacco intended for inhalation, one study of the tobacco industry concluded. It is very difficult to determine how much of increased cigarette consumption is due to advertising and how much to fashion. Tobacco firms attract new smokers, and their advertisement strategies cater to teenagers (Perry, 1999).

As with all ads, tobacco advertising mostly relies on imagery to cater to the desires of a person, and conveys very little, if any, accurate details about the product's characteristics. Advertising fulfils many of teenagers' and children's desires by successfully using themes of individuality, freedom, beauty, adventure, sophistication, glamour, fitness, social acceptability and inclusion, physical appearance, thinness, popularity, rebelliousness, and being "cool".

Although the prevalence of smoking is greater among men than women, women have a higher risk of smoking-related morbidity and mortality, and face multiple obstacles (Allen, 2014). Cigarette is often flaunted as an appropriate commodity and emblem of women's emancipation. Tobacco companies had to make sure that women would not be ridiculed for using cigarettes in public so it was "probably the most important sign" of a new sense of independence and equality for young women after the war (Fass, 1977: 292). Smoking was "a welcome source of notoriety" for the number of women attending college in the 1920s (Fass, 1977: 293). Objections to smoking by women reflected a conventional double standard, for such opposition stemmed from the twin societal beliefs that cigarettes were not virtuous and not feminine.

Smoking "implied a promiscuous equality between men and women and was an indication that women could enjoy the same vulgar habits and ultimately also the same vices as men" (Fass, 1977: 294). Though they were symbols of gender equality, cigarettes were also amorphous, making men appear more manly and women appear more womanly (Tate, 1999). Cigarette producers were initially sceptical about entering this potential new market, mindful of (and maybe sharing) those objections. As late as 1924, the editor of a tobacco trade newspaper wrote that

> all informed opinion on tobacco [found the idea of women smoking so] novel… That it would not be in the best interest of tobacco men, as individuals, to stir up a particle against or against a situation with which they had little to do at the beginning and whose end, if any, no one could foresee.
>
> *(Wessel, 1924: 6)*

And women's ads hasn't dared to imagine them actively smoking.

Caution from the tobacco industry was short-lived. The appeals to women by cigarette ads were becoming stronger. In 1926, a then controversial commercial was released by the Chesterfield Company, in which a woman encouraged a male friend to "Throw Some My Way" (Ernster, 1985: 336). In 1927, ads from

Lucky Strike featured a famous female opera star promoting Luckies to the throat as calming, and a famous actress assuring readers that Luckies did not irritate the throat. The 1927 Lucky Strike promotion also linked attractive female performers and their voices to smoking Luckies. According to Fortune magazine, Lord & Thomas used "decent, wholesome American actresses like Alice Brady" in a campaign that was "so well timed... that public cigarette smoking by women in America can be accurately dated from 1927". (Lum et al., 2008). "I use Lucky Strikes, as I feel they not only protect my voice but also provide me the greatest amount of true satisfaction, "Brady said above the title "The Captivating Voice of the Delightful Actress, Alice Brady" (Lucky Strike, 1930). In 1928, the diet-conscious slogan, "Look for a Lucky Instead of a Sweet, " was sold to women to encourage them to avoid sweets and prefer a cigarette instead (Ernster, 1985: 336).

In the late 1970s, there was controversy about the effects of smoking on the unborn child inside and outside the medical community. There have been very few studies investigating smoking and pregnancy, and no specific consensus about whether women should avoid smoking during pregnancy altogether. Although Surgeon General Studies addressed the increased risk of low birth weight and other health concerns for babies in the late 1970s, tobacco lobbyists muddled the debate by highlighting the lack of conclusive evidence that ties smoking to these problems. The pregnant woman is urged to stop smoking for mother and child's well-being in this early booklet from the American Cancer Society.

The tobacco firms opted for a large payout in the face of crippling litigation, negative press, and possible federal legislation controlling the industry. Through entering into the Master Settlement Agreement (MSA) in 1998, the five big American tobacco firms settled litigation with 46 states. The tobacco industry agreed, under the terms of the MSA, to curb pro-tobacco advertisements, pay states over $206 billion over 25 years to cover smoking-related healthcare expenses, and fund a national anti-smoking prevention programme. While it was described by tobacco companies as burdensome, many public health officials thought the settlement was much too mild, particularly because it did not require tobacco control by the Food and Drug Administration (FDA) and because the state payment system gave businesses an incentive to keep up the sales of tobacco.

Consensus from the medical establishment

With increasing feelings in and outside the medical community that there were significant risks to tobacco use, government agencies became increasingly concerned about tobacco ads that claimed health benefits to the cigarette or implied health benefits. During the 1950s, numerous orders were released by the Federal Trade Commission (FTC) against cigarette ads that made health claims. Congress also took an interest in tobacco advertisements; Representative John A. Blatnik (D-MN) conducted hearings in 1957 on misleading filter-type ads for cigarettes (Neuberger, 1963). The Surgeon General first introduced the Public Health Service onto the scene by setting up a consortium of researchers in 1956 to determine the health consequences of smoking. The research group concluded a causal association existed between heavy cigarette smoking and lung cancer. In 1957, Surgeon General Leroy E. Burney claimed that "the weight of the evidence is gradually pointing in one direction: that cigarette smoking is one of the causative factors in lung cancer" (Burney, 1958: 44).

The medical community was first reticent to join the anti-smoking crusade. The Surgeon General's 1964 report's "moral entrepreneurship" was to declare smoking a health danger rather than proclaim cancer a medical problem. Thus, armed with the findings of the Surgeon General's report, a battery of public health officials, politicians, and consumer advocates moved against the persisting social and medical problem of smoking, while organised medicine followed slowly and sometimes reluctantly in the wake, and social sceptics worried about the Orwellian implications. These attempts were eventually accepted by a broad cultural movement that distrusted medical moral entrepreneurship. The "demedicalising" movement, which aimed to make healthcare both a personal and a political issue rather than one solely under the control of physicians (Starr, 1982), advocated for a preventive rather than a solely curative approach to medicine.

In some ways, the anti-tobacco campaign is a mix of public health and advertising. It is part of a public health campaign, similar to ones aimed at ensuring the purity of food and medications, as well as the cleanliness of water supplies and air quality – movements aimed at improving the collective provision of healthy settings. However, some people interpret or characterise the anti-smoking effort as a moral reform movement because it inevitably aims to change human behaviour. "We are in the midst of one of those periodic moments of repression", One Observer writes,

> We are in the midst of one of those periodic moments of repression, when the culture, descended from Puritans, imposes its hysterical visions and enforces its guilty constraints on society, legislating moral judgments under the guise of public health, all the while expanding the power of surveillance and the reach of censorship to achieve a general restriction of freedom.
>
> We are in the midst of one of those periodic moments of repression, when the culture, descended from Puritans, imposes its hysterical visions.
>
> *(Klein, 1993: 3)*

In the late 1940s and 1950s, several studies related smoking to lung cancer. The medical community has been vigorously discussing how and why smoking has induced cancer in some but not others. Until federal involvement, non-profit groups such as the American Cancer Society and the American Lung Association led anti-smoking campaigns, all of which were concerned with the dramatic rise in lung cancer. In 1961, the president of the American Cancer Society along with members of the National Tuberculosis Association (which was later known as the American Lung Association) and others published a letter urging President Kennedy to set up a commission to examine the health risks associated with smoking. The consequence was the 1964 landmark study Smoking and

Wellbeing: Recommendation of the Public Health Service Advisory Committee to the Surgeon General. Anti-smoking advocates have been fighting smoking on the job, in public places and at home since the 1970s.

Tobacco control programmes in India

During the 11th Five-Year Plan 2007–2008, the Government of India initiated the National Tobacco Control Programme (NTCP) with the goal of increasing awareness of the harmful effects of tobacco use, reducing the production and supply of tobacco products and ensuring successful enforcement of the harmful effects of tobacco use and of the Tobacco Control Laws. The programme was approved on 28 January 2010, by the Cabinet Committee on Economic Affairs (CCEA). The NTCP developed laboratories for the testing of tobacco products, provide baseline estimates of tobacco prevalence and the implementation status of the Tobacco Control Act. The pilot step was to concentrate on 42 of the 21 state districts. It also organised exhibits, workshops, district-level banners, enforcing the anti-tobacco act in letter and spirit, submitting monthly reports on district-level anti-tobacco activities to the Ministry. At headquarters, the activities centred on promoting district-level information, education, and communication (IEC) activities and multi-sectoral participation with the support of NGOs, the Police Department, the Department of Education, and the Local Administration to enforce the Act. Many volunteer groups, such as HRIDAY-SHAN, CPAA-Cancer patient support association, Salaam Mumbai Foundation, Health Bridge, and India's Voluntary Health Association, are actively involved in tobacco control in India. In India, the World Health Organization (WHO) is actively engaged in the cultivation of tobacco. The WHO has founded a National Tobacco Control Cell in collaboration with the Ministry of Health and Family Welfare, which has activities in the various domains of tobacco control, with the main impetus for awareness raising.

The Ministry of Health and Family Welfare initiated a mass media campaign in July 2011, under the NTCP on beedi smoking and its connection with cardiovascular diseases. This is the world's first mass media advertisement funded by the government that ties beedi smoking to heart health. The campaign was established by the World Lung Foundation with the technical help. The key message is: "Quitting smoking is tough, but the result of not quitting is harder". The promotional commercial features two public service announcements – "Heartbreak" and "Surgeon". These ads were broadcasted on all major TV and radio/FM networks. The ads have been dubbed for pan-India coverage in 14 regional languages.

Every year on 31 May, the WHO and its partners observe World No Tobacco Day to raise awareness of the health dangers associated with tobacco use and to promote the adoption of measures that will significantly lower tobacco use. Every World No Tobacco Day has a different focus, such as supporting campaigns to ban tobacco advertising, promotions, and sponsorships (2013) or to deploy graphic anti-smoking health warnings on tobacco products (2009).

In India, as in many other countries, tobacco yields higher net yields per unit of land than most other cash crops, and significantly more than food crops. There are currently a few specialised crops in different areas providing similar incomes, but it is estimated that these crops will not remain remunerative if overall production is increased. The economies of alternative crops are typically based on experiments performed under optimum conditions on a small area at research stations. More extensive research work is required at the farmers' field level on a wider scale before firm decisions can be made on it. In general, most other alternative crops are not currently as remunerative as tobacco under the conditions of farmers' fields. If tobacco farmers need to diversify into other crops, they will likely face economic hardships. The tobacco industry reports that 33 million people are engaged in tobacco cultivation, of which 3.5 million are in India, according to the World Bank Report (Government and Tobacco Control Economics, 1999). Many women and children make beedis and different types of smokeless tobacco products while sitting at home. The government must provide alternative crops and alternative livelihoods to replace tobacco farming and jobs in the manufacture of tobacco products. In India, four major players in cigarettes dominate the market for cigarettes worth an estimated 60 billion rupees, viz., Indian Tobacco Company (ITC), Godfrey Phillips Limited, Golden Tobacco Company, and National Tobacco. Beedis remain a major tobacco industry, with revenue estimated at 1,031 billion beedis in 2007 (Tobacco in India). Besides these, there are a large number of smokeless tobacco products such as gutkha and pan masala that are available for as low as half a rupee in attractive, colourful small sachets, and have become increasingly popular with aggressive marketing and ads. Beedis outsell cigarettes by a ratio of eight to one accounting for about 48% of tobacco consumption in the country (Joshi et al., 2013).

References

Allen, A. M., C. Onken, and D. Hatsukami, 2014, "Women and Smoking: The Effect of Gender on the Epidemiology, Health Effects, and Cessation of Smoking", *Current Addiction Reports*, Vol. 1, No. 1, pp. 53–60. https://www.ncbi.nlm.nih.gov/pmc/articles/PMC4871621/ Accessed 10th August, 2020.

Apperson, G. L., 1916, *The Social History of Smoking*. New York: G. P. Putnam's Sons.

Best, J., 1979, "Economic Interests and The Vindication of Deviance: Tobacco in Seventeenth Century Europe", *Sociological Quarterly*, Vol. 20, Spring, pp. 171–182.

Brandt, A. M., 1990, "The Cigarette, Risk, and American Culture", *Dædalus*, Vol. 119, No. 4, pp. 155–176.

Burney, L. E., 1958, "Lung Cancer and Excessive Cigarette Smoking", Statement by Surgeon General Leroy E. Burney of the Public Health Service, Department of Health, Education, and Welfare, July 12, 1957. *CA, A Bulletin of Cancer Progress*, Vol. 8, No. 3, p. 44.

Burnham, J. C., 1989, "American Physicians and Tobacco Use: Two Surgeons General, 1929 and 1964", *Bulletin of the History of Medicine*, Vol. 63, No. 1, pp. 1–31.

Camel, 1935, R. J. Reynolds Tobacco Company, http://tobacco.stanford.edu/tobacco_main/images.php?token2=fm_st149.php&token1=fm_img4496.php&theme_file=fm_mt018.php&theme_name=Sm Accessed 12th September, 2020.

Chandler, A. D, Jr., 1977, *The Visible Hand: The Managerial Revolution in American Business.* Cambridge (MA), Harvard University Press.

Dillow, G. L., 1981, "Thank You for Not Smoking: The Hundredyear War Against the Cigarette", *American Heritage*, Vol. 32, No. 2, pp. 94–107.

Ernster, V. L., 1985, "Mixed Messages for Women: A Social History of Cigarette Smoking and Advertising", *New York State Journal of Medicine*, Vol. 85, No. 7, pp. 335–340.

Fass, P. S., 1977, *The Damned and the Beautiful: American Youth in the 1920's*, New York, Oxford University Press.

Government and the Economics of Tobacco Control, 1999, *Development in Practice. Curbing the Epidemic*, Washington (DC), A World Bank Publication.

Heckewelder, J., 1818, *History, Manners and Customs of the Indian Nations Who Once Inhabited Pennsylvania*, The Historical society of Pennsylvania, USA, https://www.gutenberg.org/files/50350/50350-h/50350-h.htm#:~:text=Heckewelder%2C%20in%201818%2C%20published%20under, and%20in%201822%20he%20prepared Accessed 12th September, 2020.

Joshi, K., M. Robins, P. Venu, and K. Mallikarjunaih, 2013, "An Epidemiological Study of Occupational Health Hazards Among Bidi Workers of Amarchinta, Andhra Pradesh", *Journal of Academic and Industrial Research*, Vol. 1, No. 9, pp. 561–564.

Junod, S. W., 1997, "Early Tobacco Regulation: Myth and Reality", *FDLI Update*, Vol. 4, No. 6, p. 8.

Klein, R., 1993, *Cigarettes Are Sublime*. Durham (NC): Duke University Press.

Lander, M., 1885, *The Tobacco Problem*, 6th ed., enlarged. Boston: Lee and Shepard.

Lucky Strike, 1930, http://tobacco.stanford.edu/tobacco_main/index.php Accessed 12th September, 2020.

Lum, K. L., J. R. Polansky, R. K. Jackler, and S. A. Glantz, 2008, "Signed, Sealed and Delivered: 'Big Tobacco' in Hollywood, 1927–1951", *Tobacco Control*, Vol. 17, pp. 313–323.

Morgan, E. S., 1975, *American Slavery, American Freedom: The Ordeal of Colonial Virginia*, New York, W. W. Norton & Company.

Neuberger, M. B., 1963, *Smoke Screen: Tobacco and the Public Welfare*, Englewood Cliffs (NJ), Prentice-Hall.

Nissenbaum, S., 1980, *Sex, Diet, and Debility in Jacksonian America: Sylvester Graham and Health Reform*, Westport (CT), Greenwood Press.

Perry, C. L., 1999, "The Tobacco Industry and Underage Youth Smoking: Tobacco Industry Documents From the Minnesota Litigation", *Archives of Pediatrics & Adolescent Medicine*, Vol. 153, No. 9, pp. 935–941. https://jamanetwork.com/journals/jamapediatrics/fullarticle/347724 Accessed 11th August, 2020.

Philip Morris, 1937, https://www.history.com/news/cigarette-ads-doctors-smoking-endorsement#:~:text=1937%20Philip%20Morris%20advertisement%20claiming,of%20the%20nose%20and%20throat.&text=Unsurprisingly%2C%20many%20doctors%20responded%20positively,medically%20better%20for%20your%20throat. Accessed 12th September, 2020.

Proctor, R. N., 2011, *Golden Holocaust: Origins of the Cigarette Catastrophe and the Case for Abolition*, Berkeley (CA), University of California Press.

Stanford Research into the Impact of Tobacco Advertising, http://tobacco.stanford.edu/tobacco_main/index.php Accessed 12th September, 2020.

Shimkhada, R., and J. W. Peabody, 2003, "Tobacco Control in India", *Bulletin of the World Health Organization*, Vol. 81, pp. 48–52.

Starr, P., 1982, *The Social Transformation of American Medicine*, New York, Basic Books.

Tate, C., 1999, *Cigarette Wars: The Triumph of "The Little White Slaver"*, New York Oxford University Press.

Tennant, R. B., 1950, *The American Cigarette Industry: A Study in Economic Analysis and Public Policy*, New Haven (CT), Yale University Press.

Tobacco in India, http://www.fao.org/3/y4997e/y4997e0h.htm#TopOfPage%20 Accessed 12th September, 2020.

Tyrrell, I., 1991, *Woman's World/Woman's Empire: The Woman's Christian Temperance Union in International Perspective 1880–1930.* Chapel Hill and London: The University of Carolina Press.

WCTU, 1884, *Woman's Christian Temperance Union*, St. Louis (MI), Convention.

Wessel, C. A., 1924, "The First Sixty Billions Are the Hardest for Cigarette Industry", *Printers' Ink*, Vol. 126, No. 5, pp. 3–6, 137–146.

6

THE REGION

The field

The current research was carried out in the Nizamabad district of Telangana, specifically in the three Mandals of Balkonda, Armoor, and Nizamabad, as well as in the metropolitan area of Hyderabad. Telangana became India's 29th and newest state in 2014, making it the country's most recent addition. It stands 11th in rank among the other states in terms of the most land area and the 12th in terms of population. Telangana was finally established in 2014 with the passage of the Andhra Pradesh State Reorganization Bill in Parliament, following decades of struggle for a separate state. Telangana is hemmed in on all sides by the states of Maharashtra and Chhattisgarh to the north, Karnataka to the west, and Andhra Pradesh to the south and east. The cities of Hyderabad, Warangal, Nizamabad, Nalgonda, Khammam, and Karimnagar are considered to be some of the most important in the state. Telugu, a Dravidian language, is the state's official language as well as the language that is spoken by the majority of the population. Urdu is spoken by a relatively small minority.

Telangana, which is located in the Deccan plateau, has a climate that can be described as semi-arid and is plagued by an extreme lack of water. Nearly half of the world's impoverished, marginalised farmers who work in semi-arid environments call the Deccan region home. Due to its history of recurrent famines and droughts, this region consistently ranks among the world's poorest (Annual Report, 1972: XX). The CMIE index, which is based on a general baseline of economic and development criteria, reveals that seven of Telangana's districts, with the exception of Hyderabad, Nizamabad proper, and Nalgonda, fall significantly below the average for the entire nation. Although some irrigation works, road construction, and electrification have taken place since the country's independence, and paddy and sugarcane cultivation have brought relative economic prosperity to a few pockets, the district as a whole continues to be backward.

DOI: 10.4324/9781003317944-7

Rural occupational structures and job patterns in Indian villages have undergone a transformation in recent decades as a consequence of changes in agricultural production patterns, the adoption of new technology, urbanisation, industrialisation, and the deterioration of earlier traditional labour relations (Shukla, 1989, 1993). The *Jajmani* production relations between the landlord and the specialist service provider have broken down as a result of the shifts that have taken place in the labour relations that exist in rural communities. As a result, the artisans are no longer required to support the landlord in order to obtain security and grains in exchange. This has led to a reduction in the reciprocal dependency and responsibilities that existed before. As a result, many of these people were deprived of their means of subsistence. Even though there are plenty of rural jobs available for men in India, the problem is more prevalent for women. Following the conclusion of the Green Revolution, labour absorption rates in agriculture declined, particularly among women (Bhalla, 1989: 68). New employment opportunities, especially for women, have emerged in recent years, particularly in the fields of construction, domestic service, and the production of beedi.

Nizamabad district prior to the independence of India in 1947 formed a part of the erstwhile state of Hyderabad under the feudal rule of Nizams. As a result in the earlier period, this area did not see the development of infrastructure facilities like roads, railways, and irrigation on the same scale as in British administered areas of the state. Up to 2 June 2014, the Nizamabad district was part of Andhra Pradesh state. After bifurcation of Telangana State, Nizamabad district became one of the districts of Telangana state. Educational backwardness that one sees today is in some senses also a historical problem. Till the early 20th century, the medium of instruction in Hyderabad State was Urdu, which meant that a large section of society did not have access to education. Unlike the districts that formed part of the British Raj (kingdom), missionary efforts as well as nationalistic efforts in the fields of education including women's education were very limited.

The practice of child marriage, *banamati* (witchcraft and sorcery), the *jogins* system (prostitution in the name of religion), and *Vetti* (bonded labour) are some of the most prominent forms of evil that can be found in the society here. Although some irrigation works, road construction, and electrification have taken place since the country's independence, and paddy and sugarcane cultivation have brought relative economic prosperity to a few pockets, the district as a whole continues to be backward.

Historical background

Telangana has a history that spans at least 2,500 years or more, in all aspects of its existence, including its economy, society, culture, and history. The presence of megalithic stone structures in this region of the country, such as cairns, cists, dolmens, and menhirs, is evidence that people lived in this area of the country 2,000 ago. The ancient roots of artisanship and tool making in Telangana date back at least 2,000 years, as evidenced by the discovery of remnants of iron ore smelting at a number of different locations. The fact that Asmaka Janapada, which is now a part of Telangana, was considered to be 1 of the 16 Janapadas in ancient India is evidence that there was a more developed stage of society in those times. According to the sources pertaining to Buddhism, Bavari, a Brahmin hailing from Badanakurti in Karimnagar, dispatched his disciples all the way to North India in order for them to study Buddhism and bring it back to this part of the country. Megasthenes, who travelled to India in the 4th century BCE and wrote about his experiences there and reported that Andhra had 30 fortified towns, the majority of which were located in Telangana.

The name Nizamabad (Nizam-a-abadi) was given to the district after the Nizam of Hyderabad, Asaf Jahi VI, who was the ruler of Deccan during the 18th century AD. Nizamabad was derived from that name. Historically, this area was referred to as INDUR, which is thought to have been derived from the name of King Indradatta, who ruled over this part of the world in the 5th century AD. When Sir Salar Jung-I was serving as Prime Minister in the year 1876 AD, the Nizam's Dominion underwent a period of district reorganisation, during which time INDUR was given the status of a district. The Telangana region, before its merger into Visalandhra – a separate state for Telugu-speaking people – witnessed the rise and fall of various dynasties. The culmination of dynastic rule was the Nizam's rule of the southern Deccan. Its pomp and pageantry spread over the period of about 200 years. The Nizam of Hyderabad came into power in 1724 and had an uninterrupted rule for more than 200 years (Kate, 1987). This area was not a homogeneous unit. This area and component parts were ruled by different dynasties through history, including: the Mauryas, Satavahanas, Chalukyas, Rashtrakutas, Kakatiyas, Bahamani Sultans, Qutub Shahis, Mughals, and Asaf Jahis (Regani, 1988). Among all these dynasties, Asaf Jahis dynasty is the most significant as far as the history and administration of Telangana is concerned.

Asaf Jahi dynasty was established in the Deccan in the year 1724, when Nizam-ul-Mulk Asaf Jahi emerged as the victor in the field of Shakarskeda against Mubariz Khan, the Mughal Emperor's nominee. He established his rule virtually independently of the Mughal Emperor. He made Golconda his capital. The Mughal Emperor accepted this with apparent good grace, he not only confirmed Nizam-ul-Mulk in the Deccan Subedari, but also bestowed on his the title of Asaf Jahi. The Asaf Jahi's ascendance to power is an important landmark in the history of the Deccan. The foundations for the destiny of the region were laid in these initial stages.

Initially the Nizam's reign constituted the areas of Maharashtra, Circar, ceded districts, and some parts of Karnataka. The Nizam of Hyderabad, in the year 1800 after the end of the fourth Mysore war, made a treaty with the East India Company. Under the conditions of the treaty, the British force at Hyderabad was to be increased further for the maintenance of peace and security in the reign. As part of this treaty, the Nizam ceded Berar, Rayalaseema, and the coastal districts in exchange for the protection and training to his contingent given by the

Company. After this treaty, the Nizam's territory was dwarfed and left only with some parts of Telangana, Maharashtra, and Carnatic districts (Regani, 1988). After the transfer of these areas to the Britishers, no further major changes were affected in the map of Nizam State. By and large, this area continued without any changes till the reorganisation of Indian states in 1956.

In Nizam's dominion, the administrative condition was not satisfactory. The government officials in charge of Taluqs, the Deshpandes and Deshmukhs, were indifferent to the welfare of the people. Therefore, there was no scope to undertake welfare programmes like health and education. There were no precedents of this kind in the history of the district anywhere, Telangana region being no exception. In 1853, Salar Jung became the Prime Minister and laid the foundations for the subsequent prosperity of the region. He made noticeable reforms in every sphere of activity. He even paid attention to the development of health and education (Regani, 1988). The Nizam of Hyderabad refused to join the Indian Union when India gained independence from the British Empire in 1947, preferring to remain independent. After a military action known as Operation Polo, the Government of India seized Hyderabad State on 17 September 17 1948. Mir Osman Ali Khan was the Nizam at that time. The Telangana Rebellion, a peasant revolt, in the Telangana regions of the Hyderabad State between 1946 and 1951, was led by the Communist Party of India (CPI).

In December of 1953, a commission known as the States Reorganization Commission (SRC) was established with the purpose of organising states according to linguistic differences. On 20 February 1956, the leaders of Telangana and Andhra came to an agreement to merge their respective states into a single entity, with commitments made to protect the interests of Telangana. After the reformation that took place in 1956, Andhra Pradesh was created by combining Telangana with Andhra State. The Andhra Pradesh state was initially established as a unitary state by the central government on 1 November 1956.

There have been various attempts to undo the Telangana-Andhra merger, with the most notable ones coming in 1969, 1972, and 2009. An initiative by the Telangana Joint Action Committee, TJAC, which includes political leadership from the Telangana area, sparked the drive for a new state in Telangana. The Indian government declared the creation of the Telangana state on 9 December 2009. People in the Coastal Andhra and Rayalaseema regions staged violent protests after this announcement, and hence, no decision could be taken, and this was put on hold on 23 December 2009 (Annual Report, 2018–2019).

In February of 2014, the Indian Parliament passed a law known as the Andhra Pradesh Reorganization Act, 2014, which made it possible for the state of Telangana to be formed out of ten districts located in the northwestern part of Andhra Pradesh. These included Hyderabad, Mahbubnagar, Ranga Reddy, Karimnagar, Medak, Adilabad, Warangal, Nizamabad, Khammam, and Nalgonda. On 1 March 2014, the bill gained the president's signature and was published in the gazette. Telangana became an independent state on 2 June 2014. Telangana's first chief minister, K. Chandrashekar Rao, was elected. Hyderabad became the combined capital of Telangana and Andhra Pradesh until the state of Andhra Pradesh decided to have Amravati as its new capital and develop it.

Boundaries and topography

Nizamabad is one of the 31 districts of Telangana. This district is surrounded by the districts of Adilabad, Karimnagar, and Medak. To the west of the Nizamabad district are the districts of Nanded and Bidar, which are located in the states of Maharashtra and Karnataka, respectively.

Physical aspects

Based on geographical factors such as rainfall, soil type, and climate, Telangana is categorised into four agro-climatic zones: (i) northern Telangana, (ii) central Telangana, (iii) southern Telangana, and (iv) high altitude and tribal zones. Telangana state is situated in a semi-arid region with a predominantly hot and dry environment. The summer season begins in March and ends in May, with average high temperatures of 42°C. The monsoon season begins in June and lasts through September, with an average rainfall of 713 mm. With little humidity and typical temperatures in the range of 22–23°C, a dry, mild winter begins in late November and lasts until early February.

On an average, the state's normal rainfall is around 905.3 mm, with the south-west monsoons accounting for almost 80% of yearly rainfall (June to September). Rainfall in the state is unpredictable, and rainfall distribution is uneven among districts. The region is drained by two large rivers, with the Godavari River catching 79% of the catchment area and the Krishna River catching 69%. Several minor rivers flow through Telangana. These include Bhima, Maneru, Manjira, and Musi.

Since Nizamabad is located in the Deccan table land, hills with a significant range are extremely uncommon in the surrounding area. There are many instances of solitary summits and rocky aggregations. The rock formations are related to those that existed during the Archean and Deccan trap formations. The Godavari, which forms the district's northern border, and the Manjira, which is the Godavari's most important tributary, are the two major rivers that flow through it. In addition to these, the region of Kamareddy Taluk is traversed by streams such as the Phulang and the Yedlakattavagu, both of which are advantageous for the purpose of irrigation. The summers in this region are typically very warm, and the weather is typically dry, with the exception of the monsoon season that occurs in the south-west. The beginning of the rainy season is marked by the beginning of the south-west monsoon, which begins in the latter half of June and lasts through the month of October. Roughly 74% of the annual average rainfall occurs during this time of year. The average annual rainfall is about 1,081 millimetres.

Important soils include red sandy loams, red loams with clay base along with very small patches of alluvial soils. The total geographical area is 112.08 lakh hectares, of which the area under forest constitutes 22.66% of the land. A total of 37.25% area is under cultivation, 14.08% is current fallow lands, 7.96% of land is put to non-agricultural uses, and 5.42% is barren and uncultivable. The remaining is under a waste land, permanent pastures and other grazing lands, and land under miscellaneous tree crops and groves are not included in the net area sown (*Statistical Year Book 2017).*

During 2015–2016, production of total food grains was recorded as 51.45 lakh tonnes in the state. Production of oil seeds was 5.79 lakh tonnes and chillies 2.28 lakh tonnes. Currently, the state is the major contributor in horticultural production, such as mango, mosambi (sweet lime), red-chilli, turmeric, marigold, and vegetables. In the state, the average size of a holding is 1.12 hectares. A total of 62.0% of the properties are marginal (less than 1 hectare), while 23.9% are small (between 1 and 2 hectares). In the state, marginal and small farms account for 85.9% of all agricultural holdings.

The central Deccan plateau with its dry deciduous forests ecoregion extends across a significant portion of Telangana state and includes the city of Hyderabad. The predominant types of vegetation are forests composed primarily of *Hardwickia binata* and *Albizia amara*. Even though more than 80% of the original forest cover has been cleared for agricultural use, timber harvesting, or cattle grazing, there are still large tracts of forest in places like the Nagarjuna Sagar-Srisailam Tiger Reserve. The Eastern Highlands are home to a more humid climate than the Eastern Ghats, which are covered in verdant deciduous forests. The Eastern Ghats are located in the eastern half of the state. A total of 27,292 square kilometres, or 24.35% of the state's total geographical area, is covered in forest. This figure takes into account social forestry as well. In terms of the total forest area, the area that is classified as reserved forest is 19,629.54 square kilometres, the area that is classified as protected forest is 6,988.95 square kilometres, and the remaining area is unclassified. The state's forests are home to a variety of high-quality timbers, including teak and eucalyptus, amongst others. Non-wood forest products, such as Sal seeds (from which an edible oil can be extracted), tendu leaves (for rolling cigarettes), gum karaya (a type of emulsifier), and bamboo, are also very important. Bamboo is a fast-growing grass that can be used in place of timber.

State economy

The growth rate of Telangana's Gross State Domestic Product, GSDP, (at constant prices) has increased from 9.4% in 2016–2017 to 10.5% in 2018–2019. Agriculture, manufacturing, and services contributed to 16%, 20%, and 65% of the Gross State Value Added (GSVA), respectively. In the same period, these sectors grew by 8.1%, 5.8%, and 11.5%, respectively. The per capita GSDP of Telangana (at constant prices) was Rs 1,61,669, which is 9.4% higher than that in 2017–2018. The share of agriculture sector to the GSVA in 2016–2017 is 15.3% at current prices. The Periodic Labour Force Survey (2017–2018), however, points out that Telangana has an unemployment rate of 7.6%, which is much higher than the all-India unemployment rate of 6.1%.

The contribution of forestry and logging sector to GSVA at current prices is 0.41% and 2.75% in the GSVA of agriculture and allied sector for the year 2015–2016. The total revenue realised during 2015–2016 is Rs 10,820.79 lakhs on sale of forest produce in the State. The Industry Sector is contributing around 20% to the GSDP of Telangana. The average annual growth of industries sector comprising mining and quarrying, manufacturing, electricity, gas and water supply and construction, between 2012–2013 and 2016–2017, is averaged at 5.24% as against GSDP growth of 12.72% in the state. Hyderabad has become known for aeronautics and other high-technology manufacturing, as well as for plants producing electrical equipment, machine tools, and pharmaceuticals. Services have become the largest contributor to Telangana's economy and tourism has been of small but growing significance.

Coal, limestone, quartz, granite, feldspar, dolomite, and barite are among Telangana's main mineral resources. The Golconda plateau's diamond mines were formerly famous for producing the Koh-i-noor diamond and other notable stones. The majority of Telangana's energy is generated by public-sector thermal generators, with hydroelectric power plants serving as a vital secondary source of energy.

Demography

According to the 2011 Census, the state's total population is around 3.50 crores. Between 2001 and 2011, the overall population growth rate was around 13.58%, compared to 17.70% nationally. The majority of the population in the state live in rural areas (61.12%), with the remaining 38.88% living in urban areas. Between 2001 and 2011, the overall population growth rate was 13.58%, compared to 18.77% in the previous decade. The population of urban regions has been growing rapidly, increasing by 38.12% between 2001 and 2011, compared to 25.13% in the previous decades. In sharp contrast, according to the 2011 Census, the state's rural population increased by only 2.13%. The state's population density, or the average number of people living per square kilometre of land, is 312 per square kilometre.

The share of working age population (15–59) has increased from 59% to 63%, and this trend could be seen across gender and location. Sex ratio for the state is 988. In the state, the sex ratio has risen steadily from 967 in 1991 to 971 in 2001 and then to 988 in 2011. The sex composition or sex ratio is one of the most important features of population demographics. The number of females per 1,000 males in a population is known as the sex ratio. If we observe the sex ratio scenario of Telangana state, we will find that the curves are either stable or is in increasing trend. This ratio for the state is 988 according to 2011 Census. A total of 21 districts out of 31 districts have the sex ratio more than the state average of 988 and 11 districts have the sex ratio with more than 1,000 female per 1,000 male which is praiseworthy. The lowest sex ratio is noticed in more urbanised districts like Hyderabad, Rangareddy, Medchal-Malkajgiri, Sangareddy, Yadadri Bhuvanagiri, Jogulamba Gadwal, Wanaparthy, Nagarkurnool, and Nalgonda and the highest sex ratio is in Nirmal district with 1,046 female per 1,000 males (*Statistical Year Book 2017: 5*).

Telangana's religious composition is around 85.1% Hindus, 12.7% Muslims, 1.3% Christians, and 0.9% other. The Muslim population in GHMC (Greater Hyderabad Municipal Corporation) is the highest, while the Muslim population in Khammam is the lowest. Scheduled Castes, Scheduled Tribes, and others make up the state's population. Scheduled Castes account for 15.45% of the total population of the state, while Scheduled Tribes account for 9.08%. The population of Scheduled Tribes has increased significantly from 2.81% in 1961 to 8.19% in 1981, and then to 9.08% in 2011 (Socioeconomic Outlook Reports, 2017–2020).

Literacy

According to the 2011 Census, the state's literacy rate is 66.54%. Men have a literacy rate of 75.04%, while women have a literacy rate of 57.99%. According to the Indian census, literate people are those who are at least 7 years old and can read and write in at least one language with comprehension. The district with the highest literacy rate (83.25%) is Hyderabad, whereas the district with the lowest literacy rate is Mahbubnagar (55.04%). However, over the past few decades the gender gap between male and female literacy rate is declining.

TABLE 6.1 Decadal Percentage of Literacy Rate Variation

Decades	*Literacy Rate*
1951–1961	16.48
1961–1971	24.60
1971–1981	27.59
1981–1991	29.27
1991–2001	18.77
2001–2011	13.58

Source: Census (2011).

TABLE 6.2 Literacy Rates Details, 2011 Census

Details (2011)	*Literacy Rate*
Urban Literacy rate (Male)	86.13
Urban Literacy rate (Female)	75.39
Rural Literacy rate (Male)	67.56
Rural Literacy rate (Female)	47.10

Source: Census (2011).

The literacy rate is the percentage of literates in the total population, excluding 0–6 years. Urban literacy rate of Telangana is 81.09%, and rural literacy rate is 57.30% (*Statistical Year Book 2015).*

Child labour

As a result of the underdeveloped state of the region, children contribute significantly to the family's overall income. The feminisation of poverty in the state is essential to understanding child labour, which must be viewed in this context. In comparison to the total population, the total child population, and the total workforce, Andhra Pradesh stands out as having the highest number of children working in labour-intensive occupations. Andhra Pradesh has a rate of child labour that is nearly 0.8% points higher than the national average of 4.26% points, which stands at 4.26%. In other words, 13% of all child labourers in India live in Andhra Pradesh. Nizamabad contributes 4.31% of child labours to this. While the male child population is growing (17.81%), there is a decline in their number as workers, but for a lesser growth in female child population (17.19%), there is a considerable increase in female child workers (29.02%). There is an increase, in the number of dropouts, with the girls dropping out of school more than the boys. We can really gauze the enormity of the problem by reminding ourselves that these are government statistics and the non-government sector would put the number much higher.

The Old City of Hyderabad

The city of Hyderabad now referred to as the Old City was planned by the Qutub Shahis' nearly 400 years ago, when Golconda fort, the then headquarters, was not able to contain the growing population. The city was planned on the road running from Golconda towards east, as far as Masaulipatnam, the famous Andhra seaport on the East Coast. This road was made to intersect a new road running from north to south crossing at a point, where the famous Charminar now stands. About 80 yards north of Charminar was the square known as Jilukhanah (now referred to as Charkaman) flanked by four large arches 50 feet in height and each arch separated from the centre by about 110 yards. There were four broad roads jutting out from the four portals of these arches.

The city of Hyderabad was constructed out of brick and lime masonry with a thick coat of plaster different from the monuments of North India build primarily with stones. Besides nearly 14,000 shops, there were mosques, hammams (public baths) ashoorkhanas, langarkhanas (to distribute food to the poor), sarais (traveller's bunglows/guesthouses), and Dar-ul-Shifa (public hospital). A number of gardens adorned these buildings.

The city of Hyderabad was then divided into four quarters by its intersecting main highways. The north-western quarter was reserved for the royal place, whereas the eastern side was allotted to the nobility. The rest of the city was divided into 12 mohallas spreading over an area of 10 square miles which was inhabited by the common people. The city also had a number of suburbs such as Karwan, Khairatabad, Bagh-e-Lingampally, and Naubat Pahad. Soon Hyderabad grew into an important trade centre. The major exports from here included diamonds, textiles, sugar, iron, and spices. The major imports included Arabian horses, pearls, porcelain, and carpets. This became the home of Dikhani language and many important writers like Nishati and Khuda rose to prominence.

The decline of Hyderabad started after the capture of Golconda fort by Aurangzeb in 1687. The Mughals had named Hyderabad as Darul Jahad (battleground). They also made Aurangabad as the capital of six subas of Deccan. Naturally now all the nobility shifted to Aurangabad and Aurangabad became the centre for all political and commercial activity. Golconda and Hyderabad were placed under the control of a Qiledar – Rustum Dil Khan. The Asaf Jahis once again tried to restore Hyderabad to its old glory, and it once again became the scene of activity.

Presently, today the Old City is divided into three circles: Circles I, II, and III. This is an overpopulated area with a high density. Majority of the people are Muslims. What is interesting to note is that though a large number of people are getting jobs in the gulf countries, but whatever money is being remitted is not being brought back into the Old City. There are a large number of instances of people migrating and building their houses in the new city of Hyderabad or in new areas around Towli Chowki, Mehidipatnam, etc. As a result, the Old City continues to deteriorate in terms of the infrastructure facilities. Some of the important trades in these areas include bangle making, zari works, agarbatti making, wooden and carpentry works, welding, auto repairs, pandan and brass industry, and leather and rexine works. We got most of our information about the Old City from the Municipal Corporation of Old City of Hyderabad.

Old Hyderabad City has 65% Muslim who constitute the majority, and 30% are Hindus. As per 2011 Census, Christians number 9,687 while Sikhs number 7,166 in Old Hyderabad City. The overall population of Hyderabad district is 39.43 lakhs, where Hindus are 20.46 lakhs (51.89%) and Muslims are 17.13 lakhs (43.35%). Households in the Old City are generally large with members varying from 10 to 15. These families are generally poor, and so each and every child of the family goes to work to contribute to the family income. Yet, the family income remains below poverty line.

In Circle I, there are 4,32,574 males and 2,88,383 female population. The total number of children in Circle I is 2,25,123. In Circle II, there are 2,82,000 males and 1,88,000 female populations and the total number of children in Circle II is 1,72,000. Due to the poverty of families, many children are deprived of the opportunity of either attending the school or continuing the studies. As a result, there are many illiterates and drop outs than those who are attending school. The number of illiterate and drop out children in Circle I is 1,57,586, whereas those children who attend school is 67,536. The number of illiterate and drop out children in Circle II is 1,20,400, whereas those attending schools is 51,600.

In the Old City, Muslim community is in majority when compared to Hindus, Christians, and others. According to the information given by MCH – Old City, the total population of Muslims in Circles I and II is around 8,33,669. The total population of Hindus is approximately 4,55,000, whereas Christians and other communities amount to around 30,000 only. Thus, Muslims are in majority in the Old City as well as particularly in Circles I and II. There are around 700 schools, both government and private, in the Old City. And there are about four to five colleges in the Old City. There are about six governmental hostels for children there. There are many non-governmental organisations working for the welfare of weaker sections of population in the Old City. There are around 100 NGOs (Non-Government Organisations) working in the Old City.

Conclusion

Telangana is a large multicultural state and with rich diversity in language, religion, and age. The state has the potential to enhance its productivity by leveraging its rich mineral and natural resources and labour force due to its suitable age demographic of 39% between 15 and 34 years. Telangana being one of the top IT exporters of India can leverage its computer-educated young population for developing the state further. Telangana development is impacted by the distress in agriculture with a high number of farmer suicides. According to a report by the National Crime Records Bureau, Telangana (1,358) has the second-highest incidence of farmer suicide in 2015, which led to the state government to introduce many measures, but there is work to be done to ensure sustainable livelihood to the large population, dependent on agriculture. Telangana stands strong at the eighth position in India in terms of its GSDP of approx. Rs 8.4 crores, but the state can further improve by fixing the long standing issues with agriculture, increasing tourism earnings and leveraging the strong ITBT infrastructure.

Once ruled by Kakatiyas and Nizams, the caste systems in the district are highly organised. Reddy and Kapu's are the dominant caste of the region. They dominate economic and political arenas of the district. Most of the agriculture is dependent on rainfall. There is no major industry in the district to its credibility except the sugar mills. Although the Scheduled Castes and backward castes population is high, their role in the economic and political spheres is highly restricted. The people who own the means of production are politically powerful. Telangana Rashtra Samithi, Congress, and the BJP are the political parties in the district. The left parties are gradually establishing their base among the people. Regarding literacy, during the Nizam's rule, education was not encouraged. Educational development took place only after independence. The district occupies a low profile in the literacy compared to the state average. There are several registered and unregistered private schools apart from the government schools in the district.

References

Annual Report, 2018–19, Government of Telangana, Department for Women, Children, Disabled & Senior Citizens, https://www.telangana.gov.in/PDFDocuments/Telangana-Women-Children-Disabled-and-Senior-Citizens-Department-Annual-Report-2018-19.pdf Accessed 10th October, 2019.

Annual Report, 1972, International Crop Research Institute for Semi Arid Tropics, Patancheru, Hyderabad, India.

Bhalla, S., 1989, "Technological Change and Women Workers: Evidence from the Expansionary Phase in Haryana Agriculture", *Economic and Political Weekly*, October 28, pp. 67–67.

Kate, P. V., 1987, *Marathwada Under the Nizams 1724–1948*, New Delhi, Mittal Publications.

Regani, S., 1988, *Nizam-British Relations 1724–1857*, New Delhi, Concept Publishing Company.

Shukla, T., 1989, "Rural Non Agricultural Employment", *Economic and Political Weekly*, Vol. 24, No. 35–36, pp. 1993–1995.

Socioeconomic Outlook Reports, 2017–2020, Government of Telangana, Planning Department, https://www.telangana.gov.in/PDFDocuments/Telangana-Socio-Economic-Outlook-2020.pdf Accessed 5th May, 2020.

Statistical Year Book 2017, Directorate of Economics and Statistics, Government of Telangana, Hyderabad, http://ecostat.telangana.gov.in/PDF/PUBLICATIONS/Statistical_Year_Book_2017.pdf Accessed 5th May, 2020.

Statistical Year Book 2015, Directorate of Economics and Statistics, Government of Telangana, Hyderabad, https://www.telangana.gov.in/PDFDocuments/Statistical-Year-Book-2015.pdf Accessed 10th October, 2018.

PART B
The study

7

THE BEEDI WORKER

Socioeconomic profile

We conducted our survey in the three Mandals of Armoor, Balkonda, and Nizamabad, and the municipal area of Hyderabad. In each Mandal, data was collected from two areas: one urban and one rural, and we had a sample of 40% from the urban areas and 60% from the rural areas. These Mandals' urban areas are also like towns and cannot be compared to a metropolitan like Hyderabad where 100% of our sample were from the urban area. We had a total sample of 1,040, out of which 665 were women and 375 were children. A child labour was understood to be one between 5 and 14 years of age. In Armoor, field work was conducted and data collected in Pipri (rural area) and Armoor town (urban area). In Balkonda Mandal, field work was conducted and data collected in Kisanagar (rural area) and Balkonda town (urban area). In Nizamabad Mandal, field work was conducted and data collected in Gaggupalle (rural area) and Nizamabad town (urban area). In Hyderabad, data was collected from six urban areas namely, Amberpet, Ramanthpur, Musheerabad, Parsigutta, Malkajgiri, and Uppal. The area chosen was based on high incidence of women and children concentration of beedi making.

According to the findings of our research, 97% of families were nuclear, 2% were joint, and 1% were extended. Out of these households, nine out of ten were headed by a male member, while the remaining 10% were led by a female member.

The household size and actual numbers are as follows (Figure 7.1).

As clearly visible in the diagram, more than 50% of the households in all four areas had four to five members in the family. There were no families with more than six members in Hyderabad and Nizamabad, while less than 2% families in Balkonda and less than 5% families in Armoor had more than six members in their family. Interestingly, this is quite contradicting to the view that most of

DOI: 10.4324/9781003317944-9

the families in rural areas and/or in the lower income group have higher fertility rates and tend to have bigger family size. More than 90% of the families in all four areas had three to six members in their families, which is an average family size found in our country (Figure 7.2).

Of the women in our sample, 83% were married, 2% were divorced, 4% were separated, 7.9% were widow, and 3% were deserted. More than 70% of women in these three areas were in the age group of 26–40 years, and almost 20% of the women were in the age group of 41–50 years and 26–30 years each. The highest number of women was in the bracket of 31–35 years, while males were more in the age group of 26–30 years. Some of the samples in our data sets also included sons and other male relatives who were staying with the family (Figure 7.3).

After talking to the beedi-making women and getting details about their families, we found out that most of them were illiterate. Around 80% of the people in these households were either illiterate or had no formal education. No women in Hyderabad and Armoor reached middle school. Almost none of the family members of all the respondents reached high school. This is not surprising

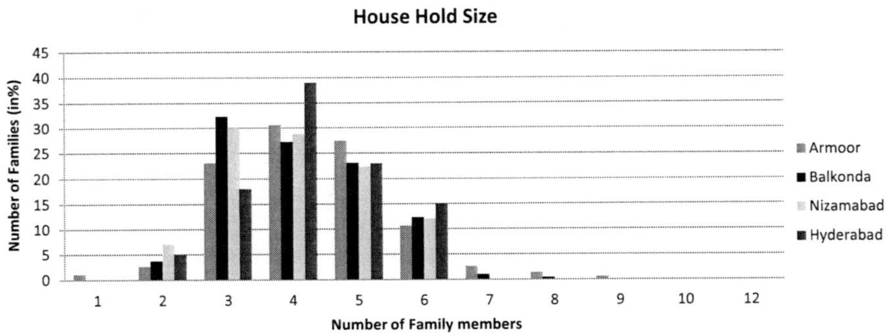

FIGURE 7.1 Household size.

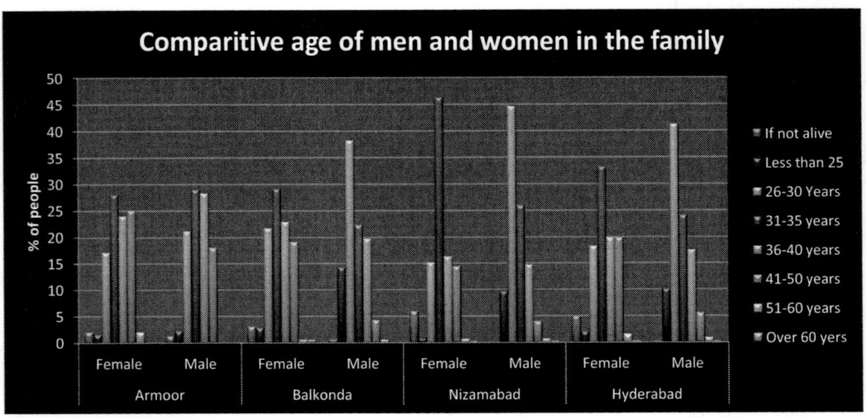

FIGURE 7.2 Comparative age women and men in the family.

TABLE 7.1 The Educational Level of the Men and Women

Status	*Armoor*		*Balkonda*		*Nizamabad*		*Hyderabad*	
	Female	*Male*	*Female*	*Male*	*Female*	*Male*	*Female*	*Male*
Not alive	5.4	0.6	3.1	0.6	2.0	0	1.0	0.3
Illiterate	74.7	63.7	68.6	56.1	65.1	66.6	69.00	64.6
Literate but no formal education/ read and write	10.9	15.7	13.3	17.1	14.3	13.0	16.70	18.7
Primary	9.0	18.0	12.0	18.2	13.6	14.3	13.3	15.4
Middle	0	2.0	3.0	8	5	5.8	0	1
High school	0	0	0	0	0	0.3	0	0
College	0	0	0	0	0	0	0	0
Technical diploma	0	0	0	0	0	0	0	0
Total	100	100	100	100	100	100	100	100

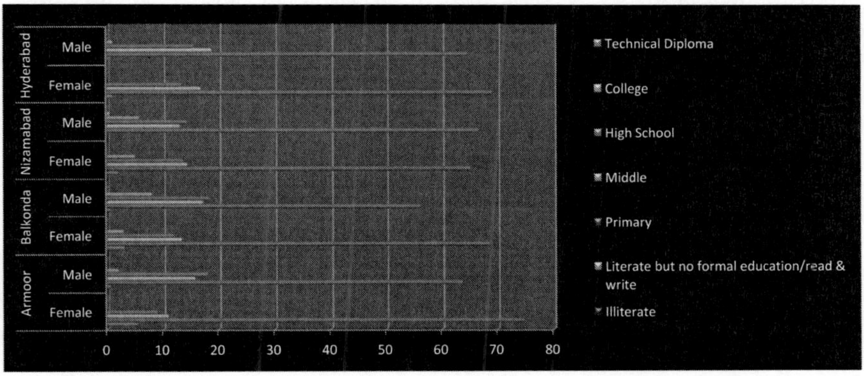

FIGURE 7.3 The educational level of the men and women.

because beedi making is primarily practiced by the people of backward classes and castes who are mostly illiterate or worked as agricultural labourers. Though many of these people are not educated, they realise the importance of education for their children but again here they give preference to a boy's education rather than that of the girl's. We found that in these families, the total number of boys attending school was 47%. As compared to this, girls attending school were 53%. The boys' dropout was 5%, and for girls, it was 10%, while boys who never went to school were 7.4%, and the girls who were illiterate were 20%. Thus, in the families that we surveyed, more girls enter primary school, but this number kept on reducing later on with the boys continuing their studies and the girls being made to sit at home after puberty or primary. The dropout rate was more for girls when compared to boys. In these families, the total number of illiterate women was much more than men. Girls amounted to 20% as compared to 7% boys.

Beedi making is primarily dominated by women and there were very few men or boys in our sample, because nearly 92% women were employed in it as compared to 12% men. The men, even if involved in beedi manufacturing, worked only in the karkhanas and were employed in labelling, baking, packaging, transporting, etc., never in making the individual beedi. The same pattern was followed for boys and girls also. While 26% of boys were employed in beedi making, the number was 70% in the case of girls (Figure 7.4).

Thus, among our respondents, majority of the men (53%) were engaged as agricultural labourers and majority of the women (97%) were working in beedi making. Since majority of the women work in beedi making and being a home-based industry, a large number of girls were also drawn into this work. The women of the households were involved in beedi-making process, but hardly 10% of the males were involved in this work. However, in Hyderabad, the trends were different from the other three areas. In Hyderabad, a good number of people were employed in the service sector (15.3%) or they were self-employed/had their own business (24.60%). In Armoor, Balkonda, and Nizamabad, more than 45% of the males were employed in agriculture, while only 7.1% of males in Hyderabad were into agriculture, mostly due to lack of agriculture fields in the area. Very few of these men were involved in cultivation. When we said cultivation, we meant having their own land for agriculture, and very few of these families had their own lands (Figure 7.5).

While compiling the total household income of the households in all the regions, we found that the majority of households in all the regions earn between 5,000 and 6,000 per month. Interestingly, here we found a trend that contrasted with the usual beliefs. Usually it is believed that people in cities earn more than the rural areas or smaller towns. However, we found that more than 95% of people in Hyderabad earned 7,000 or less than that. The maximum monthly income in Hyderabad was 9,000, while that in other areas was more than 11,000.

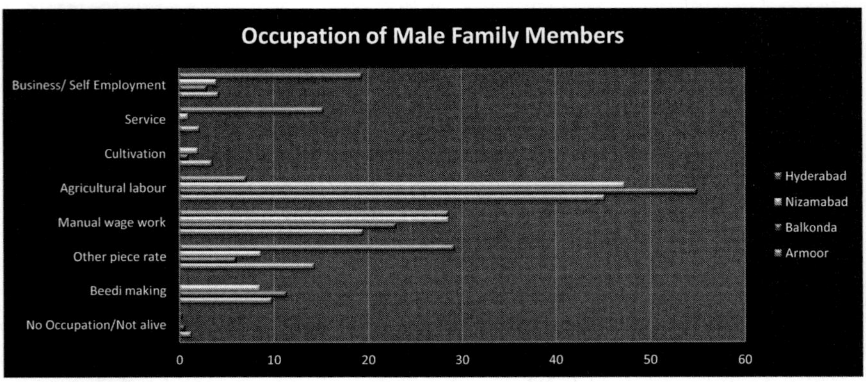

FIGURE 7.4 Occupation of the male members.

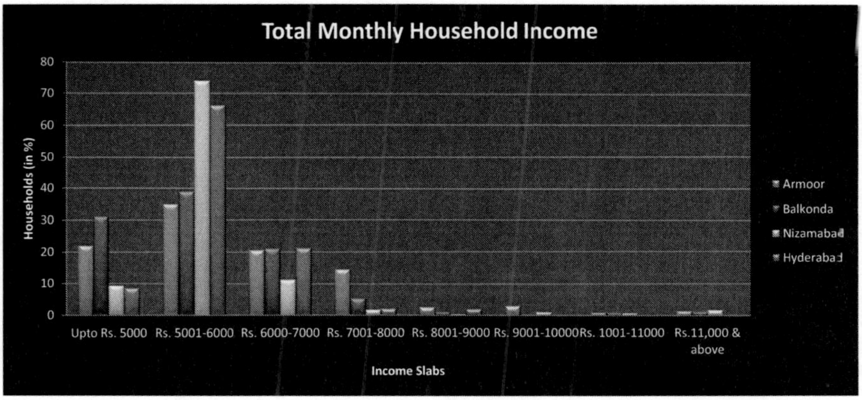

FIGURE 7.5 Total monthly household income.

Since majority of our respondents came from very backward sections of society, they had no other sources of income except beedi making. Whatever the contribution of income from agricultural land or business, receipts from family members living outside were very less. The contribution which the children made to beedi making in the family was also very substantial. In the villages and towns where we did our study, majority of the respondents get the payment monthly and only another 7% got it fortnightly. Majority (98%) of the respondents stated that they received their payment in time, and only 2% stated that there was a delay in payment or they received their payment in parts. In the majority of the cases (95%), the payment was received by the respondent herself and in 1.5% cases by the husband, 1.7% other male members, and 1.8% other female members.

When we wanted to find out about victimisation, we got a mixed response, though majority 67% of our respondents said that they were harassed. In our various conservations with the respondents and child workers, we found out that the harassment was primarily in the form of giving them the less amount of tobacco for making the beedis or giving them poor-quality leaves and then rejecting large number of beedis. Thus, through this process, the women suffered a loss in payment. The contractor weighed less tobacco, and if they filled less tobacco in the beedi, it was likely to be rejected; hence, they had to buy tobacco at their own cost from outside or suffer a cut in payment made by the contractor. They were afraid to complain to the contractor.

Though this was an everyday occurrence, they were afraid that he would stop giving them work from the next time.

Majority of our respondents felt that the situation of the family remained the same during the past five to ten years. The majority of respondents (68%) felt that during the coming few years, the situation of the family would neither improve not worsen but remain the same; the other 32% however felt that their situation would only become worst. They stated that now because the increase in prices of all commodities, they were not able to make both ends meet. Besides this, they stated that unlike the previous five to ten years, the contractors had become much more money minded, and there were lots of problems in the way tobacco is weighed. They also complained of the very poor or light quality of leaves and showed us how the leaves used to be earlier. Because of all these problems, more beedis were being rejected now. Besides this, unlike the earlier periods when work was not so much centralised, the karkhanas were open for the longer duration, but in the present circumstances, the karkhanas were closed immediately for no rhyme or reason, and they were devoid of any work or source

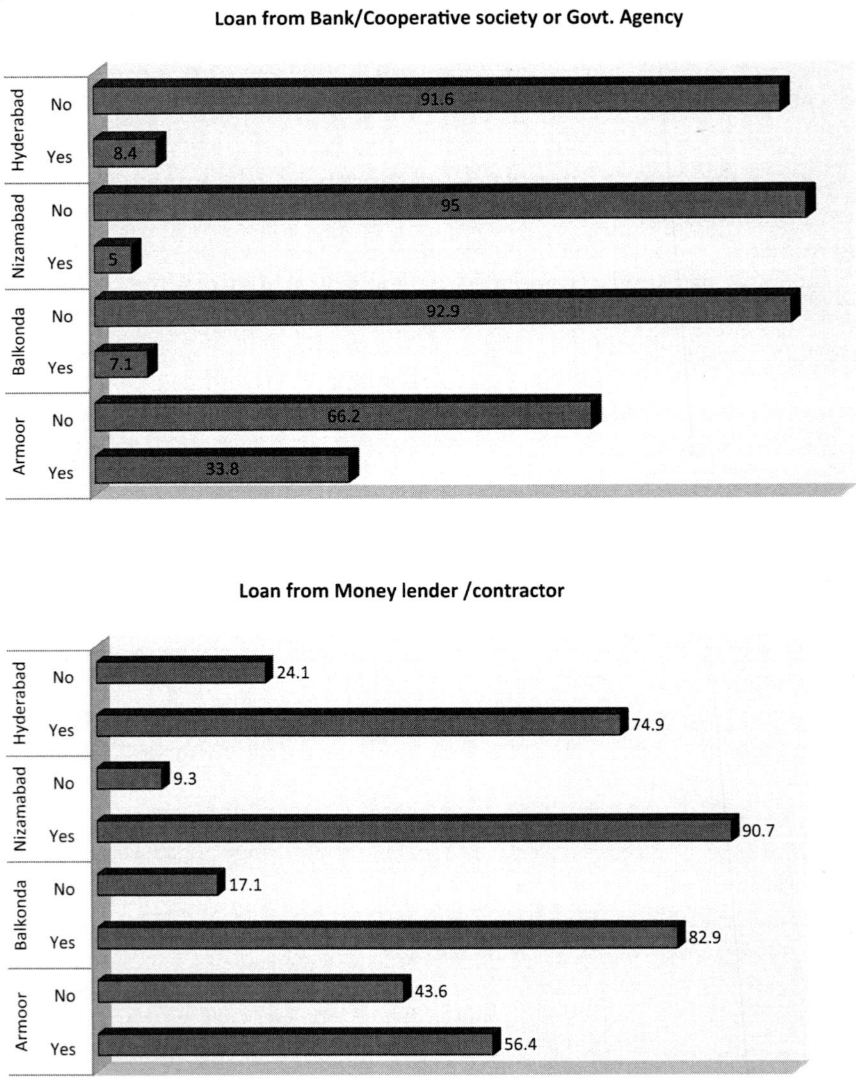

FIGURE 7.6 Family indebtedness.

of income. As far as the family indebtedness is concerned, we got the following details (Figure 7.6).

With such low monthly family income of the households and the rising inflation, it becomes very common for people to borrow money and take loans. However, as commonly known, the same problem of borrowing money existed as people prefer informal sources of taking loans than the formal ones even when the informal sources charge high interest rates. People usually prefer the informal sources because it is easier to take loans from them and it avoids the paper work and formalities in formal ones. Also, these people usually require loans to run their families and for basic facilities for which no formal source would provide loan. Interestingly, in Hyderabad, less than 10% of the families borrowed money from banks and cooperative societies, while more than 30% people in Armoor preferred the formal source, which is again shocking as we usually expect people in bigger cities to use the formal sources. One major reason could be that these people living in Hyderabad do not usually have anything to be kept as collateral which the banks usually ask for. Also, the highest number of people taking loans from money lenders was in Nizamabad while the lowest was in Armoor (Figure 7.7).

The above table shows various government-implemented schemes in all the four areas of our study. Overall, the study found that maximum number of beneficiaries of these schemes were in Nizamabad, while the least number of people using these schemes were in Hyderabad. Minimum wages were being taken by more than 35% of people in Nizamabad, while hardly 11% people in Hyderabad were availing this scheme. Smaller towns like Nizamabad and Balkonda had better health facilities in Hyderabad.

TABLE 7.2 Awareness about Government Schemes

Sr. No.	*Scheme*	*Armoor*		*Balkonda*		*Nizamabad*		*Hyderabad*	
		Yes	No	Yes	No	Yes	No	Yes	No
1.	Minimum wages	27.6	72.4	30.9	69.1	36.9	63.1	11.2	88.8
2.	Scholarship for children	9.4	90.6	6.9	93.1	17.1	82.9	8.0	92
3.	Housing	12.5	87.5	4.80	95.2	5.35	94.65	3.20	96.8
4.	IRDP	14.3	85.7	6.3	93.7	9.80	90.2	2.0	98.0
5.	Nehru Rojgar Yojana	16.3	83.7	8.0	92.0	2.3	97.7	6.8	93.2
6.	TRYSEM	10.9	89.1	11.3	88.7	12.0	88	6.6	93.4
7.	ICDS	10.3	89.7	9.9	90.1	11.5	88.5	7.9	92.1
8.	Non-formal education	2.3	97.7	6.77	93.23	17.4	82.6	2.3	97.7
9.	Community development	0.3	99.7	0.8	99.2	7.1	92.9	3.4	96.6
10.	Healthcare	1.4	98.6	7.1	92.9	6.8	93.2	4.5	95.5

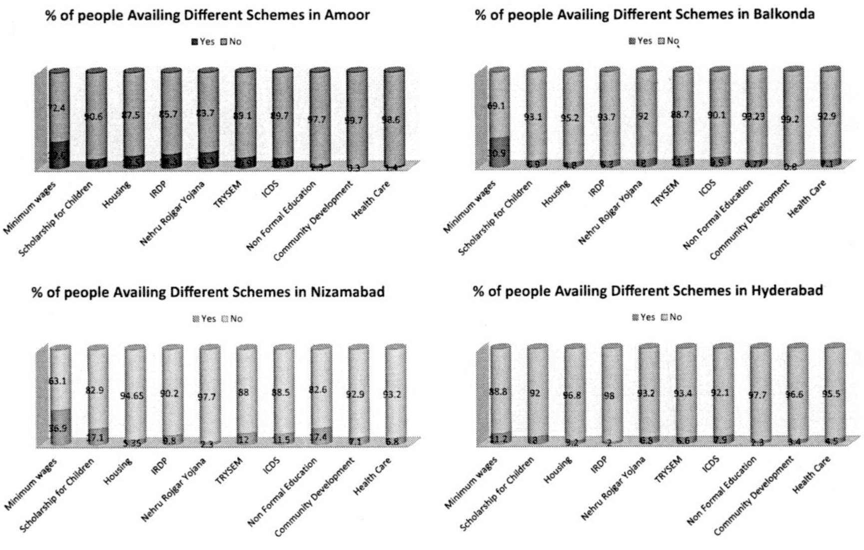

FIGURE 7.7 Awareness about government schemes.

Lactating mothers

In our study, 24% of the mothers were breast-feeding children who were less than four years of age. Many of these women had regularly fed their children on only breast milk for a period of two months and soon tried to wean their children. Nearly half of these women who were breast-feeding their children had discarded the colostrum and were not aware that it was rich in protein content, especially globulin and vitamin A. They thought that this was not fit to be fed to the child. Many stated that they did not get milk for the first few days. They had no concept of antibodies or vital nutrients being present in the milk. Usually feeding started on the second day. With a slighter old child, the women continued to breast-feed the child, while making beedis. Many health experts have attributed the decline of breast-feeding to lack of awareness and the power of advertisement of breast milk substitutes (Kumar, 1988). Therefore, the conventional approach to empower women to breast-feed has rested mainly on eradication of the supposed ignorance of mothers. Such an approach fails to recognise the multiple roles of women as workers, homemakers, and mothers. It is assumed that housewives have the time, resources, and inclination to provide a high-quality care for children (Basu and Basu, 1991). It is assumed that if women cannot afford to withdraw from market activities, work in the family enterprise or family farms will provide greater flexibility to provide better quality of care for their children (Tamang et al., 1990). Domestic responsibilities take up tremendous portion of women's time in poor areas and affect both their care of young children and participation in labour force (Jain et al., 1995). This is more so in the unorganised sectors (Kameshwari, 1992). Our study of the beedi workers clearly showed us that though much need to be done on creating awareness, the economic, social, and psychological constraints all affect the mother child proximity. Many of these women who had to drop out of infant care during breast-feeding belonged to low-income groups. The choice was between making beedis and survival or the luxury of childcare. Many of these women during the first month faced severe financial constraint, were forced to cut out a meal or two, or resort to heavy borrowing. These women hardly had any respite from domestic work and had to fetch water, do cleaning, cooking along with getting raw material, rolling beedis, and childcare. It is true that a woman's work is never done (Sharma, 1989).

Nutrition and health are inextricably linked to the quality of life and economic productivity. Many of our respondents were ignorant about the proper weight gain as one of the best criteria for judging the adequacy of breast milk. They did not consider burping of any use. There was no awareness that early weaning would lead to secondary lactation failure and more chances of gastrointestinal infection, and would result in iatrogenic malnutrition. There was a strong belief that undiluted milk was unfit for consumption by an infant and only undiluted top milk could be digested properly. There was a strong belief that fruits and fruit juices were cold products and should be avoided because it could lead to diarrhoea. It is difficult to state if the origin of these beliefs should be seen in economic milieu of the household or the cultural and traditional practices of the region. Even in the area of hygiene for breast-feeding, much was to be desired. Many a times the women did not wash their hands of the tobacco and pulled out their nipple for the child. This was due to the paucity of time. For these women, every day was a race against time to make the required beedis and get more raw materials from the contractor.

Ambitions for children

While interviewing the respondents, we wanted to assess their attitude towards their children's education, and so we had a fairly large section related to children's education. In one sample, majority of the respondents were mothers of the child workers (94%), and only 4% were fathers. It was interesting to note the social biases and attitudes which the respondents had regarding boys and girls. When we asked the respondents for their opinion as to what level the children should be educated, we got different responses for both boys and girls. We found that as far as the boys were concerned, the parent felt that collage was a must (42%), and as far as girls were concerned, they felt (21%) that high school was the only requirement. Thus, in our sample, while the mothers thought that college education was required for boys, as far as girls were concerned, it was enough if they studied up till high school. In many informal discussions with the parents and mothers, we found that as far as boys were concerned, they were very ambitious and never saw beedi making as an option. They wanted the boys to join some service or start a business. For girls, they felt even high school was enough because their ultimate ambition was to get them married. They did not look upon beedi making as a source to collect money for their daughters dowry but for day-to-day survival. If at any time education came in the way of their beedi making, education was invariable sacrificed. While parents did not mind sending their girls till primary or middle school, after puberty, they were often made to sit at home and concentrate only on beedi making.

Regarding the satisfaction at their children's education is concerned, in case of boys, 20% of parents were satisfied in Armoor Mandal, 30.3% in Balkonda Mandal, and 30% of parents in Nizamabad Mandal were satisfied with the education of boys. Some parents were satisfied somewhat with their boys' education. They amount to 24.3% in Armoor Mandal, 19.4% in Balkonda Mandal, and 21.3% in Nizamabad Mandal. Parents who were not satisfied with the education of their boys can also be found. They amount to 10.6% in Armoor Mandal, 3.4% in Balkonda Mandal, and 2.7% in Nizamabad Mandal.

The parents who were not satisfied or somewhat satisfied with their children's education were in urban areas. They were very clear that they wanted some kind of a technical training for boys. Many mentioned typing, computers, etc., which were not part of the syllabus, and the parents had to spend a lot of money to get these training through private institutions located in other urban areas. For girls, they mentioned sewing and stitching as being important but were never a part of the syllabus.

References

Basu, A. M., and K. Basu, 1991, "Women's Economic Roles and Child Survival: The Case of India", *Health Transition Review*, Vol. 1, pp. 83–101.

Jain, D., and S. Desai, 1995, "The Women Worker and Her Child", *Institute of Social Studies*, Dossier No. 4, Bangalore.

Kameshwari, J., and R. Pande, 1992, Report, Crèches in the Organized and Unorganized Sectors in Secunderabad and Hyderabad, *Department of Women and Child Welfare, Government of India*, New Delhi.

Kumar, R. (ed.), 1988, *Child Development in India,* Vol. 1, New Delhi, Ashish Publishing House.

Sharma, M., and U. Varjani, 1989, "Women's Work Is Never Done: Dairy Development and Health in the Lives of Rural Women in Rajasthan", *Economic and Political Weekly*, April 29, WS pp. 38–44.

8

BEEDI MAKING AT HOME AND AT THE WORK SHED

The survey in the different areas found that most of the families were involved in beedi making from a very long time. The study indicated that beedi making had become their permanent profession. Around 65% of the people in all the four areas have been in this profession for more than 15 years. In Armoor, 56% of the beedi-making women were doing this work from more than 21 years. Less than 5% of these people in all four regions were involved in this work from less than five years. This clearly indicates that beedi making was a stable and permanent job for them. They did not take it up as a short-term work or a part-time job. This had become the sole source of their earnings for their entire lives.

Making beedi was a very specialised kind of activity that was handed down from one generation to the next. Because they were inexperienced, the contractors frequently rejected the bids submitted by newcomers because the beedi's did not meet the required standards. As a result, there was very little room for newcomers to compete in this industry. Due to this, they suffered a significant financial setback because they were forced to buy beedis from a group of experts at a higher price and then provide it to the contractor. Therefore, newcomers sought employment in other fields, and if they did enter the beedi-making industry, it was primarily to assist others in performing certain initial tasks such as cutting the leaves, filling tobacco, and other similar activities. We discovered that the contractors also relied more on long-standing families than they did on newer families entering the field because they did not want to give work to the latter. Actually, much to our surprise, in some families involved in beedi making, daughters-in-law who had come from outside the village did not make beedis, despite the fact that the entire family was involved in beedi making (Figure 8.1).

Beedi making was thus a very specialised kinds of work, and when we asked as to what the family was doing before beedi making, we found that majority

DOI: 10.4324/9781003317944-10

of them were involved in beedi making, with 76.3% in Armoor, 75.04% in Balkonda, 72.09% in Nizamabad, and 66.90% in Hyderabad. Table 8.1 clearly shows this.

As we saw in the previous chart as well, most of the families are in the business for a very long time, and as we can see in this diagram, most of the families carry out this as their occupation for generations. More than 70% of the people in Armoor, Balkonda, and Nizamabad said that their family occupation before beedi making was also the same. Only in Hyderabad, the trend was a little different, probably because of a higher share in service sector and some of them being self-employed and/or having petty business. A total of 5–10% of people have shifted from being a casual labour to beedi making, which shows their preference.

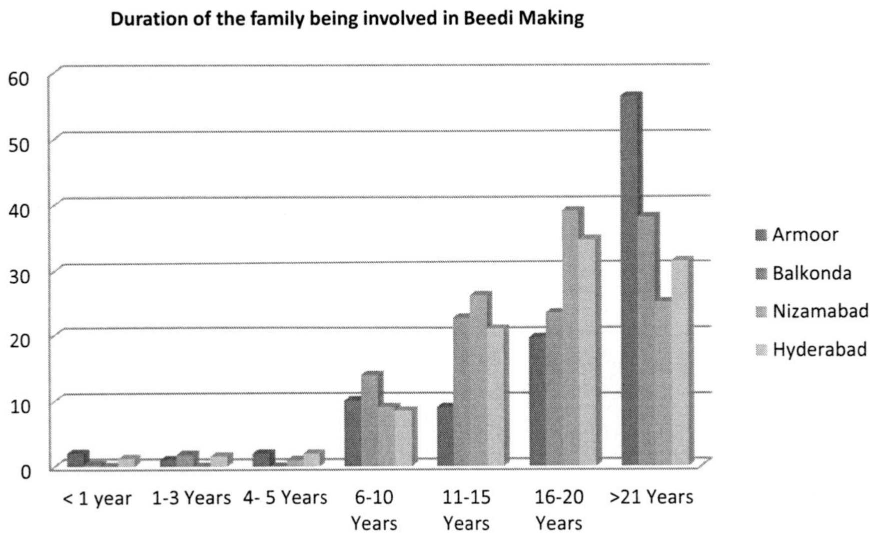

FIGURE 8.1 Duration of the family being involved in beedi making.

TABLE 8.1 Family Occupation before Beedi Making

Occupation	*Armoor*	*Balkonda*	*Nizamabad*	*Hyderabad*
Beedi making	76.03	75.04	72.09	66.90
Cultivation	1.2	1.2	0	3.7
Casual labour	7.1	6.1	8.5	5.0
Piece-rated work	11.97	8.4	7.04	7.20
Petty business/self-employed	1.1	4.0	0.2	5.20
Manuel wage work	2.0	4.6	7.0	5.0
Service	0.6	0.30	2.2	7.0
Total	100	100	100	100

These people prefer beedi making to casual labour, maybe because this gives them more freedom than being a casual labour, and here they are their own boss.

When we asked the reason for the family to get involved in beedi making, majority of our respondents, 96.6%, said that there was no other source of income, 1.6% stated that their family was traditionally involved in this work, and 9% said they had no other skill other than beedi making. Of our respondents, 95% were involved in beedi making even before their marriage, and only 3.9% were not engaged in this work prior to their marriage. Thus, on an average, the family is engaged in beedi making for a period of eight to nine months. However, it is not that this work is done continuously. Most of the time the karkhanas are closed and the contractor does not provide raw material, and the women cannot do any work for 10–15 days in a month. So the women felt that on an average, they were engaged in beedi making for about nine months. When we asked them as to what they did when they were not involved in beedi making, we found that majority of our respondents, i.e., 94%, did not do any other work and only 41% did the work of agricultural labour. The main reason we found for this was that the beedi workers were not free for a continuous period of time. They became free any time of the week due to non-availability of raw material or the *karkhana* being closed or the contractors not being available in town. Since, all these were very unpredictable, they could not find any other work, and only few went out to work as agricultural labourer. What we found was that the beedi workers would go to the *karkhana* or the contractor every day to get work and in between suddenly for a day or two, there was no work and they had no other option but to sit at home.

We found that majority of our respondents had been issue identity cards 85.7%, and only 14.2% did not have identity cards. Most of these cards (81%) were in the name of the respondent, and 3.3% were in the name of other female member in the family. About 86% of our respondents had a passbook issued to them, and only 13.8% did not have a passbook. Majority of the people stated that it was kept up to date. In fact, in many villages, women very proudly showed us their passbooks. This was their prized possession. We found that an entry was made every day on the number of beedis made by the respondent and then monthly or weekly wages calculated accordingly.

Majority of our respondents, 98.9%, complained to us that the raw material supplied to them was insufficient for the number of beedis they were expected to make. In fact, many of the women in the village showed us the raw material supplied to them; some of it was not up to the mark, the leaves not being of proper shape, tobacco being weighed less. They told us that the contractor benefited doubly by this method. He would charge them for more raw material and pay less amount for the lesser number of beedis. Often the women incurred much loss for they had to purchase beedis or raw material from outside. Though most of the women were very agitated on this account, they could not do anything because they feared that if they complaint to the contractor, he would stop giving them work, and they will not have any other sources of income.

The work shed

A very important feature of beedi making in Nizamabad district is the work shed, where many of the women and children sit together and make beedis. We found a large number of these work sheds in all the three places of our study. However, our data could not reflect this quite correctly because we wanted to interview the mother and child simultaneously. In these work sheds, the mother would be present at one time and the daughter would be present another. Hence, we had to go home to the house of the beedi makers in the evening in order to get both mother and daughter, and they were recorded as working at home. Yet we could interview 41 mothers and daughters working in the work shed. These work sheds were not strictly *karkhanas* or factories but more or less a common space given either by the contractor or the village panchayat to work. Many women told us that though these work sheds did not have any facilities, they preferred to sit here and make beedis because they could make more beedis, not being disturbed by housework. They also did not get bored with their work because they would continue to sing, chat, and gossip while making beedis. However, it was not an absolute necessity that the women come to the shed. If they had more work at home, they would sit at home and make beedis and come to the work shed only when it suited them. The children came back from school and joined their mothers in the evening. Other children who were not going to school were in the work shed for a longer duration of time.

Most of these sheds are at a walking distance of 2% of our respondents, and the other 8% had to walk 1–2 km to reach the work shed. Some of these sheds had drinking water and toilet facilities, but there was no facility of rest, lunch time, medical, or paid holiday. But working in the shed, the child worker could earn up to Rs 100 (0.2%), Rs 101–150(1.4%), Rs 151–209 (6%), and Rs 210–300 (0.2%). Most of them received their own payment (1.6%). Payment was made monthly, and it was often on time. Most of them got this work through other family members and known person, and the others got it through an agent or contractor of the children who work in the work shed. A total of 9% also make beedis at home, and 1.3% do not make beedis at home. As mentioned earlier, many of them preferred working in the work shed, because there was no monotony in the work, and they could make more beedis without being distracted by housework etc. and at the same time, chat with their friends. Of these, 1.2% said that they were victimised, while 1.1% said that they were not victimised. The major form of victimisation or harassment was that there was a cut in payment, and there was a demand for extra beedis. However, we found that the work shed functioned more or less very informally with the women and children coming on the days it suited them and staying there for the full day. Most of the women and children did agree that they were able to make more number of beedis by sitting at the work shed rather than at home. At home, the work was done individually and combined with household chores, but in the work shed, it was done in a group and along with friends (Figure 8.2).

As the graph clearly depicts, maximum number of families in all the areas made 501–1,000 beedis per day. Majority of the people in all the regions made less than 1,000 beedis. It was with a lot of input from the children, and if two women were making beedis in some families, they could make more than 1,000 beedis (Figure 8.3).

When we collected the data of their incomes to see how much they earned by beedi making, we found another interesting detail. Although Hyderabad produced lesser number of beedis per day, still the income earned by beedi making was higher in Hyderabad. Although majority of the people in all four regions

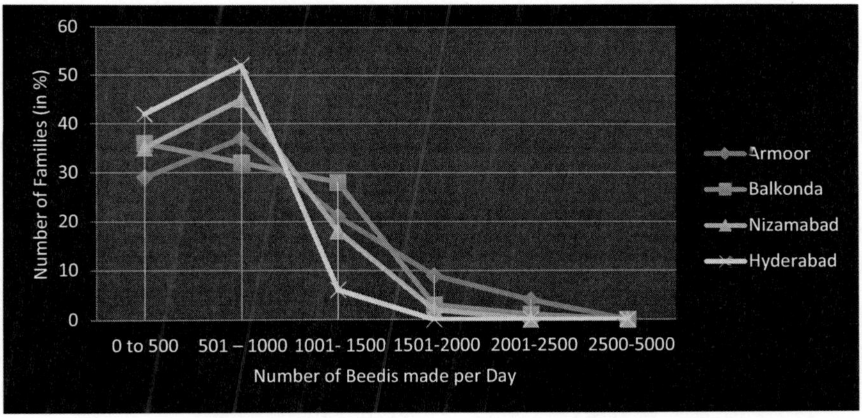

FIGURE 8.2 Number of beedis made per day.

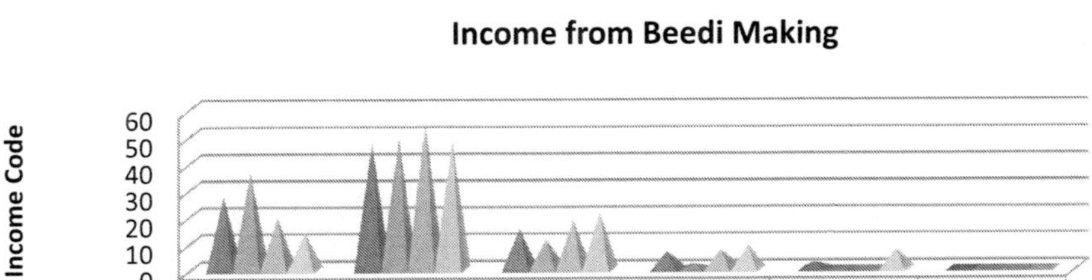

	Rs. 1000-2000	Rs. 2001-3000	Rs. 3001-4000	Rs. 4001-5000	Rs. 5001-6000	Rs. 6001-7000
Armoor	27.7	47.2	15.1	6.7	2.6	0.7
Balkonda	36.6	49.2	11.4	2.1	0.5	0.2
Nizamabad	19.5	54.7	18.3	7.5	0	0
Hyderabad	13.95	47.9	21.39	8.9	7.4	0.46

FIGURE 8.3 Income from beedi making.

earned between Rs 2,001 and 3,000, but higher income was being earned in Hyderabad. Interestingly, Armoor and Balkonda were the areas where families were producing higher number of beedis per day, but these were also the regions where close to 30% of the people earned less than Rs 2,000. We saw that none of the families in Hyderabad could produce more than 1,500 beedis per day, yet while calculating the income generated, maximum people in the higher income bracket were from Hyderabad. Hardly 3% in Armoor, less than 1% in Balkonda, and 0% in Nizamabad earned more than Rs 5,000, but around 8% of families in Hyderabad earned that amount. This means that the number of families earning more than Rs 5,000 in Hyderabad was more than the number of families earning the same amount in all the other three regions combined. This difference could be because of two reasons. Either the quality of beedis being prepared in Hyderabad was superior to the other regions or the Hyderabad beedi makers were earning the benefit of being in a bigger city and being closer to the markets.

9

INVISIBLE LABOUR

The girl child worker

Our study consisted of 375 children within the age group of 5–14 years. Of these, like their mothers, 60% were from the rural areas and 40% were from the urban areas. We did not have any sample of child workers from Hyderabad. Most of the children were going to school here.

The male/female division among the children in the family was as follows (Table 9.1).

Though we had 15.4% of boy child workers from Armoor, 28.64% from Balkonda, and 33.0% from Nizamabad in our sample, this field was dominated by girls. We found that beedi making was a very gendered kind of work. While the girls made beedis at home, the boys were doing it if they were less than 12 years of age. Boys who were 12 years and above worked in the factory and did works like packaging and labelling. In fact, many boys looked down upon beedi making as only a women's work. We found a number of boys between 13 and 15 just loafing around, neither studying nor doing any other kind of job, but they did not make beedi because they were clear that this is not a man's work. Most of the boys worked in the factory and helped the family by bringing raw material or taking the ready-made beedis to the contractor. We focused mostly on the girls making beedis and did not focus on the boys.

TABLE 9.1 Sex of the Child Beedi Workers

Sl. No.	*Sex*	*Armoor*	*Balkonda*	*Nizamabad*
1	Male	15.4	28.6	33.0
2	Female	84.6	71.4	67.0
	Total	100.0	100.0	100.0

DOI: 10.4324/9781003317944-11

The age division among the girl child workers was as follows (Figure 9.1).

Thus, we had a fairly representative sample with 9% of our child workers being of 7 years, 11% of 8 years, 1.0% of being of 9 years, another 11% being of 10 year, nearly 12% being of 12 and 13 years, 16% being of 14 years, and 13% being of 15 years of age.

The birth order of these children was a follows (Figure 9.2).

Thus, majority of the child workers (67%) were first born, and 20% were second born. So these children if they were girls had the added responsibility of sibling care besides doing household work.

Majority of the children in our sample, 92%, spoke Telugu and 5% spoke Urdu. Other Urdu-speaking Muslim children were very comfortable with Telugu and used this language as a medium of communication.

Of our sample, 95% were unmarried, 2% were married, 2% divorced, and 1% were deserted. The educational status of the children was as follows (Figure 9.3).

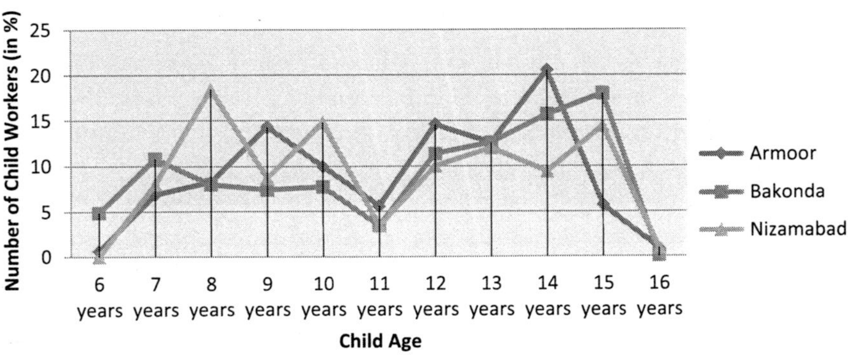

FIGURE 9.1 Actual age of the child worker.

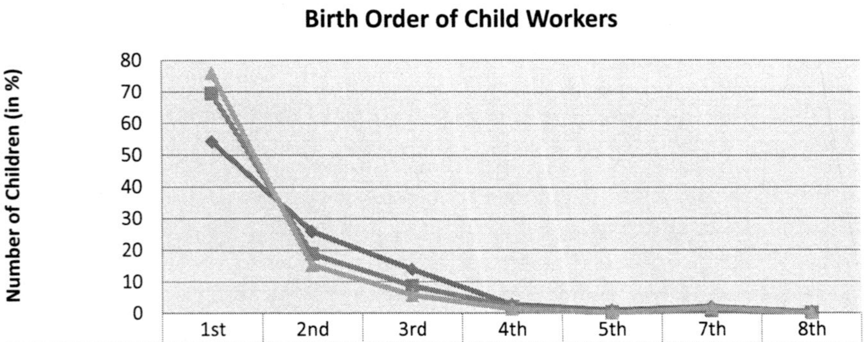

	1st	2nd	3rd	4th	5th	7th	8th
Armoor	54.2	26	13.9	2.7	0.9	2	0.3
Balkonda	69.4	18.9	8.6	2	0.3	0.8	0
Nizamabad	76	15.3	5.7	1.3	0	1.7	0

FIGURE 9.2 Birth order of the girl child worker.

Though 24% of our sample was illiterate, 45% were studying in primary school and 22% in high school.

Following is the current status of the child (Table 9.2).

Of our sample, 13% from Armoor, 9.1% from Balkonda, and 9.4% from Nizamabad were dropouts, and 16.9% from Armoor, 11.4% from Balkonda, and 12.6% from Nizamabad had never been to school. By and large, the girls were attending school and did beedi making after they came back from school and during holidays.

We were very much interested in knowing the reasons for the child to drop out of school or never having gone to schools, so we had asked a number of questions related to this. We found that only 3% of the children did not go to school because they did not like studies, but 14% did not go to school because the parents were too poor to afford education, and 3% had to supplement the family income. A total of 3.3% could not attend school because there was too much household work or family obligation. When we asked, if given the facilities, would they like to go to school? Only 5% said yes and 21% said no. Of those who said yes when we asked them what kind of facilities they would like to have, many said convenient school timings and other 4% stated a combination of mid-day meal, books, conventional timings, etc.

When we enquired the others who said that they did not want to go to school, the reason for this, majority of them, 7%, said that they find it awkward to go to

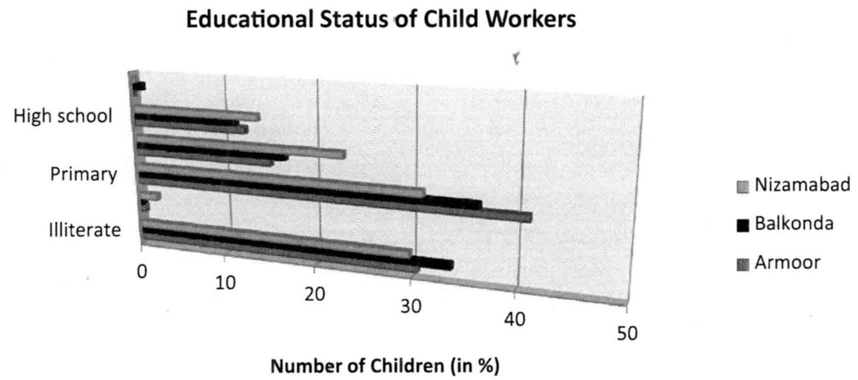

FIGURE 9.3 Educational status of the child workers.

TABLE 9.2 Current Educational Status of the Child

Sl. No.	*Status*	*Armoor*	*Balkonda*	*Nizamabad*
1	Currently attending school	70.1	79.3	78.0
2	Dropout	13.0	9.1	9.4
3	Never went to school	16.9	11.4	12.6
	Total	100	100	100

school at this age, 5% said that they had to supplement the family income, and 2% said that there was too much household work and family obligation. In the various conversations we had with the child workers, we found that many of them wanted to go to school, but since they did not know reading and writing, they had to start at the beginning which would be very awkward in a regular school with their present age. Many children were excited with the idea of a non-formal system of education which would equip them with reading and writing skills.

Child workers who dropped out

In our sample, we had 11% of our child workers who had dropped school at the age of 12 years, another 3% at the age of 13 years, 2% at the age of 14, and another 2% at 11 years. Parents educated the girls until the time they reached puberty and as soon as they matured, be it at 12, 13, or 14, they were made to sit at home and concentrate on beedi making only. Of these children, nearly 10% were studying in a coeducational school, and 8% in an only-girls school. Majority of these girls were studying in 6th/7th class when they dropped out of school. Their medium of instruction was Telugu only. Majority of the girls stated that the reasons they had stopped going to school was because they had to supplement family income, and there was too much household work and family obligation. Few mentioned puberty and education not being valued by their parents as the reason for their dropping out of school.

Of these girls, 8% said that they would not like to go to school, and only 3% said that they would like to go back to school. They mentioned the fact that they had to supplement the family income (3.4%), there was too much household work (2%), and 3% stated finding it very awkward to go to school at this age. Many of these families needed the income earned by the girls for their day-to-day survival, and they could not afford a luxury like education (Figure 9.4).

When parents were asked that if all facilities, support was provided, would they send their children to school? A total of 17.4% in Armoor Mandal replied positively. The reply was positive even in Balkonda 99.75) and Nizamabad (11.3%) Mandal. Some parents did not want to send their children to school even in facilities were provided. They amount to 26.3% in Armoor Mandal and 22.9% and 16.3% in Balkonda and Nizamabad Mandals, respectively. When we spoke to these parents, we found their day-to-day basis for survival, and therefore, education was a luxury which they could not value. Most of these families were below poverty line, and since they did not have any land or other means of livelihood, they needed all the hands they could to help in beedi making.

Child workers who were attending school

Of our sample, 66% of the children were attending school. The mid-day meal scheme also attracted a large number of children to school. Following are the details about the type of school they were attending. Thus, majority of the

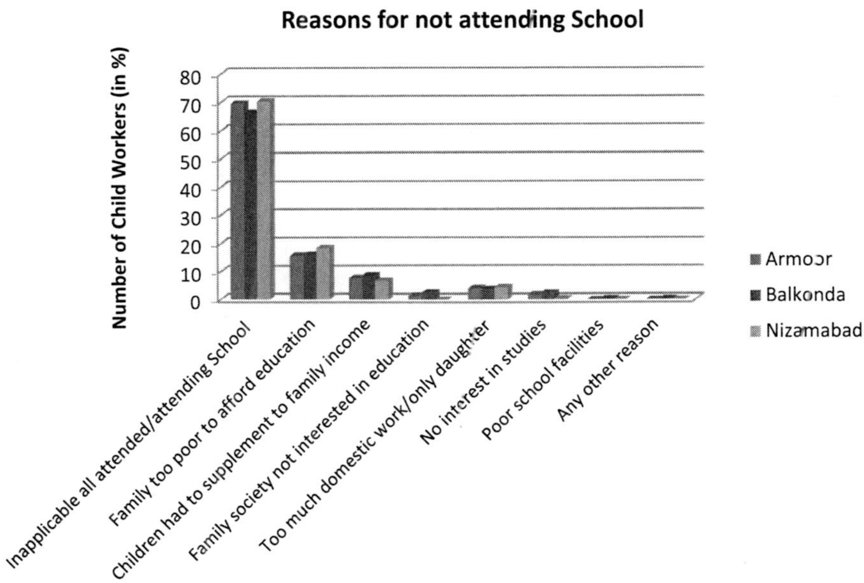

FIGURE 9.4 Reasons for discontinuing or never going to school.

children were studying in coeducational school. We found that in all these Mandals, the primarily schools were coeducational only and children studied there. Of our sample, 74% of the children were generally able to complete their homework, and only 4% could not complete their homework in time.

Most of the schools were at a walking distance. Most of the children walked to the school which was nearby and only 4% of the children had to travel 2 km. Since the school was at a walkable distance, none of the children had any problem while travelling to school. Of our sample, 55% said that they liked their studies very much, only 11% said that they liked studies only somewhat, and 3% did not like studies at all. Thus, most of the children would like to study up to high school and college. Many of the girls asked us why we were asking this question to them, because it was their parents who would decide as to how much they can study. Given the choice, many of them wanted to go to college, because they thought that a college degree is a must to get a good job.

When we asked our respondents if some children between 6 and 15 years have discontinued studies or have never gone to school, we found that it was inapplicable in majority of the cases (71%), because they had attended or were attending school. Among the rest, majority (24%) mentioned family being too poor to afford education as the reason for children discontinuing or never attending school and 6% mentioned that children have to supplement family income.

Given a choice of acquiring general school education or technical/vocational training for their children, only 1.4% parents in Armoor Mandal responded in favour of general education, and the number is meagre in the other too, i.e., a total of 6% favoured general education. But for the technical/vocational training, the response is overwhelming: 72.9% in Armoor Mandal, 64% in Balkonda Mandal, and 51.3% in Nizamabad Mandal favoured for it, i.e., a total of 63.4%. Most parents felt that if they wanted technical training, they had to send their children to private institutions in Nizamabad city which involved a lot of expenditure; there were no facilities like computer courses in Armoor and Balkonda. For girls, they wanted stitching, cutting, and embroidery classes to be held in their villages. We even saw some stitching machines in few houses, but they were not in much use because the girls did not know cutting.

We also wanted to assess the ambitions of the parents for their children, and so we asked specific questions regarding their children and their ambitions for them. The following chart illustrates the results. Therefore, parents (19%) ranked having a good job and more income for boys as being important followed by (15%) feeling that having their own business or being self-employed was important for boys. As far as the girls were concerned, majority of the parents (94.5%) felt that getting them married was their only ambition. Having business or getting a good job was nowhere in their list of ambition for girls. We found most of the mothers being very much influenced by the social reality which they see around them and the continuous harping of the idea of women the homemaker being portrayed through television, and they pass on the same values to their daughters.

Child workers and beedi making

Our study showed that while the mothers had been involved in beedi making for a long time, for about ten years or more, the majority of the child workers were involved in beedi making for the last two or four years. The following table shows the number of years the child workers were involved in beedi making (Figure 9.5).

Most of the child workers were involved in this work from last two to five years. There were some child workers who were involved in this work from nine to ten years and even more, which means they started working when they were hardly five to six years old. The children working at such minor age of five to seven years are much more prone to catch infections and can also get some severe life-threatening disease in the future. Majority of the child workers, 98%, worked in the home or in the neighbourhood. These child workers were doing various kinds of tasks in beedi making as shown by the following table (Figure 9.6).

When a child worker was a beginner in beedi making and had been initiated into it for only a year or so, they primarily rolled the beedis, cut the leaves, or tied the thread. However, once they had been in beedi making for more than two years or so, they performed more than one activity (54%) and often made the complete beedi. This is what we discovered. The majority of the workers were women and children, and in order to maximise efficiency, they would cut all of the leaves at once before moving on to the next step in the process of making beedi.

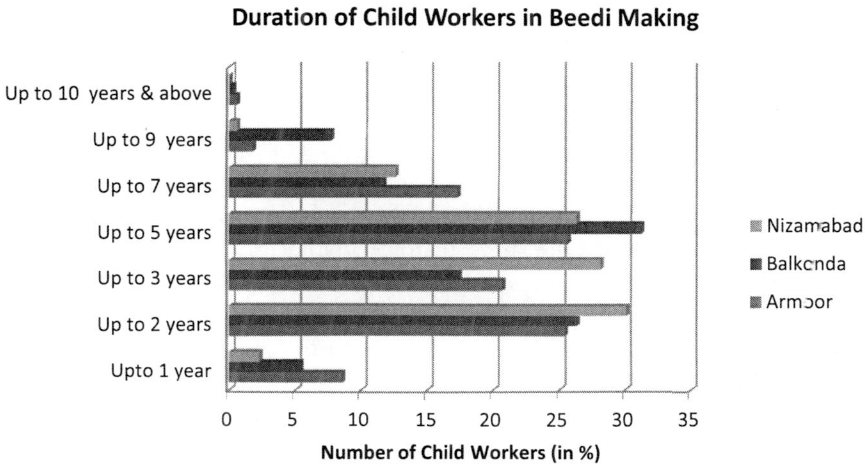

FIGURE 9.5 Duration of child worker in beedi making.

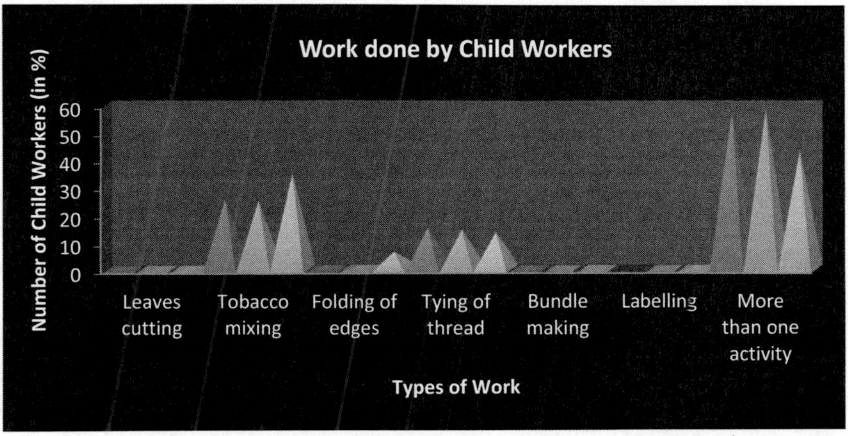

FIGURE 9.6 Kind of work done by the child worker.

On enquiring the work done by the child workers since they were too young, we got to know that around 55% of them did more than one activity. This was a very clear-cut indicator that these children learnt the entire process of beedi making and were capable of doing any part of it. As we have seen, the child workers join the process at a young age of six to seven years. After working for two to three years, they are totally aware of the entire process and are capable to take up any work of beedi making. Other than this, most of the child workers said that they were into tobacco mixing and tying of thread. This is mostly done by the younger children. Since leaves cutting required experience of knowing which leaves are to be chosen and bundle making and labelling required the person to be very careful, these works were not done much by the child workers and were usually taken up by the elders in the family.

Most of the child workers spend two to four hours in beedi making as many of them were going to school and came from school and did this work. The following table shows the time spent by the child worker in beedi making (Figure 9.7).

Majority of the child workers spent two to four hours in beedi making probably because they go to school, and in the remaining time, they help their family in the work. There were very few children who were working more than six hours. There were hardly any children in Nizamabad who were working more than 4 hours, but there were more than 10% children in Armoor who were working for more than 10 hours. In previous chapter, we saw that Armoor was the place where maximum numbers of beedis were being made and where the income was the least. Probably this is the reason that children were also asked to work for more time in order to make more beedis, and thus, they drop out from school.

What we discovered was that on the one hand, young children between the ages of 8 and 11 who were also attending school spent two to four hours making beedi. On the other hand, we found that girls who had reached puberty and were either not going to school or had dropped out spent more time making beedi. The vast majority of these children completed their work in the evenings, as well as in the mornings, evenings, and both times in between before going to school and after returning from school. Majority of the child workers, 66%, said that they liked their work. When we probed the reasons for this, we were amazed to see the level of maturity among these small children. They were very proud of the fact that while other children were only going to school, they were sharing the responsibilities of their parents and assisting them in earning a livelihood. Only 34% of our child workers stated that they did not like their work, and many of them stated body pain and no time to play and study as a reason for this. The following table shows this.

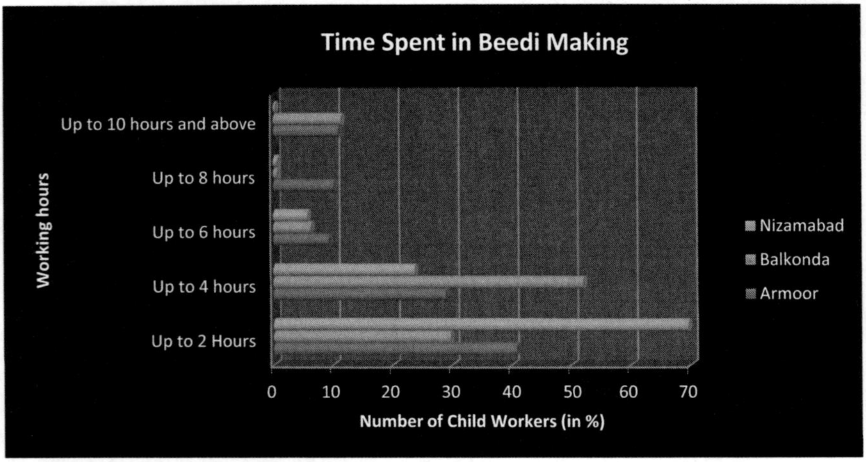

FIGURE 9.7 Time spent in beedi making.

Majority of our child workers (24%) made 101–150 per day, and 20% made 201–250 beedis per day. The following table shows this (Figure 9.8).

In all the three regions, around 50% of the child workers make less than 200 beedis per day. In Armoor, there were slightly more than 10% child workers who were making more than 500 beedis per day while less than 5% children in Nizamabad and Balkonda made more than 500 beedis. Above, we had seen that child workers in Armoor give more time in beedi making as compared to child workers in other regions due to various reasons. This is the main reason why more number of beedis was being prepared by children in Armoor.

What we found was that children who were going to school regularly and worked only after school hours made 100–250 beedis per day and children who made more than 250 beedis per day had either dropped out of school or never went to school and were engaged in beedi making for the whole day. When we asked the child workers if they did not do as much work as was expected from them, what punishment was given? A total of 53% said that there was no punishment given and 47% said that they were scolded. We came across very few cases where severe beating (0.3%) was given or they were denied food (0.3%). This was primarily in families which were very poor and the fathers did not take any responsibility of the house being a drunkard, and the house was run primarily by the mothers who had more than one problem on her hand. When we asked the child workers that if they did more work than was expected from them, what was the reward they received? A total of 16% said that there was no reward, and 84% said they were appreciated, praised, and loved. Only 0.2% said they were given reward in the form of cash, and 0.1% said they were given special food (Figure 9.9).

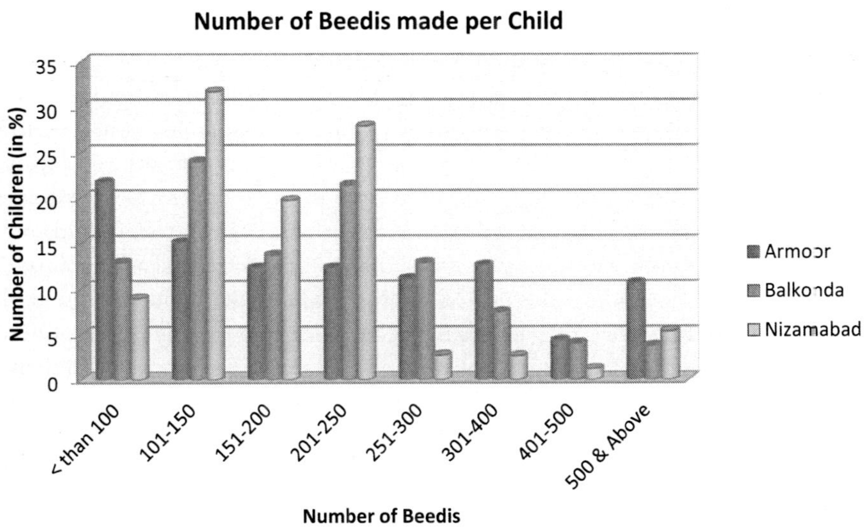

FIGURE 9.8 Number of beedis made per day by child workers.

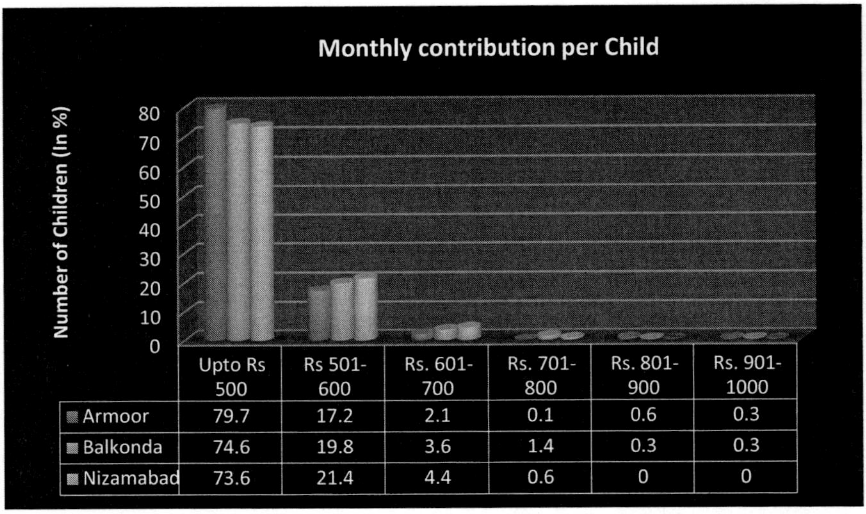

FIGURE 9.9 The child's monthly contribution in monetary terms.

The trend was almost same in all the regions when we studied the contribution made per child. Around 95% of the child workers could contribute less than Rs 600 per month. There were less than 1% children in Armoor and Balkonda who contributed more than Rs 800 per month, while there was no child worker in Nizamabad contributing above Rs 800.

We also wanted to find out if these children got any money out of their earnings to spend on their own, and we found that children who were below 10 or 11 were not given any cash in hand, but children over the age of 11 often got cash in hand. Since most of these workers were girls, we also found that besides beedi making, they also assisted in household chores. We saw that even if the child was going to school, they would clean the house, wash the utensils, and bring in water from outside the house. Girls who were doing beedi making full time did a lot of house work which also included cooking, cleaning, washing, and taking care of the siblings. In our conversations with the child workers, we found that they were not even willing to accept housework as work and only regarded beedi making as work. We found that housework varied a lot with age, and tasks were clearly delegated based on age. Most of the child workers took care of their sibling when their mothers did beedi making or other works. Often the child worker did a lot of household chores, thus relieving the mother and giving her more time, so that she could make more beedis. The speed of the mother was much more than the child worker. In fact by the end of our study, we got quite used to seeing the mother and daughter continuously making beedis and carrying on the day-to-day work in the house. Beedi making when it was being done was hardly stopped for a minute either while cooking or talking to us. We found that beedi making was not something which was done after the household works were completed. Both were done simultaneously. Wherever the women or the girls was, a small basket containing the raw materials for making beedis was always with them. They would keep it aside, wash the rice and put it on the fire, start making beedis, clean the dal and put in on the fire, and then continue with beedi making. We were really amazed at how these people could do more than one task at a time. What was interesting was that many child workers had their basket of raw materials in front of them even while reading or writing (Figure 9.10).

Shockingly, majority of the children were happy and satisfied with the work. The percentage of such children was as high as 83% in Nizamabad. This came as a huge shock because despite knowing the problems and diseases associated with beedi making and also the exploitation leading to financial issues in this profession, they were still happy, which means that they would continue doing the work. This brings us to the same point again; the importance of education and the guidance required by these children. Besides this, the children felt very happy that they were contributing to the family income.

Of the 34% of our child workers who did not like beedi making, 10% said it was because they could not study, 10.5% said they could not study and play, and 11.4% said because of body pain. Most of these children were below 12 years. Though these children were young, they made immense contribution to the family by making a large number of beedis.

When we asked the respondents if beedi making improved the marriage prospects of their children in any way, the majority of our respondents (99%) felt that it did not and only 1% felt that it improved the marriage prospects. Beedi making, the parents say, will not improve the marriage prospects of children in

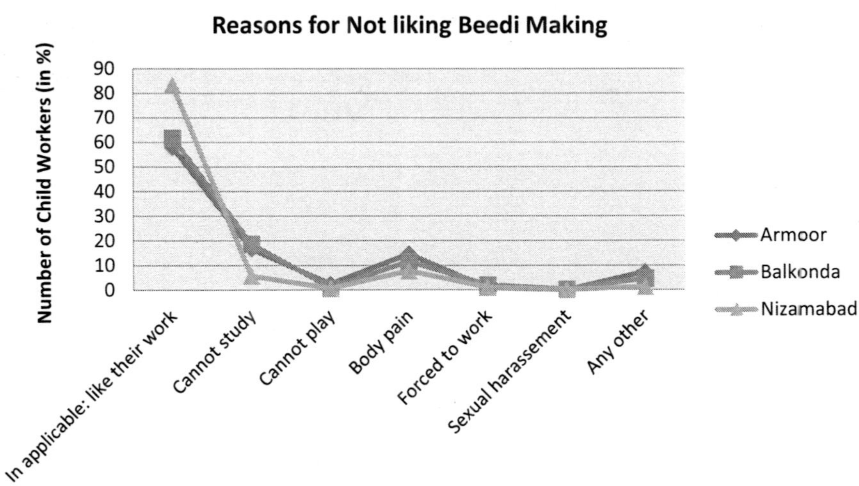

FIGURE 9.10 Reasons for not liking beedi making.

TABLE 9.3 Beedi Making Improving Marriage Prospects

	Armoor	*Balkonda*	*Nizamabad*
Yes	2.6	3.1	0.7
No	97.4	96.9	99.3
Total	100	100	100

any way. Only 2.6% of the parents in Armoor Mandal said it would improve the prospects (Table 9.3).

These parents looked upon Beedi making primarily as a source of making money for their daily needs. All of them complained that they could hardly save any of this money for their daughters' dowry. They knew perfectly well that if their daughters were more educated and had good jobs, their marriage prospects would be better, but since this was not possible in their day-to-day fight for survival, they continued to make beedis without any other option and got the girls married as and when the opportunity came.

We also wanted to find out if our respondents were aware of government schemes for the betterment of families like theirs. We posed similar questions to the child worker and found that there was a lot of difference between the urban areas and the rural areas regarding awareness. Even trade union activity was primarily concentrated in pockets of urban area and had very little impact in rural areas. Majority of our respondents though aware of many of the government schemes and legislations had not benefited out of them. The following table shows comparison of the level of awareness between the mothers and child workers. What we found was that the women were more aware than the child workers regarding government schemes for the betterment of families. In Nizamabad, we found 98.3% of our respondents replying in affirmative about their awareness of schemes. This was probably due to the fact that a lot of union activity was concentrated in and around Nizamabad and that the parents and children were much more exposed to these than the respondent children of the other two Mandals. Many unions had put up posters for awareness.

Recreation

We also wanted to know how much time the child worker spent on recreation and what were their ambitions, so we asked a number of questions to the child workers. What we found was that since beedi making did not go on continuously throughout the month, the children were free on these days and continued to play throughout the evening. So they did find some time to play. Children thoroughly enjoyed this break; though children above 11 years were a bit unhappy that this break had cut across their earnings. the younger children could not care less. We participated in a number of games played by the children and found that these games were clearly gendered. Some of the games played by the boys are:

1. **Golli Koyelu**: Where a long stick is used to hit a small stick, and one has to run the distance covered by the stick. This is the popular *Gulli Danda* in Hindi.
2. **Kota Kommachi:** All the boys would climb a tree, and one would throw a stick down which the other boys had to catch.

Besides these games which were clearly boys' games, some of the games played exclusively by the girls were as follows.

1. **Uppalla Kuppamma**: Where the children would hold their hands criss-cross and turn around in a roundabout manner in a circle.
2. **Gaccha Kayelu:** This is the five stones played by girls seated in a circle. Small round stones of the same size are thrown down, and by throwing up one stone, a person has to pick up one, two, or three stones in different formations.
3. **Kunti Billa**: This is the game of stapoo where squares are drawn on the ground and one has to cross them in one leg or two.
4. **Astha Chamma**: This is like a board game where tamarind seeds are used as dice, and the game is drawn on the ground in the form of square.

We found that whenever free, children played both outdoor and indoor games. Thus, majority of the children played both indoor and outdoor games, though we found children above 12 years especially girls hardly participating or playing any games. When they were not making beedis, they would be doing housework or sitting in a group and chatting with their friends. On the days when there was no work of beedi making, children would watch TV. Parents did not encourage their children to watch television while making beedis, because then they would pay more attention to the TV and not concentrate on beedis. We found Star TV connections also in many houses of beedi makers in Nizamabad, and the neighbours told us that since six to seven people were making beedis per day in that particular family, and they had prospered a lot. Majority of the children, 93%, went to fairs festivals some times, and 39% of the children went to their friends and neighbours quite often, and the other 60% went sometimes only.

We were keen on knowing the ambitions of these children and also assess their parents' ambitions for them, as per their perceptions. We found that children below ten years rarely had an idea as to what they wanted to become or what was their parent ambition for them. But 20% of our child workers wanted to become teacher, and another 20% wanted to study and improve their technical skill. Nearly 19% of our child workers parents wanted them to get married and be a housewife as against only 13% of the child workers. Nearly 18% of the children saw themselves continuing to make beedis against 14% of the mothers. We found that as far as the values attached to education were concerned, there was a clear-cut division between the rural and the urban areas. Girls were being educated in urban areas and they combined beedi making with studying. Their aspirations were also higher, and many of them wanted to be teachers and improve their skill. Though marriage was uppermost in the minds of parents, they saw education of their daughters increasingly as opening more opportunities for job and making the girl independent.

The following table shows the child workers perception about education (Figure 9.11).

While majority of the people in all the three regions believed that education improves employment and economic opportunities, there were almost 20–30% of children who believed that education does not provide any advantage. This is a very high percentage because if children lose motivation and are not guided and shown the right path, these children will not be able to come out of the poverty and economic condition that they live in and will continue to work in beedi making, which is not good for their health and their family. The percentage of children believing that it improves social status, improves marriage prospects, gives confidence, and improves competency is almost the same in all the three regions. Despite knowing these benefits, there were hardly any child workers who studied beyond high school, and in fact, more than 70% did not even reach till high school.

There was a lot of difference between Armoor and Balkonda (which are not yet urbanised to the extent of Nizamabad) and Nizamabad, as far as values attached to education are concerned. While in Armoor 24% and in Balkonda 31% of the children saw no advantage in education, this was only 23% in Nizamabad.

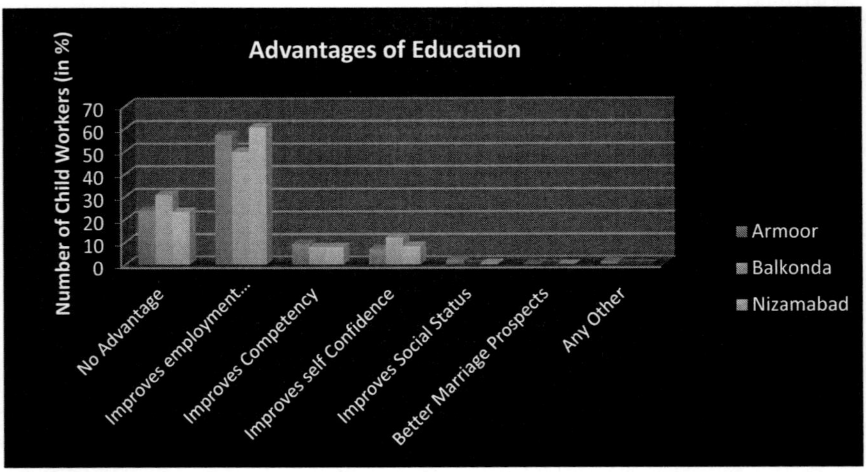

FIGURE 9.11 Perception on advantages of being educated.

In Armoor, only 57% of the child workers and 50% in Balkonda saw education improving their employment opportunities, but this percentage was 77% in Nizamabad. When we asked our child workers if they would like to have some vocational or technical training, 78% of them replied yes. Though majority of the child workers (97%) did not have any other skill other than beedi making, we found that they were very vocal in their demand for having technical or vocational training which would improve their skill. Tailoring was given a high preference (35%) followed by typing, 28%, and knitting and embroidery/weaving being 13%. We found that many houses had stitching machines, but they were lying waste, because the girl did not know cutting.

10

BEEDI MAKING, HEALTH, AND DISEASE

When we asked our respondents if beedi making led to any disease or it made no difference, we were shocked to see that majority of them (99.7%) knew that it leads to diseases and only 0.3% said that it makes no difference. The respondents felt that knowing this reality they continued to be in beedi making because there was no other option open to them since they did not have land or were not educated enough to have some other kind of job. It was interesting to note that when we asked the same question to the child workers, also we got the same response because majority (99.2%) of our child workers said yes and only 0.6% said that it made no difference (Figure 10.1).

We asked the women beedi makers and the child workers whether they were aware that beedi making leads to diseases. More than 75% of women in all regions except Armoor were aware that beedi making leads to diseases. Only 60% of the women in Armoor were aware of the same. This shows the lack of information and literacy level of women in Armoor. Hyderabad had the highest number of women who were aware of the diseases associated with beedi making. Interestingly, the child workers were more aware of the harmful effects of beedi making. Close to 99% of child workers in all the three regions were aware that beedi making leads to diseases. On the one hand, it was good news to see that the child workers were aware of the diseases and the harmful effects of making beedis, but on the other hand, it was a sad state to see the plight of the children who were aware of the diseases but still had no option but to continue working.

When we asked them in detail as to what diseases they could get, we got the following response as this table shows (Figure 10.1).

We spoke with the females of the house who were into beedi making and asked them whether they were aware of the diseases that were associated with beedi making or the diseases which they might have to face by making beedis.

DOI: 10.4324/9781003317944-12

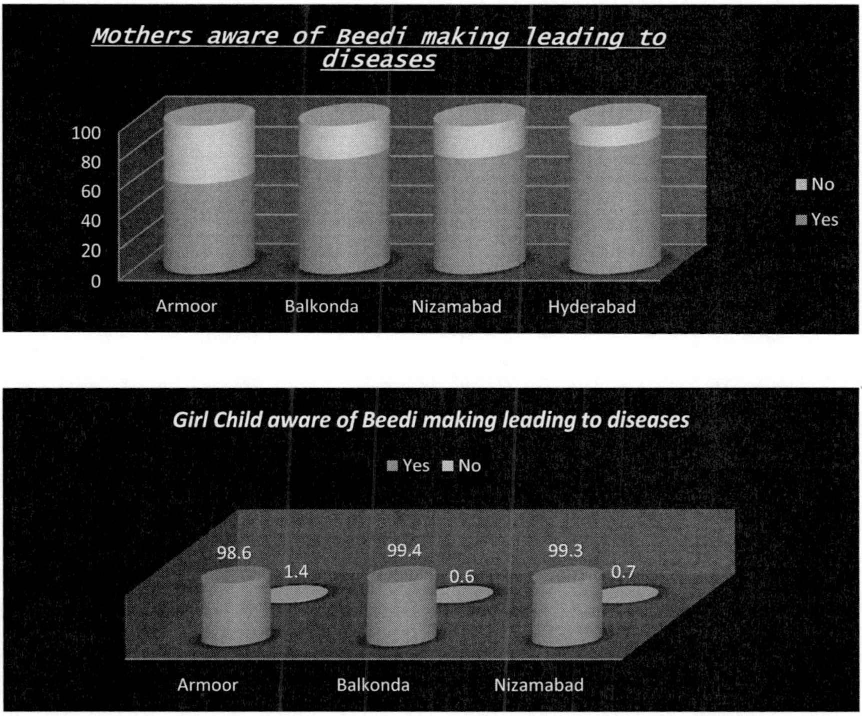

FIGURE 10.1 Beedi making leading to diseases.

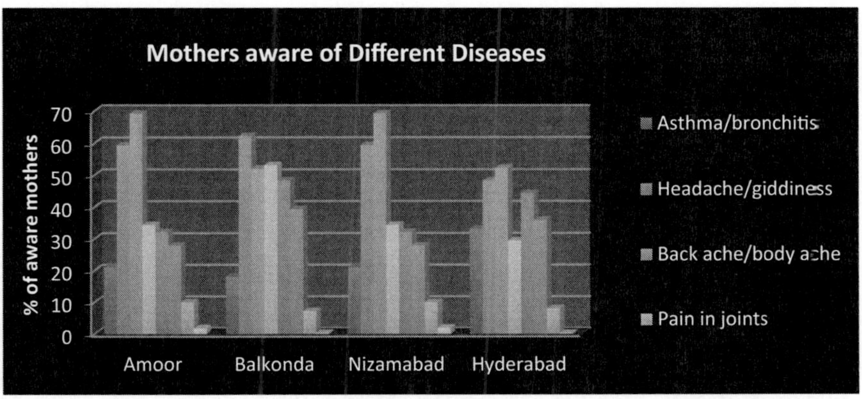

FIGURE 10.2 Mother's awareness of different diseases due to beedi making.

In all the four regions, majority of the people were aware of headache/giddiness and back ache/body ache. These two problems were known by majority of the women probably because they are facing these problems already. Life-threatening diseases or severe organ problems usually start showing up gradually and over a period of time, but these smaller issues come up very soon as you start making beedis. Around 20% of women in Armoor, Balkonda, and Nizamabad were aware of beedi making leading to asthma/bronchitis, but more than 33% of women in Hyderabad were aware of this disease probably because of being in a developed city. As expected, very few women were aware of diseases like TB and cancer. Comparatively, more number of women in Hyderabad and Nizamabad were aware of these two diseases, but the number was still less than 10%. This raises very alarming questions about the lack of information that these people have. These people deserve to know that they are playing with their lives by getting into beedi making that is exposing them to such life-threatening diseases (Figure 10.3).

The same exercise was repeated with child workers in Armoor, Nizamabad, and Balkonda. As we all know that the skin and eyes of small children are very delicate and sensitive, they are much more prone to getting rashes on skin and itchy eyes. The children in all the three regions were aware of the harms that come with beedi making to their skin and their eyes. Close to 70% of the children were aware of body aches and back pains. These problems are known to children as well because they have to face this everyday while making beedis. They were not aware of the joint pains probably because they haven't faced it yet as their bones were young and strong. Children in Balkonda were comparatively more aware of diseases like joint pains, asthma, and body pains. Interestingly, more number of children were aware of cancer than their mothers in all the three districts (Table 10.1).

Our study clearly shows that most of the respondents as well as the child workers suffered from many of the diseases cited above. It is true that in the informal sector, it is not always possible to isolate occupational causes from other interrelated factors like living conditions, nutrition, discrimination, and lack of opportunities which directly or indirectly affect women's and girls' health. The main occupational hazard in the beedi industry is due to tobacco dust, causing

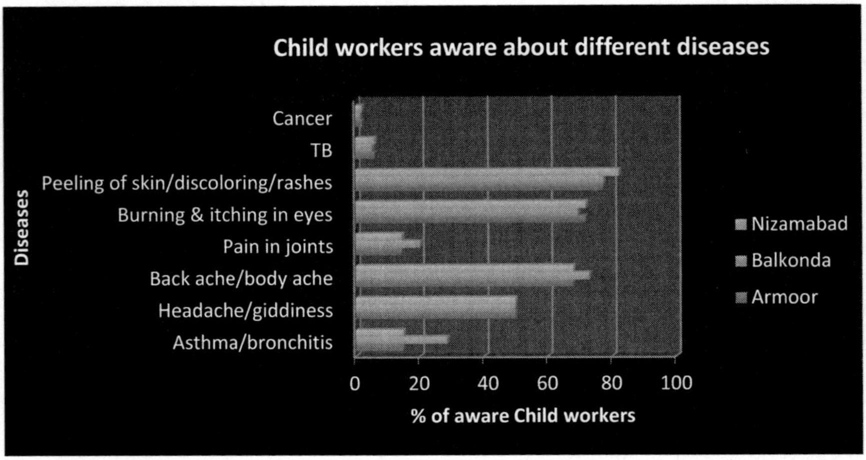

FIGURE 10.3 Children's awareness of different diseases due to beedi making.

TABLE 10.1 Beedi Making and Health Hazard

Disease	*Balkonda*											
	Yes	*No*	*Total*	*Yes*	*No*	*Total*	*Yes*	*No*	*Total*	*Yes*	*No*	*Total*
Asthma/bronchitis	21.0	79.0	100	14.9	85.1	100	18.10	81.90	100	28.4	71.6	100
Headache/giddiness	59.4	40.6	100	49.8	50.2	100	62.3	37.7	100	49.7	50.3	100
Back ache/body ache	69.2	30.8	100	67.82	32.18	100	52.6	47.4	100	72.80	27.2	100
Pain in joints	34.4	65.6	100	14.4	85.6	100	53.20	46.8	100	20.10	79.90	100
Burning and itching in eyes	32.2	67.8	100	71.7	28.3	100	49.0	53.0	100	69.30	30.7	100
Peeling of skin/discolouring/rashes	27.9	72.1	100	72.0	28.0	100	39.4	60.60	100	77.35	22.65	100
TB	10.0	90.0	100	6.0	94.0	100	7.2	92.8	100	5.3	94.7	100
Cancer	1.9	98.1	100	2.0	98.0	100	.4	99.6	100	1.5	98.5	100

Disease	*Nizamabad*			*Hyderabad*					
	Mother		*Total*	*Child worker*		*Total*	*Mother*		*Total*
	Yes	*No*		*Yes*	*No*		*Yes*	*No*	
Asthma/bronchitis	21.0	79.0	100	14.9	85.1	100	33.2	66.8	100
Headache/giddiness	59.4	40.6	100	49.8	50.2	100	48.3	51.7	100
Back ache/body ache	69.2	30.8	100	67.82	32.18	100	52.3	47.7	100
Pain in joints	34.4	65.6	100	14.4	85.6	100	29.50	70.5	100
Burning and itching in eyes	32.2	67.8	100	71.7	28.3	100	44.40	55.60	100
Peeling of skin/discolouring/rashes	27.9	72.1	100	82.0	18.0	100	36.0	64	100
TB	10.0	90.0	100	6.0	94.0	100	8.0	92	100
Cancer	1.7	98.1	100	2.0	98.0	100	.35	99.65	100

burning of eyes, conjunctivitis, rhinitis, mucous dryness including of the genital tract, occupational dermatitis, bronchitis, emphysema, and dystonic.

A significant number of tasks are completed while sitting, either on the floor with the legs crossed, with either the right or left leg bent at the knee, or with both legs extended. When you sit for an extended period of time with your trunk bent forward, you cause a sustained static contraction of the back muscle. As a result, a significant number of workers experienced problems with their backs and joints. We learned about a number of different friends and other neighbours who had suffered from a variety of symptoms over the course of their lives. A significant number of the respondents demonstrate what they are claiming by showing us their hands and fingernails. A good number of them have reported feeling giddy. What we discovered was that both the respondent and the child worker did not believe that beedi making was responsible for asthma, bronchitis, tuberculosis, or cancer. However, they did believe that beedi making was largely responsible for minor ailments (as they call it), such as headaches, giddiness, body aches, pains in the joints, burning and itching in the eyes, a feeling of the skin, and the development of skin rashes. Concerning the issue of minor ailments, we engaged in lengthy conversations with both the respondents and the child workers. They were clear that illnesses such as cancer, tuberculosis, asthma, and other similar conditions were serious because patients had to be laid in bed and could not perform any work. However, the ailments from which they suffered were minor because they only caused irritation and discomfort, and they did not prevent them from making beedi because they did not have to be laid in bed for an extended period of time.

When we asked our respondents where they would take a member of their family if that member became seriously ill, we found that 98% of them went to the government dispensary, 0.8% went to a private hospital, and 1.1% went to a private allopathic doctor. Since they did not have a lot of other options, the vast majority of people went to the government dispensary. The government dispensary did not have very good facilities, and the majority of the time, the medications that were needed were not even stocked there. If given the choice, they would go to a private doctor or hospital if they could afford it, but given their financial situation, that option is out of the question. However, the majority of respondents (51%) were required to get treatment for the patient within their own village, while only 39% had to walk up to 5 kilometres to get treatment for the patient.

Malnourishment

The poor socioeconomic conditions of the people living in rural areas, combined with malnutrition and an environment that is both unsanitary and unhygienic, contribute to the people's poor health status. It is estimated that approximately 50% of Indians suffer from malnutrition because they cannot afford a diet that provides the minimum amount of energy required for a healthy and active lifestyle. The majority of women show signs of anaemia, which is caused by an inadequate intake of dietary nutrients and a poor environment. There was a vicious cycle in which the girl child worked more than her brother did but ate less than her brother did. Her precarious nutritional status puts her at risk for anaemia and other nutritional deficiencies as well as infections; despite the fact that she was more ill than her brother, she was only occasionally taken to the hospital for medical care. These differences are only made worse by poverty; the underlying problem is not so much a lack of food as it is the value attached to the boy child over the girl child. She eventually marries at a young age and gives birth to a number of babies who are typically born with a low birth weight. The cycle of nutritional depletion is finished when a young mother passes away while giving birth to her child.

In our sample, majority of the girls were attending school, 70.1% in Armoor, 79.3% in Balkonda, and 78% in Nizamabad. There were a large number of girls in the primary school, but this number kept on reducing later with the boys continuing their studies and the girls being made to sit at home after primary school or after puberty. Beedi making was very gendered because only girls made beedis and boys made beedis only if they were less than 12 years. Boys looked down upon beedi making as women's work. Many of the girls in our sample were first born, and hence, they had added responsibility of doing household chores, taking care of the siblings besides making beedis. Majority of our respondents (66%) said they liked their work because they were proud that they were not just going to school like other children but also were earning and adding to the family income. A total of 34% of the children who did not like their work said that this was because they had a lot of body pains and did not get time to play.

Health consequences of rolling beedis

We found that there was a high prevalence of illness among households of beedi workers. There is no physical partition separating the workspace from other areas of the home, such as the kitchen, which is one of the most significant characteristics of home-based beedi work. This is one of the factors that contribute to the poor health of girls. The high incidence of illness may, to some extent, be attributable to poverty and a poor health status independent of tobacco work; however, it appears to be exacerbated by the continuous contact that beedi workers have with tobacco.

It is possible for workers in the beedi industry to develop bronchitis, asthma, cancer, and dust-related allergies such as conjunctivitis and occupational dermatitis as a result of their consistent contact with tobacco and inhalation of tobacco dust while on the job. An infection of the conjunctiva, or the white part of the eyelid, is known as conjunctivitis. It causes the eyes to become red and swollen, in addition to itching and burning. Redness, itching, scaling, and blistering of the skin are all signs that an individual may have occupational dermatitis (skin rashes). The majority of people can make a full recovery from dermatitis if it is diagnosed at an early stage and appropriate preventative measures are taken. However, the sensitisation will prevent full recovery for some individuals. Green tobacco sickness can be caused when nicotine is absorbed through the skin after coming into contact with wet tobacco leaves. Workers who harvested tobacco were the first people to report symptoms of green tobacco sickness. At the time of harvest, the typical worker in the field could be exposed to as much as 600 millilitres of dew or rain on the tobacco plants. This is roughly equivalent to the nicotine content of 36 cigarettes in the United States (Campaign for Tobacco Free Kids, 2000). The idea that tuberculosis is extremely common among beedi workers is not supported by the fact that an individual can only contract tuberculosis if they are an alcoholic or do not adhere to healthy dietary practices.

Many girls complained of back ache, nausea, and giddiness. This was primarily because they were seated in a same posture for a long time and absorbed tobacco dust. Many complained of itching in the eyes and peeling of the skin and development of skin rashes. Since these ailments only caused irritation and discomfort and never came in the way of beedi making, and they were not laid in bed for a long time, in the absence of any other alternative, these girls continued to make beedis. With prolonged involvement of beedi making, an activity involving a repetitive movement and long hours of sitting in a particular posture, beedi workers also develop problems like back ache, joint pain, and arthritis. Fingers lose sensation and become numb. Many of our beedi making girls did not think that beedi making is responsible for asthma, bronchitis, or cancer. They actually report on symptoms and attribute the development of minor ailments (as they refer to them) to the act of making beedi, including headaches, giddiness, body aches, pains in the joints, burning and itching in the eyes, peeling of the skin, and the formation of skin rashes.

Care-seeking behaviour

Beedi workers usually only seek help when their health problems start to affect their work. The beedi workers' dispensaries are free of charge; however, many workers are not aware of these facilities. In addition, many of those who are aware report not using them. Irregularity and carelessness of the doctors are reported as reasons for the abandoning of these hospitals. The workers prefer using private doctors, but end up spending a lot more money than they would have had to if the doctors in the government hospitals were reliable (Hirji, 2000). When it comes to accessing medical facilities, distance is obviously another very important factor to consider. Beedi workers are under a significant time crunch, and as a result, they are unable to spare the necessary time and resources to travel to distant medical facilities. In addition to this, many of these young ladies were also enrolled in classes, which meant that they were extremely pressed for time.

The state of the workers' health must be understood in the larger context of the situation, which can be characterised as one of extreme exploitation in the case of beedi workers. It is impossible to consider health in isolation from political and economic structures. The enhancement of one's quality of life should be the primary focus of efforts to better one's health conditions. Consequently, it is necessary for programmes dealing with health to have direct connections with programmes dealing with protected water supplies, environmental sanitation, hygiene, nutrition, family planning, and maternity and child welfare.

Employment concerns

During the conversations with the beedi workers in the villages of Pipri, Armoor, Kisanagar, and Gopanpally, the workers stated that they do not have as much work as they did in the past. The amount of work that needs to be done each week now only requires a maximum of two to three days rather than the previous four to six. When we asked why there is less work available, we were given a number of different explanations, including because of a prohibition on smoking in public places (tobacco control measures), competition from mini-cigarettes, the import of beedis from Pakistan and Bangladesh, beedi companies are moving to another state when beedi workers become more organised, export restrictions, and companies are closing down. These explanations are confirmed partly by a variety of other sources.

An article in the Indian Express on 22 August 1999 reported, "The recent Kerala High Court Judgement which has banned smoking in public places has hit the private beedi manufacturers hard. They are now trying to gain respite by escaping to neighbouring Karnataka or taking up other businesses". On 13 May 2001, the South Nexus read:

> District Beedi Workers Federation president K. Vasudeva has called for the removal of the ban on smoking in public places to be enforced soon. He said that the livelihood of several lakh beedi workers would be affected if the ban comes into force.

The recent trends of globalisation, urbanisation, and increased per capita income are expected to make people shift from beedi consumption to consumption of mini-cigarettes.

There are five distinct sub-markets within the cigarette industry: micros, plains, regular filters, longs, and king-size filters. These sub-markets cater to consumers who have varying levels of disposable income. In terms of cost, it is a step up from what beedis offers. It is estimated that there are over eight people who smoke beedis for every person who smokes cigarettes. Because of this, cigarette manufacturers have a significant financial interest in getting people to start smoking their products. Because of the significant price difference between beedis and cigarettes (which was primarily caused by the higher excise duty component of cigarettes), cigarette manufacturers were unable to offer beedi smokers a low-cost alternative until the year 1994.

Under the guise of safeguarding the rights of workers and the health and safety of children, the government of the United States imposed a trade sanction on the beedi industry in India during the round of WTO negotiations that took place in Seattle. Recently in Seattle, workers' organisations, trade unions, and developing countries vehemently opposed this move, while the United States wanted to push through the issue regardless of their opposition. According to the opinions of various analysts, the issue of linking labour standards with trade is not merely a matter of human rights, as the developed world likes to bring up every so often. The true intention behind it is to seize a larger share of the market in developing nations, which is necessary because many businesses are struggling in the developed northern countries.

If workers begin organising themselves or if the market continues to contract, manufacturers may choose to relocate their operations to another state. More and more manufacturers are leaving the state in search of better opportunities and higher returns in order to escape the state's worsening economic climate, which includes a contracting market, difficult labour conditions, and dwindling political influence. The new manufacturing hubs are emerging in the economically disadvantaged regions of West Bengal, Bihar, Orissa, Andhra Pradesh, Tamil Nadu, and Karnataka, where the cost of labour is lower and the quality of craftsmanship is higher. The elimination of plants and machinery has made the moving process much simpler. According to the manufacturers, the main reason for the declining market is the changing smoking habits in rural areas. This could be due to an increased awareness about the dangers of smoking or simply a growing preference for other forms of tobacco, such as cigarettes and *paan masala*. In addition to this, the collection of tendu leaves in the state, which accounts for nearly 60% of the country's supply, was rather low at 40 lakh bags prior to the beginning of the monsoon… The quality of the leaves has also diminished in recent times. It is an industry in which there is little supervision, where it is difficult to eradicate child labour, and where the final product has been shown to be harmful to one's health.

There is a possibility that new policy directions regarding tobacco control will have an effect on employment in the beedi industry. In February of 2001, the Indian cabinet gave its approval to the Cigarettes and other Tobacco Products (Prohibition of Advertisement and Regulation of Trade and Commerce, Production, Supply, and Distribution) Bill, which had been a hotly anticipated piece of legislation for quite some time. The bill will make it illegal to advertise tobacco products, will make it unlawful to smoke in public places, and will provide consumers with more comprehensive health warnings. Additionally, the legislation will make it illegal for anyone under the age of 18 to purchase tobacco products and will prohibit tobacco companies from sponsoring any kind of sporting or cultural event. The government has mandated that health warnings on tobacco products be more explicit and must be prominently printed in both English and the Indian language. When it comes to a provision that prohibits smoking in public places, effectiveness is a very important issue to consider.

In this case, it is not so much the existence of a law as it is the enforcement of that law that is the most important thing. A second inquiry concerns the characteristics of a public location. The scope of the bill's potential impact is another important consideration. When it comes to other tobacco products, however, it will only apply to four states: Goa, Punjab, Uttar Pradesh, and West Bengal. This is in contrast to the fact that it will apply to the entire country in the case of cigarettes. These four have voted in favour of a resolution that makes it possible for Parliament to enact a law that regulates other types of tobacco products. In order for the legislation to be truly effective across the entirety of the country, it is necessary for the other states to follow suit. Concerning the prohibition on advertising, there is scepticism regarding the efficacy of any legislation in preventing businesses from employing the time-honoured tactic of promoting the brand through thinly disguised surrogates. This tactic has been around for a long time.

11

NARRATIVES OF VULNERABILITY AND EXPLOITATION

Here we present few case studies of the women and child workers from different villages, so that we are able to move from mere numbers and become a part of the world of these working people.

Women workers

Case 1

Balamma is around 90 years old. She cannot remember her age exactly, but this is what she thinks. It was never of importance anyway. Her eyes are weak, she can't see well. She now walks with the help of a stick. When she stands, she stoops. However, she is a proud woman with a small body of 5 ft. height. All her life, she has been making beedis. She cannot remember the days when she did not make beedis. On an average, she made around 1,000 beedis a day. Those were the days when a thousand beedis fetched Rs 2. She was very disciplined in her work. She was known for not gossiping or wiling away time. Her concentration was always on her work. She would go from interiors of Secunderabad to Kawadiguda to purchase material directly from the factory owner. Middlemen were not reliable in those times. Her pride however comes from the fact that she has single-handedly raised her family of seven children – four daughters and three sons. All four daughters were married from the savings she could make from beedi making. Her three sons are now well settled with own houses. She lives with one of the sons. Her days are now spent in reminiscing about the old days. She misses not being able to make beedis anymore but is satisfied.

DOI: 10.4324/9781003317944-13

Case 2

Rama is a 60-year-old woman. She is lean and tall in appearance. She comes across as a very intelligent woman. Unlike other women following this occupation, she is very well aware of the current affairs. Politics in general and the government policies regarding beedi industry and workers are of great interest to her. Her knowledge in this regard is astonishing. Her strong personality is reflected in her mannerisms, the drape of her saree, and her walking style. She has been making beedis since childhood. She continued this activity even after marriage. She is now a widow. She is a very self-respecting person. Even when her husband was alive, she earned through beedi making. Her savings contributed to the family income. She does not want to be under anybody's control. She has two sons but prefers to live alone. Making beedis 30 years back was not a lucrative occupation. They were paid very less and had to toil for long hours. They had to get the raw materials directly from the factories as middlemen were very few in those days. They were also not reliable. They also tried to control the women workers and exploit them. According to her, these circumstances have changed in recent times. Rama is a special woman among her category because she did not think of only her benefit. Rather she strove for all women who made beedis. Early in life she realised that unless women unite and demand better terms and conditions, they will not get a fair share. She was one of the first women to attend union meetings and take part in *dharnas*. This went on for many years. It took a lot of courage and time on her part. She is now proud of the fact that the struggle she along with her colleagues undertook has borne fruit. Under her watchful eye, beedi rates rose from Rs 20 to 155 per 1,000 beedis. Further political struggle ensued pension and provident fund for women making beedis. She has been at the forefront of these struggles and acted as a leader in many cases, especially in bringing women to such political congregations. The women in her area now receive pensions, medical facilities from the government. They also have a provident fund. She continues to make beedis to take care of her day-to-day expenses and provides guidance to young women who seek her advice.

Case 3

Kali is a young woman. She is around 40 of age. She is an illiterate. However, lack of education is not a deterrent for furthering her ambition. Her personality is both strong as well as fierce. She can be very aggressive if the situation demands it. Her personality is a reflection of the circumstances she has been through in her life. Extreme poverty and lack of support has been a major factor in her life. Her mother was a beedi maker and a single mother. Her father deserted his family quiet early. This left a deep impact on the children, Kali and her four siblings. With no financial support, she too was thrown into making beedis. Back then child labour was very common. Parents were not aware of the benefits of educating their children. Instead they thought education was a waste of time. So the girl child was involved in money making. Kali being a girl, her education was never important for her mother. Kali has been making beedis since childhood. She is very fast and efficient in her work. She could make 3,000–4,000 beedis in a day and contribute to family income. She continued to do the same work after marriage as well. Her husband is a daily wage earner. His income is not stable. Sometimes he gets more and sometimes less, depending on the number of days he gets work. This situation compels Kali to contribute to family income in the only way she knows: beedi making. However, she is not a pessimistic person. She has put her skills to best use. Besides making beedis herself, she now is the head of a collection centre. She manages some 250–300 workers who sell beedis to factories from this centre. According to her, leadership abilities, management skills, and sharp intelligence got recognised by the factory owner, and she was offered this job. She has the added ability of knowing three languages that enables her to deal with different groups of women. She is happy that her efforts and qualities get recognition. More importantly, this position adds to her income. Her income is now almost doubled. Her ambition in life is to facilitate her two children's education and give them a good life.

Case 4

Satyamma is a middle-aged woman who refuses to reveal her age. She looks like an experienced and wise lady. Her husband is an auto-rickshaw driver. He has his own auto which he uses mainly to transport school children. This ensures some assured income. She is illiterate and resents the fact very much. According to her, no amount of intelligence can compensate for lack of formal education. In her opinion, occupational opportunities become constricted without education. "Will a Government job open up for you unless one is educated", she tells me, "Hence, we have to earn a living with what ever job is available". Benefits accruing from government also do not reach uneducated people as they are largely unaware of their policies, and middlemen exploit the situation to their advantage. Only those people who are close to such middlemen get benefitted, others are left to fend for themselves. Her husband too is uneducated. This makes life unstable for Satyamma and her family. Piece meal jobs are the only option for such men. Even these are limited. Hailing from a higher caste category of weavers, neither she nor her husband can undertake menial jobs like labour in construction industry or domestic services in well to do families. Social restrictions play a big part in determining the kind of work one does in India. Despite gloomy prospects of income earning capacity, Satyamma has to stick to beedi making. She has been a beedi maker since childhood. As it often happens with most girls in beedi-making villages, she too was thrown into beedi making early in her life. She used to lend a hand to her mother who was into this occupation and gradually it became her mainstay. It has now been 35 years since she started making beedis. She was then married to Ramanna who migrated to Hyderabad for work. She was 12 years old then. She has four children, three daughters and a son. Her son did not complete graduation. "We spent a lot of money and we were hoping that he will be educated and get a good job, but unfortunately he was not interested in studies", Satyamma tells me. He now works as a salesman in an electronics shop. He is married and has a 4-year-old daughter. They all live together. Satyamma is efficient in making beedis. Earlier she made 1,000 beedis in a day. With age and added responsibilities, her ability to make beedis has come down. Now she has other distractions and demands on her time. Since last 20 years, she has been heading a collection centre. She operates from her own house where all women of her area gather and submit the beedis they make. After selecting the good beedis and counting them, she makes entry into the cards provided to beedi makers. They are paid accordingly. This activity is undertaken two times in a week. The contractor comes to her house to collect the beedis and also give raw materials like *tendu* leaves and tobacco. Satyamma has a dedicated godown-like place to store these raw materials. This activity fetches her extra income, which inspires her to work hard. She has the cooperation of her co-workers as she is soft spoken and wise. She also provides useful advice to these women as and when required. In earlier days, she also took part in dharnas and attended meetings demanding for better pay for beedi makers. She continues to be in touch with political and grass root activists. She is surprisingly very well informed of the government policies and latest developments on this front. Though not satisfied with her situation in life, she has a positive and cheerful attitude towards life.

Case 5

Saraswati is a young woman. She is a mother of two children, elder a girl and younger one a boy. She has the company of her ailing mother who constantly keeps complaining about life. It is difficult for her to keep her household running. Her father died while she was still a young girl. Her mother was a beedi maker. She does not make any now. Saraswati learnt making beedis while still a small girl. Going to school was a luxury she could not afford. Not being educated, she had little prospects to gain skills for well-paying jobs. Domestic chores or working in shops is beneath her caste status. Therefore, she could not undertake these jobs, though they are better paying. Caste is an essential social status marker even if it is not economically beneficial. Thus, beedi making is the only viable option for her. Living in urban places like Hyderabad has its own burdens. She has to rent a space as she has no house of her own. She also has to abide by the rules and regulations of the land lord. Her husband was a daily wage earner. He deserted them when her son was an infant. Since then she has been the sole bread winner of her family. She finds the occupation of beedi making different in urban areas from rural areas. Here she has to get the raw material from the middleman and make beedis at home itself. There is no factory or area where she can sit and finish her work. Also she has no friend or well-wisher who can provide her moral support. She feels lonely. The occupation also does not provide her much financial support as she is not very efficient in making large number of beedis. This has started taking a toll on her health as well. She faces multiple issues like blood pressure, weakness, frequent headaches and anxiety-related problems. Buying medicines too is a burden. In addition her mother too faces several medical issues. She recently underwent a surgery. This compelled Saraswati to shell out savings. Her mother too needs medicines which are expensive. There is no way she can meet these expenses. Both her children are intelligent. Her daughter is exceptionally good in studies. But paying school fees has been a problem too. However, recently she received help on this front from a local NGO working for the upliftment of girl child. Thus, she need not worry about her education and books now. She however has to look after her son's welfare. Being a boy, there is no organisation which supports his education or other needs. Thus, even though she is willing to work and has some skills, she has limited opportunities. The constraints she faces are either circumstantial or social. Beedi making remains her best option. However, she is unable to concentrate on this work as well. Thus, she produces a minimal number of beedis and ends up earning little. Her pessimistic attitude makes life look bleak.

Case 6

Sheetal is in her mid-30s. She is a well-educated woman. She could complete her master's degree and obtain a lecturer's job in a private college. Originally hailing from Nizamabad, she finished her education from Bombay and then migrated to Hyderabad after her marriage to a bank employee. Sheetal is a success story for a beedi worker's family. Her mother was a beedi worker. Her father was a class four employee in a bank in Bombay. Their family had migrated to Bombay many years before. Hailing from Nizamabad, her mother Bharti was skilled in making beedis. She continued doing the same in Bombay post her marriage. In this way, she could contribute to the family income and save something for a rainy day. She was proud of her skills. Sheetal too made beedis while she was young. She would make beedis before and after school hours. Though not required she made beedis to help her mother meet the numbers. Gradually she became skilled and efficient in this work. Later as she grew up and the demands of studying also increased, she backtracked from beedi-related work. Her mother continued to make it. She started developing health issues. Back ache was a common problem as she would sit for long hours for making beedis. Also she became addicted to consuming tobacco while sitting with other women. Beedi making in those days was a group activity. Some 12–15 women would sit in the courtyard and make beedis while chatting with each other. Chewing tobacco also relieved stress leading to addiction. Later they realised that Bharti developed cancer due to constant exposure to tobacco. She suffered from this disease and had to forego making beedis. Her last days were full of suffering and regret. Sheetal lost her mother while she was still in her 20s. She cannot overcome the feeling that her loss was because of beedi making and resents the occupation. However, for the women making beedis, she is a role model as despite all the drawbacks and financial difficulties, she could complete her education. She also grabbed a respectable teaching job. This makes Sheetal swell with pride. She asserts that it was her mother who always encouraged her to study and go ahead in life.

Case 7

Gauri is in her mid-50s. She lives in Hyderabad. Originally hailing from Sholapur, her family shifted in search of better work opportunities. In Sholapur, she was comfortable. They had a joint family and a house of their own. Her sons wanted to explore and believed that better opportunities would present themselves in a city like Hyderabad. Gauri's husband is a saree vendor. He roams around the city selling sarees on his bicycle. He does not make much money, but there is hardly anything else he can do. His skills are limited. He is illiterate and not very intelligent or street smart. He is also not a very healthy person. Lacking in stamina, he tends to fall ill often. Excess stress can have a toll as well. City life is a bit overwhelming for him. Her two sons are tenth pass. Not being interested in studies, they stopped college education midway. Back home there was not much they could do. Her, one son is working as a salesman and another as a driver. He runs taxis. However, he does it for others. Having own taxi would require huge investment which he cannot at present manage. Both are married and have a child each. The daughters-in-law too make beedis and add to the income their mother-in-law makes. Gauri is herself unhappy for having migrated. At this age, she wanted to relax and enjoy with familiar people. Life in urban areas is very different from district places. There the neighbourhood consisted of all beedi-making women. Once the men of the house went out for work, all women would sit together and make beedis while having a chit chat. Here the neighbours are not very welcoming. Also not everybody is involved in making beedis. Those who don't make beedis don't mingle with Gauri and her family. They consider it beneath their status. They think that inhaling tobacco can lead to diseases like cancer. So they don't want to associate with her. This kind of ostracising is new to Gauri. She also suffers from health issues like diabetes, weakness, and anxiety. She also resents the fact that being recently migrated, she does not get pension or provident fund benefits from the state governments, something which she got in her village. Gauri is therefore unhappy and regretful. Her children however insist this life is way better than what they had back home.

Girl children workers

Case 1

Hashmat Begum is from Armoor town in Armoor Mandal. She is 11 years of age, weighing about 35 kg, and is about 4.2 ft. in height. She is the fourth child in the family of four children. She has been involved in beedi making for two years now and works for four to five hours per day. She also does all the household chores after coming back from school. Her mother Zahira Begum informs us that if she is relieved of housework, she can concentrate more on beedi making. Zahira Begum's husband is a piece-rated worker and is illiterate. They have three sons Sabir, Nazir, and Zahir aged 20, 18, and 16, respectively. The eldest has studied up to intermediate and other two up to SSC. They are all unmarried and unemployed. The sons do not want to do any piece-rated job (the father puts plastic linings for beds, chairs, etc.), because they feel it is beyond their dignity. The family is facing a lot of financial issues for the father's job is not regular, and the sons are unemployed and yet the sons do not help in making beedis. According to the elder son, "This is a women's work and we do not want to be the but of laughter in our neighborhood". They want to do some kind of service, and not getting one, they pass their time roaming here and there looking for jobs. In the absence of any permanent source of income, the family has to depend only on beedi making primarily done by the mother and the daughter. The job the sons perform is that they bring the raw material for beedi making from the karkhana/contractor daily or as and when it is available. They take the beedis prepared by the mother and daughter for selling every week to the contractor and collect the money and get it entered in the passbook which they carry. Because of strict purdah, the woman/girl do not go to the contractor who is also a Muslim gentleman. They live in a very dilapidated one-room house and have no other property. They have borrowed Rs 20,000 from the private money lender to finance a trip for their elder son to Saudi Arabia last year. But this did not materialise, and they were cheated by the agent and the son did not go to Saudi Arabia. They have a big tension of returning the money to the money lender and tell us that the interest is piling up. Presently the girl is studying in seventh class, but the mother is clear that after puberty and once she learns beedi making perfectly, she would leave school and make beedis full time. Somehow the mother thinks that running a home is the responsibility of herself and her daughter and one cannot blame the sons for not doing anything. "They are after all educated and cannot work like 'Anapadh Gawar' (illiterate, uneducated) people", according to the mother. Her only ambition in life is to see her sons get a job and the daughter married. The daughter is also not very ambitious and thinks she can do nothing on her own except following the wishes of her parents. The mother was very pessimistic about life, and its expectation and has passed on the same values to her daughter.

Case 2

Ganga Mutu is from Pipri village in Armoor Mandal. She is 12 years of age, weighing about 35 kg and is 4 ft. in height. She is the third child in a family of six children. She has never been to school and is involved in beedi making for the last six years. She works seven to eight hours per day throughout the day and then does housework, which includes washing, cooking, cleaning, and looking after the siblings. Her parents did not send her to school because they are very poor. The parents of Ganga Mutu are illiterate, and the mother combines agricultural labourer's work with beedi making. The father is also an agricultural labourer. The elder two sisters of Ganga Mutu are married. They live in a Kutcha house and have no other property. Ganga Mutu suffers from severe back ache, and there are big white patches on her skin but she continues to make beedis, because someone has to be at home, do the work, and look after the siblings. Ganga Mutu's greatest fear is that she will not be able to make 600 beedis per day. She sees no change in her life. She values education and thinks that if she was educated, she would be able to get a better job like that of a teacher and earn good money and have a better standard of life. She sees no future for herself, but she thinks that if she gets an opportunity, she would like to learn to read and write, but sees no way how she can find the time. She knows for a fact that education does bring in a change in one's life, but it seems to be beyond her. Here is a case of a girl who would like to change her life but is so caught in the web of life and its day-to-day struggle for survival that she sees no way out of it.

Case 3

Swapna Rani is from Kisanagar village in Balkonda Mandal. She comes from a backward caste of Devagulu. She is eight years of age and is currently attending school and studying in second class. She weighs about 25 kg and must be 3 ft. in height. She appears to be a clean child, though the environment in and around the home is not clean.

Swapna's mother Donda Laxmi is 30 years of age and makes beedis. Her husband Nagabushan is 35 years of age and works as an agricultural labourer. They are both illiterate. They have only two children, Swapna and another daughter Sandhya Rani, who is five years and presently studying in class one. The family has no other property and live in a one room Kutcha mud house which is rented. Though both parents are illiterate, they have high hopes on education and want both their daughters educated at least up to intermediate. Though presently both the daughters make beedis and assist the mother, she thinks that may be after attaining education, her daughters may get some service as a teacher and leave beedi making. Swapna has been involved in beedi making for the last three years. Though she started only by cutting leaves and tying the thread (which her younger sister does now), she soon mastered the art and presently makes the complete beedi by herself. She makes about 251–300 beedis per day and does this work mostly in the evenings and late evenings. She also assists her mother in household work by bringing water, cleaning, and at times even cooking. She is not very aware of what government is doing for people like them. She suffers from frequent cold, coughs, fever body ache, and pain in the joints but tends to ignore it because she has to help her mother in making the maximum number of beedis. Swapna, though young in age, seems quite mature and is quite clear that her life and her parents' life can only change if they are educated and they have a good job. Though the family does not have any boys, they are not very keen because, "This is not in our hands", and they would want to take care of these two children properly. Though the mother is clear that ultimately girls have to marry, she would not like to force her daughter into marriage at a very early age. She wants her daughter to study as far as she can and as far as the parents can afford. She knows that once children are not educated, their lives would also be like theirs (parents) where they have to labour for long hours and be without any earnings during some parts of the year and month. Though the parents do not understand anything which is taught in school, they feel very happy when they see their children reading books. Swapna is a very interesting case for in spite of financial constraints because of which she has to make beedis, her parents value education and want a better social environment and future for their children. Because the parents are so ambitious, the children have also acquired these values and want a better life for themselves, though the social environment around them has not changed. There is every hope that despite the economic hardship Swapna will have opportunity to develop as an individual.

Case 4

M. Krishnamma is nine years of age and comes from the OBC community of Berta in Balkonda Mandal. She is married to Ranganna who is 14 years of age, but he and his family have nothing to do with her. Krishnamma has studied only till class 1 and had to leave school to get married. When we met Krishnamma, she was staying with her maternal grandmothers, who makes beedis. Krishnamma's mother had died recently, and the father had left her and gone to another village and remarried. Krishnamma makes about 301–400 beedis a day and both the grandmother and she survive on this earnings. They live in a hut/jhopri and have no other property or means of livelihood. Krishnamma knows the value of education, but feels it is too late for her to go back to school for she will feel awkward at this age. Besides she has to be involved in beedi making full time for survival. Both the grandmother and she feel very-very threatened when there is no raw material available for making beedis. On these days, they go to the karkhana and do some cleaning etc. for the contractor. Krishnamma felt that she had no control over her life, and since her parents married her off, she wanted to adjust well in this life. Unfortunately the groom's side was not very happy with the dowry, and they did not even bother to take the bride or come and enquire about her after marriage. She was seven years at that time. She does not want to get married again but continues making beedis. She knew the value of education but thinks it is beyond her. She however welcomes the idea of non-formal education, but it is not sure how she will find the time or what purpose if will serve now. Krishnamma and her grandmother are not aware of any government schemes for their benefit. Due to the peculiar circumstances of which she is a victim both she and her grandmother have a very pessimistic view of life without any hope for future.

Case 5

Narayana is 13 years of age and comes from Pipri in Armoor Mandal. He is third among his brothers and belongs to Veeramursti caste which an ST. He works in the karkhana in the package section. His whole family of father, mother, and two elder brothers are illiterate, and while the mother makes beedis at home, the father and sons work in the karkhana.

Narayana has never been to school, and the parents do not see the need for education. The family was too poor to afford education, and now they think it is beyond them. They are contented lot with working in the karkhana. Narayana works from morning to evening. His job is to put the beedis bundles in the tray from where it is taken to be baked. He often also helps in packaging where a large number of beedis are packed into huge brown paper packets and then transported to other states like Maharashtra and Karnataka. Being surrounded by tobacco, all the time Narayana coughs continuously but ignores it and accepts it as a part of life. He does not care much for the pain in his limbs because he can continue to work and it does not make him immobile by being laid in bed. He works continuously for eight hours and more throughout the day earning between Rs 250 and 400 per month. The family lives in a Kutcha/mud house and has no other property. Among themselves, the family's total household income is between Rs 1,000 and 1,500 per month, and they feel they are better off than many other beedi workers. Working in the karkhana is a big status symbol for them and they are very happy with the karkhana owner for they get their payments on time and do not face any kind of harassment. The family seems contended a lot without any great ambitions. They don't see any change in their circumstances and hope they will have enough money to get all their three sons married comfortably. They are keen to get daughters in-law who are already familiar with beedi making. They are not aware of various legislation and schemes for their benefit but know very well that children below 15 are not allowed to work in the karkhana. They are confident that nothing will happen because, "the government can make any rule but it is they who have to fight for survival". The other two sons who are now 15 and 16 years, respectively, had also started working in the karkhana much before and nothing happened. They are thankful that instead of just roaming around, all their sons are engaged in work and contribute to the family income.

Case 6

Sheerin Zeenath comes from Nizamabad town and is nine years of age. She is the third child in her family of one brother and two sisters. Their mothers Ishad Banu is educated till fifth class and presently makes beedis at home. Their father Allauddin is educated till SSC and has his own cycle repair shop. The family seems more aware. They are very unhappy that their son could not pass SSC and now assists his father at the cycle repair shop. Sheerin's elder sister Moshin Zeenath is 12 years of age and studying in eighth class, and she studies in fifth class. Both these girls come back from school and after doing their homework, immediately start making beedis. Sheerin works up to four hours per day and is able to make 250–300 beedis. The whole evening is spent in beedi making, and so she does not find time to play. She makes the complete beedi and has been involved in beedi making for the last three years. She wants to be a teacher when she grows up. The fact that the parents are educated has made a lot of difference in their attitude and perceptions about life. The mother would want to get her daughters married but not before they are educated at least till the intermediate level. The family earns between Rs 1,001 and 1,500 per month. "Education makes one self confident and one can get a good job or service", according to the mother. They are aware of some of the laws and schemes of the government regarding beedi workers, though they have not benefited from these schemes in any way. She only hopes that for her daughters, beedi making is only a stop-gap arrangement, and once they are educated enough to get a good match and good service, they will leave beedi making for better alternatives. Sheerin's family is very optimistic about life and has passed on this optimism to their children.

Case 7

Chowti Lalitha is 13 years of age and is from Gopanpally in Nizamabad Mandal. She belongs to OBC of Padmasali. She has been married for three years now to a boy who has passed his high school and helps a tailor for his livelihood. Lalitha stays with her in-laws where her mother-in-law Ramayamma is a beedi maker. Her father-in-law was an agricultural labourer and died one year ago. Presently in the family, there is Ramayamma, her two daughters aged 10 and 9, and the young couple. Except for the son, all are illiterate. They live in a Kutcha mud house which is rented and has two very small rooms. They have no other property or land. They have borrowed Rs 4,000 to incur the expenditure on the wedding of their son and other funeral expenditures. Chowti Lalitha has now been making beedis for the last six years. She makes nearly 501–600 beedis per day and does it the whole day as and when she gets time. She did not go to school because her parents, agricultural labourers, were too poor to afford it. She cannot think of education now because it would be too awkward at this age. She thinks life was no different for her earlier and will continue to be the same, and she will continue to make beedis. She is interested in learning tailoring but gets no encouragement from her husband. One can see visible signs of illness in her eyes which continuously water and she complaints of a lot of joint pain, because she is often seated in one posture. But she sees no way out of her plight. Here is a child who has not seen any childhood and has been working for livelihood from a very young age. She is locked in this world and sees no alternative for herself.

12

CONCLUSIONS AND THE WAY FORWARD

Our sample consisted of an urban sample of 40% and a rural component of 60%. There was a total sample of 1,040 with 665 women and 375 children. In Armoor, field work was conducted and data collected in Pipri (rural area) and Armoor town (urban area). In Balkonda Mandal, field work was conducted and data collected in Kisanagar (rural area) and Balkond town (urban area). In Nizamabad Mandal, field work was conducted and data collected in Gaggupalle (rural area) and Nizamabad town (urban area). In Hyderabad, data was collected from six urban areas namely, Amberpet, Ramanthpur, Musheerabad, Parsigutta, Mallikajgiri, and Uppal.

In our study, of the selected 1,040 household, majority of these were Hindus followed by Muslims and then Christians, Sikhs, and others. Majority of the women were married and about 17% of the women in our sample were divorced, separated, deserted, and widowed. In the absence of any land with them, the men worked as agricultural labourers and the women worked in beedi making. Majority of these households came from backward communities and were Schedule Castes and Schedule tribes by caste. Beedi making is dominated by the backward castes, which are below the poverty line. Most of these household had migrated into Nizamabad over 15 years and remembered always living there. We had very few households less than 1%–2% who had migrated less than a year were or between six and ten years. Making beedis was a specialised job, and newcomers rarely joined this work because, not being experts, their beedis were frequently rejected by the contractor, causing them to incur a financial loss as a result, they preferred to assist in some aspect of making beedis rather than making it completely on their own.

Most of the household in our sample were nuclear families, the mothers were in the age group of 26–30 years, 24.1% were in the age group of 31–35

DOI: 10.4324/9781003317944-14

years, and 17.5% were in the age group of 36–40 years. Precisely, 18.1% of the fathers were between 26 and 30 years, 33.2% were between 31 and 35 years, and 19.8% were between 36 and 40 years. Precisely, 62% fathers and 88% mothers were illiterate. Of the 375 girls in our sample, the actual age of majority of our respondent child workers was between 7–9 years and 12–13 years. Precisely, 66.6% of these girls were first born and 20.1% were second born. Hence, they had to also look after their siblings and assist in household works too.

Only young boys, those younger than ten years old, made beedis. Boys who were older than this age did not participate in the production of beedis; rather, they were employed in the factory or the firm and participated in activities such as packaging, transportation, and so on. Even when they were unemployed and could not find work in the factory, the boys would either just loaf around or bring the material from the contractor and return the finished beedis (especially in Muslim households), but they would never make beedis themselves because they looked down on the practice. We heard from a lot of older boys that this was considered "women's work", and that other people would make fun of them if they made beedis. The vast majority of our young workers attended some form of formal education. A great number of children were forced to leave school in order to help contribute to the family's income or to take care of the household responsibilities, while their mothers made beedis. A large number of children attended school due to the *Midday meal scheme*, of the Government, whereby school children are provided with a midday meal. The schools we saw had a dearth of prerequisites such as qualified and well-paid teachers, adequate school building, playground facilities, books, boards, and slates. We found that the children who went to school regularly and worked only after school hours made between 100 and 250 beedis per day. Children who made more than 250 beedis per day had either dropped out of school or never went to school and made beedis for the whole day.

Human rights being gender-specific

There is a gender component to human rights. Theoretical understanding and actual application were two very different things. Even though equality is enshrined in our constitution, in practice there was a great deal of exploitation of the women who made the beedis. According to the findings of our study, the women who made beedis tend to be young, uneducated, and come from landless families. Because the husband's job was unpredictable and his earnings were meagre, the majority of the responsibility for supporting their large families fell on the shoulders of the wives. The girl child helped out around the house, which resulted in her dropping out of school. The women and the child, in addition to performing domestic duties, spent nine to ten hours actually making beedi and performing activities related to it. These activities included gathering the raw materials, cutting the leaves, soaking them, and cleaning them, as well as delivering the finished products to the contractor.

The poor socioeconomic conditions

The majority of the girls and women who participated in our research were in extremely poor health. The poor socioeconomic conditions of the people living in rural areas, combined with malnutrition and an environment that is unsanitary and unhygienic, are contributors to the rural population's poor health status (Singh, 1979). It is estimated that roughly half of all Indians are undernourished and unable to afford a diet that provides them with the minimum amount of energy they require for a healthy and active life (Rao, 1990). The majority of women show signs of anaemia, which can be attributed to insufficient dietary intake as well as a poor environment (Gupta et al., 1983). There was a vicious cycle in which the girl child worked more than her brother but ate less than her brother did. Her precarious nutritional status puts her at risk for anaemia and other nutritional deficiencies as well as infections; despite the fact that she was more ill than her brother, she was only occasionally taken to the hospital for medical care. These differences are only made worse by poverty, but the underlying problem is not so much a lack of food as it is the importance placed on the male child over the female child (Pande et al., 1993). She eventually marries at a young age and gives birth to a number of babies who are typically born with a low birth weight. The cycle of nutritional depletion is finished when a young mother passes away while giving birth to her child (Chatterjee, 1988).

Nutrition and health

Nutrition and health are closely linked to the economic productivity and quality of Life. Many of our respondents were ignorant about the proper weight gain as one of the best criteria for judging the adequacy of breast milk. They did not consider burping of any use. There was no awareness that early weaning would lead to secondary lactation failure and more chances of gastrointestinal infection and would result in iatrogenic malnutrition. There was a strong belief that undiluted milk was unfit for consumption by an infant and only undiluted top milk could be digested properly. There was a strong belief that fruits and fruit juices were cold products and should be avoided because it could lead to diarrhoea. It is difficult to state if the origin of these beliefs should be seen in economic milieu of the household or the cultural and traditional practices of the region. Even in the area of hygiene for breast-feeding, much was to be desired. Many a times the women did not wash their hands of the tobacco and pulled out their nipple for the child. This was due to the paucity of time. For these women, every day was a race against time to make the required beedis and get more raw materials from the contractor.

In our study, 24% of the mothers were breast-feeding children who were less than four years of age. Many of these women had regularly fed their children on only breastmilk for a period of two months and soon tried to wean their children. Nearly half of these women who were breast-feeding their children had discarded the colostrum and were not aware that it was rich in protein content, especially globulin and vitamin A. They thought that this was not fit to be fed to the child. Many stated that they did not get milk for the first few days. They had no concept of antibodies or vital nutrients being present in the milk. Usually, feeding started on the second day. With a slighter old child, the women continued to breast-feed the child while making beedis. Many health experts have attributed the decline of breast-feeding to lack of awareness, the power of advertisement of breastmilk substitutes (Kumar, 1988). Therefore, the conventional approach to empower women to breast-feed has rested mainly on eradication of the supposed ignorance of mothers. Such an approach fails to recognise the multiple roles of women as workers, homemakers, and mothers. It is assumed that housewives have the time, resources, and inclination to provide a high-quality care for children (Basu and Basu, 1991). It is assumed that if women cannot afford to withdraw from market activities, work in the family enterprise or family farms will provide greater flexibility to provide better quality of care for their children (Tamang et al., 1990). Domestic responsibilities take up tremendous portion of women's time in poor areas and affect both their care of young children and participation in labour force (Jain et al., 1995). This is more so in the unorganised sectors (Kameshwari, 1992). Our study of the beedi workers clearly showed us that though much needs to be done on creating awareness, the economic, social, and psychological constraints all affect the mother child proximity. Many of these women who had to drop out of infant care during breast-feeding belonged to low-income groups. The choice was between making beedis and survival or the luxury of childcare. Many of these women during the first month faced severe financial constraint and were forced to cut out a meal or two or resort to heavy borrowing. These women hardly had any respite from domestic work and had to fetch water, do cleaning, cooking along with getting raw material, rolling beedis and childcare. It is true that a women's work is never done (Sharma, 1989).

Occupational risks hazards

We found that many of our respondents were suffering from ill health as a result of their prolonged involvement in the process of beedi production as well as their confinement in the dim, small, and enclosed space of the hut or the workshop. It is well known that women are less likely to participate effectively and for an extended period of time in healthcare activities if those activities involve repetitive movement (Leslie, 1989). The enclosed atmosphere, the overcrowding in the *karkhanas* or huts, along with the odour of the wet leaf and tobacco, adds to the already poor ventilation and makes the environment in which the beedi maker works extremely unhealthy.

There was a lot of burning of the eyes, conjunctivitis, rhinitis, mucous dryness, and bronchitis as a result of inhaling tobacco dust, to which the worker is continuously exposed. Because the work involved in making beedi is so repetitive and monotonous, the work eventually becomes mechanised after a few years of doing it. There is no room for creativity or innovation in this environment. Because of the nature of the work, a worker cannot afford to take even the brief break from what she is doing if she expects to produce the required quantity of beedis in a given day. The eyesight of these women suffers as a direct consequence of this, particularly as they get older. We became aware of a number of accounts involving friends and neighbours who had suffered from a variety of signs and symptoms associated with poor health. As evidence of the skin rashes they were experiencing, a number of the workers presented us with their yellow-coloured nails and hands.

A large number of the steps in the process of making beedi are carried out while the maker is seated, either on the floor with their legs crossed, with either their right or left leg bent at the knee, or with their legs extended. When seated for an extended period of time with the trunk bent forward, sustained static construction of the back muscle occurs. As a consequence of this, a number of the workers experienced back aches.

It is a well-established fact that prolonged exposure to tobacco causes a greater absorption of nicotine, which, in turn, causes long-term damage to the respiratory, circulatory, and reproductive systems. Women who worked in the beedi industry experienced a variety of reproductive issues, including abortions, stillbirths, and infections of the reproductive tract. A significant number of the women reported to us that, in comparison to other women who had worked in agricultural labour, they had significantly fewer labour pains and shorter labour times. A great number of women had the impression that their thighs and legs did not receive sufficient blood flow because they spent the majority of their time seated with their legs bent or folded. Because of this, they had the impression that they experienced more difficulties during childbirth in comparison to women who worked in the fields.

In India, occupational health hazards have never been the focus of either legislation or implementation, and they are generally ignored. This is the case across the country (Durvasula, 1992). Both the mother and the child worker denied that the act of making beedi was to blame for any of their illnesses, including asthma, bronchitis, T.B., or cancer. They believed that the process of making beedis was largely to blame for a variety of what they referred to as "minor ailments", including headaches, giddiness, body aches, pains in the joints, burning and etching in the eyes, peeling away of the skin, and the development of skin rashes. These respondents were clear that while conditions such as cancer, asthma, and tuberculosis were serious because they caused one to be laid in bed and unable to do any work, the ailments from which they suffered were minor because it only caused irritation and discomfort but never came in the way of beedi making because they were not laid in bed for a long time. The people who made beedis put off going to the doctor for as long as they could, but when they became incapacitated to the point where they could no longer produce beedis, they had no choice but to seek medical attention. This occurred a little bit too often we could see. The vast majority of them visited public health clinics, while only a few went to private hospitals or saw private physicians. Because they had no other option, a good number of the people who made beedi went to the government dispensary. The government hospital didn't have very good facilities, and most of the time they didn't have any of the medicines that patients needed. If given the option, they would choose to see a private doctor, who in some instances would even provide the necessary medications; however, this option was prohibitively expensive for them, and they declined it. The vast majority of people in the village received their medical care at one of the facilities found within the village, while the patient was forced to travel between five and eight kilometres outside of the village to receive treatment. These villages did not appear to have any mobile dispensaries that we could locate. When it comes to accessing medical facilities, distance is obviously a very important factor to consider. Due to the time constraints placed on them, beedi workers are unable to spare the necessary time and resources to travel to a faraway location in order to make use of the medical facilities there.

Intervention

The worker in the beedi industry do their job in a dangerous industry, in an environment of exploitation due to the way the industry is organised and the gender relations that exist. There is a great deal of structural violence in this sector of the economy. The majority of Dalit women and girls are not forced into beedi making; rather, they participate because they are grateful for the opportunity. This is the fundamental reason for people's poor health. In light of the complexity of the situation, no single action will be effective. Education and awareness will result in the emergence of demands for improved working conditions, higher wages, and additional welfare measures.

There are no time saving, organised healthcare facilities specifically for the beedi-making women. The manufacturers have not demonstrated any interest in either corrective or preventative measures at any point. Women are aware of the health risks, but they choose to suffer in silence because they lack the time and resources to seek help. It is imperative that a comprehensive analysis of the health of women be conducted. We are of the firm belief that diseases such as bronchitis, asthma, and tuberculosis cannot be detected in a timely manner in order for treatment to be administered if regular medical surveys are not carried out. In spite of the fact that there is a provision for a mobile medical unit facility, there is no indication that this will ever be used. The owners of the factory as well as the contractors have a duty to accept responsibility. In order to prevent women and children from handling tobacco with their bare hands, alternative methods of handling tobacco need to be developed as soon as possible. When making beedis, people ought to be required to wear protective eyewear and face coverings at all times. This needs to be strictly enforced by raising awareness about the significant risks to people's health posed by the production of beedi.

When it comes to the beedi workers, the structural violence has its origins in the class, caste, and sexist nature of society. As a result of these factors, women are consistently devalued and discriminated against in every aspect of their lives All of this results in the women having a very poor self-image, and as a result, they internalise many of these values and notions, which they then pass on to their daughters, thereby perpetuating the vicious cycle. Women's health can be negatively impacted by a variety of factors, including the type of work, the social environment, the amount of work, and stresses and strains. It is impossible to examine human rights in isolation from the socioeconomic structures that are currently in place. The enhancement of the current status of human rights should focus primarily on the enhancement of the existing standard of living. Due to the fact that the majority of girls assist their mothers in the production of beedi, they quickly become a group that is exploited, and their work is not even acknowledged as work. In addition to working excessive hours and barely scraping by, the vast majority of these women and children struggle with a variety of health issues.

As a result, human rights and health programmes need to be linked together and need to have direct links with programmes for protected water supply, environmental, sanitation and hygiene, nutrition and education, family planning, and maternity and child welfare programmes. The topic of health cannot be reduced to the question of curing illness or preventing illness alone. The right to health would encompass not only the absence of illness but also the right to a state of complete mental, emotional, and physical well-being as well. The concept of human rights encompasses every aspect of a person's life, including the type of housing one resides in, the diet one consumes, and the occupation one pursues. It is impossible to separate issues of class, caste, and gender from those pertaining to human rights.

Recommendations and suggestions

According to the findings of our research, the majority of the women and children who are employed in the beedi industry do so primarily due to the fact that their work is essential for ensuring their continued survival. Women and children from low-income groups who live below the poverty line are most likely to make beedis. This includes women and children from OBCs, SCs, and STs. These women and children are placed in a very subordinate position as a result of the social and cultural constructions of gender relations, the power relations that already exist in the society, as well as the disadvantages of the putting-out system in the informal manufacturing system. All of these factors work together to give these women and children this position. Because this is such a significant problem, it needs to be addressed on its own. Because the production of beedis is necessary for the continued existence of a great number of households, in the absence of any other means of earning a living, under the current circumstances, in the short run, the focus should not be on the elimination of child labour and the confiscation of the children's earnings; rather, the goal should be to rehabilitate the children in some industry that does not pose a risk to their health and safety, or, until that goal is accomplished, to improve the working conditions of the children and it is very challenging to separate the girls from their mothers and the rest of their families because the vast majority of the beedi workers in our case are female. As a result, even a small change in the circumstances of the family as a whole and the mother in particular will have a significant impact on the quality of life of the child labourer.

Some of the broad areas where we would like to make recommendations and suggestions are as follows.

Poverty alleviation

After the formation of a national commitment to the development of effective poverty alleviation and other policy measures to reduce the population living below the poverty line, one can begin to discuss the abolition of child labour. However, this cannot happen until after the formation of the commitment. This requires a commitment on the part of the nation as a whole as well as a clearly defined ideological commitment on the part of the ruling elite. After this objective has been accomplished, and only then, will it make sense to discuss doing away with child labour completely.

Education

Though majority of our respondents were going to school, there was much to be desired. There is a need to recognise the importance of education as a means of obtaining the improvement in the quality of life. All planning and policy making should rest on this premise. The schools we saw had a dearth in basic prerequisites such as qualified and well-paid teachers, adequate school building, playground facilities, books, boards, and slates. Education must be made exciting with a mobilisation of community resources and more societal involvement. We found teaching methods to be very dogmatic. Little was done to encourage questioning, critical thinking, or an interest in self-education beyond the school. Learning is by rote. Most of the children come from social settings that cannot afford books, periodicals etc. There could be a lessening of centralisation and increased control of school administration and finances by the local residents. Residential schools should be established to cater to the need of children who are taken away from beedi making. Non-formal centres providing education to working children and mothers must be increased. Primary schools at village level, ZPPP (Zilla Parishad Primary Pathshala), and other local schools should be given the autonomy to change their working hours and months to suit the local economy's requirements. The midday meal scheme is a strong incentive for parents to send their children to school. This should be implemented in many rural areas.

Health

It is impossible to consider health in isolation from the socioeconomic system that is currently in place. The improvement of people's health conditions is primarily concerned with the enhancement of people's overall quality of life. As a result, it is imperative that programmes pertaining to health have a direct connection with those pertaining to the provision of safe drinking water, the environment, sanitation and hygiene, nutrition and education, family planning, maternity care, and child welfare. It is possible to conduct routine medical surveys in order to detect conditions such as bronchitis, asthma, and tuberculosis in a timely manner and administer treatment for them. It is necessary to increase the size of the government hospital's staff as well as the size of its physical facilities. Due to the fact that it is necessary to travel to Nizamabad for medical care, the surrounding villages are too far away. To satisfy the needs of the community in terms of medical care, there ought to be made available a facility in the form of a mobile medical unit. When making beedis, people ought to be required to wear protective eyewear and face coverings at all times. Since the majority of beedi production takes place in people's homes, the workers who make the product should be made aware of the risks to their health, and an emphasis should be placed on the use of protective gear like goggles and masks to keep themselves safe.

Legal

Most of the women beedi workers work at home with their children and are only contractual labour. Hence, they do not get any benefits of the government legislation. These benefits should be extended to them. The labour law–enforcing authorities should also accelerate their pace in implementing the various legislations effectively. Labour inspectors must be periodically trained and informed to the changes and amendments in legislation. They must be required to maintain progress reports of the activity for elimination of child labour. Labour inspectors should through social workers, interact with education, school inspectors, and NGO's to ensure that rehabilitated children go to school and do not return to work.

A comprehensive state level child labour Act applicable to both the workers at home and at the karkhana is required. The Beedi and Cigar Workers (conditions of Employment) Rules should be strictly implemented so that the evil of not registering the name of the workers manufacturing beedi at home is eradicated. The regional provident fund commissioner should strictly enforce the rule and see to it that all the members are covered. We found out that the contractor labour system, which is regarded to be undispensable to this trade, led to a lot of exploitation. This area has to be regulated and the workers under the contractual system should also be brought under the purview of law, so that they get the benefits of legislation. The welfare fund set up for the beedi workers should be properly administered and in the case of the death of a workman, appropriate assistance should be extended from the fund to his dependents.

Non-government Organisations (NGOs)

Beedi making is dominated by women who are assisted by the girls of the household. These people have a very weak bargaining position being home-based workers. There is also a non-recognition by both the employer and trade union organisations, to regard these women as an important segment of labour force. Since there is a total lack of organisation of any kind of fight for their rights. There is a need to help these women to help themselves. There is a need to facilitate an awareness of their shared problems and arrange a forum where understanding and solidarity can develop and the same can be extended to the girl child. The initiative has to come from some NGO. Besides arranging a forum, the NGO's can also help in organising collective action, where women and girls take the lead and decided by themselves the kind of action needed to improve their life and situation.

There are a large number of girls who are working full time in the beedi industry and hence are illiterate or have dropped out of school at a very early age. Some NGO can take a lead in organising non-formal education centres. These should be designed to suit the requirement of the beedi workers and must concentrate their efforts during the closure of the karkhana's when these girls are relatively free.

Some NGO should be identified for formulation and implementation of welfare programmes at the grass root level. A clear-cut national networking system of NGO's needs to be developed, in which the power structure and channels of communication between government and individual NGO need to be identified.

The government

Our research has unequivocally demonstrated that the vast majority of children who are employed in the beedi industry do so primarily due to the fact that their work is essential to their continued existence. Women and children from low-income groups who live below the poverty line are most likely to make beedis. This includes women and children from OBCs, SCs, and STs. These women and children are placed in a very subordinate position as a result of the social and cultural constructions of gender relations, the power relations that already exist in the society, as well as the disadvantages of the putting-out system in the informal manufacturing system. All of these factors work together to give these women and children this position. The worker in the beedi industry do their job in a dangerous industry, in an environment of exploitation due to the way the industry is organised and the gender relations that exist. There is a great deal of structural violence in this sector of the economy. The majority of Dalit women and girls participate in beedi production out of necessity rather than choice; however, they are thankful that it is an option. Yet, in the modern era, even this line of work is in jeopardy because of the government's crackdown on tobacco and the increased public consciousness regarding health concerns.

At the outset, we would like to emphasise that the prevalence of child labour in the beedi industry is not due to the absence of any legislation or welfare schemes but due to the specific role of the child in the familial economy. We found a total lack of awareness about government programmes and a general disdain for government measures with the general opinion that it involved a lot of paperwork and the benefits are cornered by only few influential people. There should be an attempt to decrease the paperwork and initiative should be taken to promote more awareness about government schemes. The IRDP (Integrated Rural Development Program) is also not as successful as expected in achieving the goals of integrated rural development. One can clearly see the vast difference in the Harijan *bastis* and other areas of the village. Integrated rural socioeconomic development has to form the basis of the programmes and their implementation strategies. Housing schemes for all the beedi workers may be formulated. Though the government is giving certain land sites and housing loans of Rs. 10,000, this was not being received by the real needy ones. There is a need to identify the real needy beneficiaries through a mechanism of involving the village people. Many of the families working in beedi industry did not have any other source of livelihood besides beedi. Such families could be identified and be given waste and uncultivable land that agriculture is developed and children are withdrawn from beedi making. It is also necessary for the government to invest in irrigation and thereby boost the agricultural output leading to generation of more income and employment.

Rehabilitation

We did not come across any rehabilitation programme for child labour, except midday meal scheme in a school to bring in more children to school. Some rehabilitation programmes should be designed to take away children from beedi making. We found a lot of interest and demand for some kind of a training centre for sewing. Such a centre could be established for the girls to make a livelihood by stitching clothes. Some incentive could be provided for making *papads*, *achars*, etc. and a proper network established to market these products. It is also recommended that stipend be given to working children as an incentive to join some training in the rehabilitation centre.

Involvement of local personal

The private sector, local entrepreneurs, and trade associations should be called to share the cost of rehabilitation of child workers, along with the government. This will give the local personnel a sense of involvement beside sharing in the cost and participating in the training of an educated and skilled work force. There is a need to monitor any programme in order to achieve any success. A committee of eminent members should be nominated with in the Mandal to monitor the various rehabilitation and governmental programmes. This committee should consist of doctors, lawyers, academicians, and activists besides representatives of government. This committee should meet once in six months and submit reports from time to time on the rehabilitation programmes. The gram panchayats which have been established to bring about a democratic decentralisation by transference of authority to the local community could take an initiative and be the link between the government agencies and the village community.

Public awareness

Public awareness has to be created at two levels for the people working in the beedi industry and the general public. We found a total lack of awareness about government programmes, in the rural area. The Television has a lot of impact in these areas and a large number of families collected together in a house having television to watch the programmes. This medium could be fully utilised for creating awareness on issues related to child labour. The beedi workers and children also have to be made aware of the health hazards they are facing in making beedis that they are able to protect themselves till they are rehabilitated. There is a need to investigate the various aspects of the phenomenon of urban child labour through critical research and seminars, workshops, and informal meetings with the target groups, their parent, and other related groups. Public awareness could also be created through child labour campaigns model.

Some models which can be used are,

1. **Investigation:** This is the first step of acquiring information through research by mass media, NGOs, trade unions, universities, government agencies, and international agencies.
2. **Analysis:** The information needs processing to arrive at plausible explanations concerning causes, consequences, and measures to be taken.
3. **Exposure:** Such interpretations need a public airing through publications, etc.
4. **Dissemination:** Wider dissemination is then needed via the mass media, trade union education structures, etc. to generate greater public awareness.
5. **Mobilisation:** Of those groups most likely to act, such as trade unions, NGOs, and churches
6. **Pressure:** Through campaigns, pressure is put on the authorities to act to eradicate the worst abuses of child labour and to protest and improve the welfare of child workers in line with internally agreed standards.
7. **Action:** Positive action which can be anticipated would include adoption of ILO standards, better labour inspection, punitive measures against employers guilty of the worst practices, improved provision of health, welfare and educational services for those children most at risk.
8. **Evaluation:** All action needs evaluation, especially if, as is often the case, it is not successful the first time. Once we find out what went wrong with the campaign, we can marshal new information and "look back" again with a fresh attempt at dissemination and mobilisation.

The way forward

Today the Tobacco industry is at cross roads and the women and children making beedis find themselves in a catch 22 situation. On the one hand, due to the rising awareness on health issues, there are various curbs on this industry and work is being reduced for these women. Yet this work is very essential for these women. How do we make policies that protect the interests of these women who are marginalised and poor. Tobacco is used both in a smokeless form and a smoking form. Tobacco use is not uniform across regions, genders, or ages in Indian society, despite the fact that there have been numerous pieces of legislation passed at varying times over the course of Indian history. It is necessary to investigate the connection that exists between low income, poor health, and the state of the environment. Poor women are the most vulnerable members of society because they are at a disadvantage and tend to have less access to education, support services, empowerment, and political power, all of which are important factors that can protect their health. There is a significant divide between the global concern for the health of women and the actual practice of putting this concern into action.

In India, there are a total of 44 federal labour laws and 387 state labour laws, 67 federal labour filings and 1,333 state labour filings, and 674 federal labour compliances and 26,484 state labour compliances. Because of the proliferation of laws, the proliferation of enforcement authorities, and the proliferation of licences, registrations, and returns, we have created an environment that encourages non-compliance and lowers the guard on the very section we intend to protect and safeguard, which has caused millions of citizens to seek employment in the informal sector. To achieve the goals of having labour laws that are comprehensive, effective, and easy to comply with, what is required is their simplification, rationalisation, and digitisation. The first step we have taken in that direction is to consolidate all of our labour laws into four distinct labour codes based on their relative importance. Following the passage of the Bill to Revise the Code on Wages, all focus has shifted to revising the Social Security code.

The Framework Convention on Tobacco Control (FCTC), which was the first global health treaty to be negotiated under the auspices of the World Health Organisation (WHO), has been of great assistance to the worldwide effort to lessen the negative effects of tobacco use. In 2015, according to the WHO, the WHO FCTC is the first international treaty pertaining to public health. The right of all individuals to the highest possible level of health is reaffirmed in this legally binding document that is based on scientific evidence. The WHO FCTC was developed as a response by countries to the globalisation of the tobacco epidemic. Tobacco advertising, promotion, and sponsorship beyond national borders, as well as illegal trade in tobacco products, are some of the issues that this initiative intends to address. Additionally, it seeks to combat some of the factors that contribute to the complex nature of the epidemic and its spread across the globe, such as trade liberalisation and direct foreign investment. Even though the United States has not yet signed on, more than 170 other countries have already ratified the FCTC. Following ratification of the treaty, countries will be required to enact a comprehensive set of policies, some of which include increased taxes, clearer health warning labels, and policies prohibiting smoking in public places (50). The tobacco industry is persistent in its opposition to efforts by governments to adopt policies that will effectively restrict the marketing of cigarettes and protect public health.

Tobacco control policy

The National Health Mission (NHM) comprises its two Sub-Missions, which are the National Rural Health Mission (NRHM) and the National Urban Health Mission (NUHM), which was just recently initiated. The main programmatic components consist of Reproductive-Maternal-Neonatal-Child and Adolescent Health (RMNCH+A), Communicable and Non-Communicable Diseases, and Strengthening Health Systems in Rural and Urban Areas. The National Health Maintenance Organization aspires to realise its vision of achieving universal access to equitable, affordable, and high-quality healthcare services that are accountable to people and sensitive to their requirements. Public spaces is a crime that carries a penalty if you are caught doing it. Advertising of tobacco products, either directly or indirectly, in any form, including sponsorship and promotion, is against the law and constitutes a criminal offence. It is illegal for anyone younger than 18 years old, including minors, to buy or sell tobacco products, and doing so is considered a criminal offence. Within 100 yards of a school or other educational facility, it is against the law and considered a criminal offence to sell tobacco products. On all packages of tobacco products, the graphic health warnings must be displayed as required by law.

So while these may be important, it is also necessary to protect these women and children who are involved in the beedi industry.

References

Basu, A. M., and K. Basu, 1991, "Women's Economic Roles and Child Survival: The Case of India", *Health Transition Review*, Vol. 1, pp. 1–20.

Chatterjee, M., 1988, "Both Gender and Age Against Them", *Mimeo Report*, NIPCCD, New Delhi.

Durvasula, R., 1992, "Occupational Health Information's Systems in India", in M. R. Reich and T Okubo (eds), *Protecting Workers Health in the Third World, National and International Strategies*, New York, Auburn House, pp. 103–134.

Gupta, S. D., R. Gupta, A. Zafar, D. K. Mangal and R. Sharma, 1983, "Control of Anaemia Among Pregnant Women by Iron Supplementations", *Indian Journal of Public Health*, Vol. 27, No. 1, pp. 28–31.

Jain, D., and S. Desai, 1995, "The Women Worker and Her Child", *Institute of Social Studies,* Dossier No. 4, Bangalore.

Kameshwari, J., and R. Pande, 1992, Report, *Crèches in the Organized and Unorganized Sectors in Secunderabad and Hyderabad*, Department of women and child welfare, New Delhi, Government of India.

Kumar, R., ed., 1988, *Child Development in India*, Vol. 1, New Delhi, Ashish Publishing House.

Leslie, J., 1989, "Women's Work and Child Nutrition in the Third World", in J. Leslie and M. Paolisso (eds), *Women Work and Child Welfare in the Third World*, Boulder (CO), Westview Press, pp. 19–58.

Pande, R., and J. Kameshwari, 1993, Report, *Girl Child and family in Telangana*, Department of Women and Child Welfare, New Delhi, Government of India.

Rao, V., G. Radhaiah, V. Narayana, and P. V. Sukhatme, ed., 1990, "How Poor Can Help the Poor", *Statistics in Health and Nutrition*, Hyderabad, National Institute of Nutrition, Indian Council of Medical Research.

Sharma, M., and U. Varjani, 1989, "Women's Work Is Never Done: Dairy Development and Health in the Lives of Rural Women in Rajasthan", *Economic and Political Weekly*, April 29, WS, pp. 38–44.

Singh, I. J., 1979, "A Study of Morbidity Pattern in Rural Community", *Health and Population Perspectives and Issues*, Vol. 2, pp. 193–206.

Tamang, D., 1990, "Indigenous Forest Management Systems in Nepal: A Review. Research Report Series – HMG Ministry of Agriculture, Nepal/Winrock International", *Policy Analysis in Agriculture and Related Resource Management*, No. 12, pp. x + 47.

BIBLIOGRAPHY

I. Books

Abbott, G., 1938, *The Child and the State*, vol. I and vol. II. Chicago (IL), University of Chicago Press.

Abraham, T. M., 1965, *Handicraft in India*, New Delhi, New Delhi Press.

Agrawal, S. P., and N. Kanta, 1990, *Child Education in India: Index to Scholarly Writings in Indian Educational Journals and Newspapers since Independence Including Constitutional Provision and Basic Indicators of Child Growth*, New Delhi, Concept Publication.

Apperson, G. L., 1916, *The Social History of Smoking*, New York, G. P. Putnam's Sons.

Aries, P., 1962, *Centuries of Childhood: A Social History of Family Life*. Trans. R. Baldick, New York, Random House.

Astige, S. B., 2006, *Role and Status of Working Women*, New Delhi, Anmol Publications Pvt. Ltd.

Banerjee, N. (ed.), 1991, *Women in a Changing Industrial Scenario, Indo Dutch Studies on Development Alternatives*, New Delhi, Sage Publication.

Bequela, A., and J. Boyden, eds., 1988, *Combating Child Labour*, Geneva, International Labour Organisation.

Beneria, L., and M. Roldan, 1987, *The Crossroads of Class and Gender*, Chicago (IL), University of Chicago.

Baxi, U., 1988, *Law and Poverty – Critical Essay*, Bombay, N. M. Tripathi Private Limited.

Bhasin, K., 2003, *Understanding Gender*, New Delhi, Women Unlimited.

Bhatty, Z., 1981, *Economic Role and Status of Women in the Bidi Industry in Allahabad*, Geneva, ILO.

Boserup, E., 1970, *Woman's Role in Economic Development*, New Work, St. Martin's Press.

Bromley, R., and C. Gerry (eds), 1979, *Casual Work and Poverty in Third World Cities*, New York, Chichester, John Wiley.

Bullock, S., 1994, *Women and Work*, London and New Jersey, Zed Books Ltd.

Buvinic, M., M. A. Lycette and W. P. Mc Greevey, 1983, *Women and Poverty in the Third World*, London, John Hopkins Press.

Chandler, A. D. Jr., 1977, *The Visible Hand: The Managerial Revolution in American Business*, Cambridge (MA), Harvard University Press.

Chandola, L. M., 1985, *Women in the Unorganised Sector*, New Delhi, Radiant Publishers.

Charms, J., 1998, *Estimation and Survey Methods for the Informal Sector*. University of Versailles, St. Quentin en Yvelines. Centre of Economics and Ethics for Environment and Development, France, https://www.stat.fi/isi99/proceedings/arkisto/varasto/char0883.pdf Accessed 4th May, 2020.

Chen, M., J. Vanek and M. Carr, 2004, *Mainstreaming Informal Employment and Gender in Poverty Reduction: A Handbook for Policymakers and Other Stakeholders*, London, Commonwealth Secretariat.

Chen, M. A., 2012, *The Informal Economy: Definitions, Theories and Policies*, Manchester, Cambridge, United Kingdom Women in Informal Employment: Globalizing and Organizing (WIEGO).

Choudhury, U., 2006, *Informal Sector in a Developing Economy*, New Delhi, Anmol Publication.

Datar, C., 1989, *Waging Change, Women Tobacco*, New Delhi, Kali for Women.

Desai, N., and M. Krishnaraj, 1990, *Women and Society in India*, Jawahar Nagar, New Delhi, Ajanta Publication.

de Soto, H., 2000, *The Mystery of Capital: Why Capitalism Triumphs in the West and Fails Everywhere Else*, New York, Basic Books.

De Souza, A., 1979, *Children in India: Critical Issues in Human Development*, Delhi, Manohar Publication.

Dingwaney, M., S. Dogra, R. Vidyasagar, and R. Gupta, 1988, *Children of Darkness—A Manual of Child Labour in India*, New Delhi, New Age Publication.

Dogramaci, I., 1981, *Child Labour in World Health*, Geneva, World Health Organisation.

Dreze, J., and S. Amartya (eds), 1991, *Social Securities in Developing Countries*, Oxford, Oxford University Press.

Ennew, J., 1986, *The Sex Exploitation of Children*, Cambridge, Polity Press.

Erikson, E., 1963, *Childhood and Society*, New York, Norton.

Everett, J., and S. Mira, 1994, *Women and Organizations in the Informal Sector*, Bombay, Himalaya Publishing House.

Fass, P. S., 1977, *The Damned and the Beautiful: American Youth in the 1920's*, New York, Oxford University Press.

Forde, B., 1979, *Children at Work*, Copenhagen, Danish Association for International Cooperation.

Franklin, B. (ed.), 1956, *The Rights of Children*, Oxford, Basil Blackwell.

Freire, P., 1985, *Pedagogy of the Oppressed*, London, Pelican.

Fuller, E., 1928, *The International Handbook of Child Care and Protection*, London, Longman.

Fuller, R. G., 1974, *Child Labour and the Constitution*, New York, Arno.

Fyfe, A., 1989, *Child Labour*, Cambridge, Cambridge University Press.

Fyfe, A., 1985, *All Work and No Play, Child Labour Today*, London, Trade Union Congress.

Gangrade, K. D., 1982, *Child Labour in India*, Delhi, Delhi School of Social Work.

Gangrade, K. D., 1978, *Social Legislation in India*, vol. I and II, New Delhi, Concept Publishing House Co.

Gangrade, K. D., and J. Gathia, 1983, *Women and Child Workers in Unorganised Sector*, New Delhi, Concept Publishing House.

George, I., 1990, *Child Labour and Child Work*, New Delhi, Ashish Publishing House.

Ghosh, J. (ed.), 2021, *Informal Women Workers in the Global South: Policies and Practices for the Formalisation of Women's Employment in Developing Economies*, New York, Routledge, Taylor & Francis Group.

Giri, N., 1990, "Beedila Kaaluthunna Bhatukulu," (Telugu), Tarakam, Bojja, (ed.), *Nela Nagali Mudeddulu*, Hyderabad, Book Trust Publications.

Grossfeld, S., 1989, *The State of the Child in India*, Boston, Globe.

Gupta, M., 2007, *Labour Welfare and Social Security in Unorganised Sector*, New Delhi, Deep and Deep Publications Pvt. Ltd.

Gupta, M., and V. Klaus (eds), 1987, *Young Hands at Work: Child Labour in India*, New Delhi, Atma Ram and Sons.

Hamilton, R., and M. Barrett (eds), 1986, *The Politics of Diversity: Feminism, Marxism and Nationalism*, London, Versa.

Hasan, N, 1972, *The Social Security System of India*, New Delhi, S. Chand and Co. (Pvt.) Ltd.

Herse-Biber, S., and G. L. Carter, 2000, *Working Women in America, Split Dream*, New York, Oxford University Press.

Hill, E., 2010, *Worker Identity, Agency and Economic Development: Women's Empowerment in the Indian Informal Economy*, New York, Routledge, Taylor and Francis.

Hirway, I., J. Collyn, and P. Pandya, 1991, *Towards Eradication of Child Labour*, Ahmedabad, Gandhi Labour Institute.

Hull, T. H., 1979, *Perspectives and Methods in the Study of Children's Work*, Geneva, ILO.

Irene, T., and M. B. Bramsen, 1976, *Women and World Development*, Washington (DC), Overseas Development Council.

Jenkes, C., 1982, *The Sociology of Childhood*, London, Batsford.

Joshi, M. V., 1999, *Women Rural Labourers, Problems and Prospects*, New Delhi, A.P.H. Publishing Corporation.

John, R. M., R. K. Rao, M. G. Rao, J. Moore, R. S. Deshpande, J. Sengupta, S. Selvaraj, F. J. Chaloupka and P. Jha, 2010, *The Economics of Tobacco and Tobacco Taxation in India*, Paris, France, International Union Against Tuberculosis and Lung Disease.

Kabeer, N., 1994, *Reversed Realities*, London, Verso.

Kalpagam, U., 1994, *Labour and Gender: Survival in Urban India*, New Delhi, Sage Publications.

Kanbargi, R. (ed.), 1991, *Child Labour in the Indian Subcontinent*, New Delhi, Sage.

Karve, I., 1968, *Kinship Organization in India*, 3rd ed., Bombay, Asia Publishing House.

Kate, P. V., 1987, *Marathwada Under the Nizams 1724–1948*, New Delhi, Mittal Publications.

Kaushik, S., 1985, *Women's Oppression*, New Delhi, Vikas Publishing House.

Kinyanjui, M. N., 2014, *Women and the Informal Economy in Urban Africa: From the Margins to the Centre*, London, Zed Books.

Klein, R., 1993, *Cigarettes Are Sublime*, Durham (NC), Duke University Press.

Kulshreshtha, J. C., 1978, *Child Labour in India*, New Delhi, Ashish.

Kumar, R. (ed.), 1988, *Child Development in India,* vol. 1, New Delhi, Ashish Publishing House.

Lander, M., 1885, *The Tobacco Problem*, 6th ed., Enlarged, Boston, Lee and Shepard.

Lebra, J., J. Paulson and J. Everett (eds), 1985, *Women and Work in India*, New Delhi, Promilla and Co Publishers.

Luxton, M., and J. Corman, 2001, *Getting by in Hard Times: Gendered Labour at Home and on the Job*. Toronto, Canada, University of Toronto Press.

Maitriya, C., 1971, *Child Labour in India*, Susses, Institute of Development Studies, University of Sussex. Mandal, A., 2005, *Women Workers in Brick Factory*, New Delhi, Northern Book Centre.

Mathew, E. T., 2006, *Employment and Unemployment in India*, New Delhi, Sage Publications India Pvt. Ltd.

Mathew, M. J., 2007, *Industrial and Labour Laws*, Jaipur, University Book House (P) Ltd.

Mehta, P. L., and S. S. Jaswal, 1996, *Child Labour and The Law*, New Delhi, Deep and Deep Publications.

Mehta, R., 1987, *Socio-Legal Status of Women in India*, New Delhi, Mittal Publications.

Mendelievich, E., 1979, *Child Labour at Work*, Geneva, International Labour Organization.

Mies, M., 1987, *India Women in Subsistence and Agricultural Labour*, New Delhi, Vistar Publications.

Morgan, E. S., 1975, *American Slavery, American Freedom: The Ordeal of Colonial Virginia*, New York, W.W. Norton & Company.

Mukherjee, R., 1997, *Legal Status and Remedies for Women in India*, New Delhi, Deep and Deep Publication.

Neuberger, M. B., 1963, *Smoke Screen: Tobacco and the Public Welfare*, Englewood Cliffs (NJ), Prentice-Hall.

Nissenbaum, S., 1980, *Sex, Diet, and Debility in Jacksonian America: Sylvester Graham and Health Reform*, Westport (CT), Greenwood Press.

Omvedt, G., 1981, *Effects of Agricultural Development in the Status of Women*, Pune, Maharashtra, Commissionerate of Agriculture.

Pachauri, S. K., 1999, *Women and Human Rights*, New Delhi, A. P. H. Publishing Corporation.

Pai, G. B., 2001, *Labour Law in India*, vol. 1 and 2, New Delhi, Butterworths India.

Pandhe, M. K. (ed.), 1977, *Child Labour in India*, Calcutta, India Book Exchange.

Pollock, L. A. 1983, Forgotten *Children: Parent-Child Relations from 1500 to 1900*, Cambridge, Cambridge University Press.

Pandey, J. N., 2002, *Constitutional Law of India*, Allahabad, Central Law Agency.

Pandey, P. N., and T. S. Papola, 1985, *Women Khadi Workers: A Study of Economic Conditions and Status of Women Spinners in U. P.*, Lucknow, Giri Institute of Development Studies.

Pati, R. M, 1991, *Rehabilitation of Child labourers in India*, New Delhi, Ashish Publishing House.

Piore, M., and C. Sabel, 1984, *The Second Industrial Divide*, New York, Basic Books.

Portes, A., M. Castells and L. A. Benton (eds), 1989, *The Informal Economy: Studies in Advanced and Less Developed Countries*, Baltimore (MD), John Hopkins University Press.

Proctor, R. N., 2011, *Golden Holocaust: Origins of the Cigarette Catastrophe and the Case for Abolition*, Berkeley, University of California Press.

Rai, C. P., 2002, *Working Women in India*, vol. 2., New Delhi, Anmol Publications Pvt. Ltd.

Ramakrishnan, S. (ed.), 1987, *Child Labour in Indian Industries*, Delhi, Alpha.

Rameshwari, P., and S. Patel, 2021, A *Study on Problems of Women in Unorganized Sector in Vadodara*, New Delhi, Author Press.

Reddy, Papi T., 1990, *Agrarian Unrest, Peasant Struggles and Social Change: A Study in Telangana*, Warangal, Sony Publications.

Regani, S., 1988, *Nizam-British Relations 1724–1857*, New Delhi, Concept Publishing Company.

Rodrik, D., 1997, *Has Globalization Gone Too Far?* Washington (DC), Institute for International Economics.

Roger, S., 1988, Children *Enslaved*, London, Routledge.

Saksena, A., 2004, *Gender and Human Rights: Status of Women Workers in India*, New Delhi, Shipra Publications.

Samanta, R. K. (ed.), 1998, *Women in Agriculture*, New Delhi, M. D. Publications.

Saradamoni, K., 1991, *Filling the Rice Bowl, Women in Paddy Cultivation*, Hyderabad, Sangam Books.

Saran, A. B., and A. N. Sandhwar, 1990, *Problems of Women Workers in Unorganised Sectors*, New Delhi, Northern Book Centre.

Sarika, P., and R. Pandya, 2010, *Women in the Unorganized Sector of India: Including a Case Study of Women in the Embroidery Industry in Surat City*, New Delhi, New Century Publications.

Savara, M., 1986, *Changing Trends in Women's Employment—A Case Study of the Textile in Bombay*, Bombay, Himalayan Publishing house.

Seccombe, W., 1992, *A Millennium of Family Change: Feudalism to Capitalism in Northern Europe*, London, Versao.

Shah, N. A., 1992, *Child Labour in India*, Delhi, Anmol.

Shahar, S., 1990, *Childhood in the Middle Ages*, London, Routledge.

Sharma, B., 1987, *My Home My Work Place*, Ahmedabad, Mahila Sewa Trust.

Sharma, U., 2006, *Female Labour in India*, New Delhi, Mittal Publications.

Shiva, V., 1991, *The Violence of the Green Revolution: Ecological Degradation and Political Conflict in Punjab*, London, Zed Books.

Siddiqui, M. I., 2004, *Women Workers*, New Delhi, Anamika Publishers and Distributors (P) Ltd.

Singh, A. N., 2001, *Women Domestic Workers*, New Delhi, Shipra Publications.

Singh, D. P., 2005, *Women Workers in Unorganised Sector*, New Delhi, Deep and Deep Publications.

Singh, A. N., 1990, *Child Labour in India: Socio-economic Perspectives*, Delhi, Shipra.

Srivastava, s. c., 1980, reprint, 2017, *Labour Laws Relating to Children in Employment, Their Impact and Implementation*, Chandigarh, Universal Law Publishing & Lexis Nexis; 2012, 6th Edition, New Delhi, Vikas Publishing House; 2017, Universal Law Publishing & Lexis Nexis.

Standing, G., 1999, *Global Labour Flexibility: Seeking Distributive Justice*, New York, St. Martin's Press.

Starr, P., 1982, *The Social Transformation of American Medicine*, New York, Basic Books.

Suguna Kumari, G., K. Nishi and K. Mukesh, 1997, *Women in India, A Statistical Profile, Department of Women and Child Welfare*, New Delhi, Ministry of Human Resources, Government of India.

Tate, C., 1999, *Cigarette Wars: The Triumph of "The Little White Slaver*, New York, Oxford University Press.

Tennant, R. B., 1950, *The American Cigarette Industry: A Study in Economic Analysis and Public Policy*, New Haven (CT), Yale University Press.

Tinker, I., and M. B. Bramsen, 1976, *Women and World Development*, Washington (DC), Overseas Development Council.

Tripathi, M. S., 1989, *Child Labour in India*, New Delhi, Discovery.

Tyrrell, I., 1991, *Woman's World/Woman's Empire: The Woman's Christian Temperance Union in International Perspective 1880–1930*, Chapel Hill and London, The University of Carolina Press.

UNICEF, 1989, *The Invisible Adjustment—Poor Women and the Economic Crisis*, Santiago, UNICEF.

Usharao, N. J., 1985, *Women in a Developing Society*, New Delhi, Ashish Publishing House.

Valle, T. D., 1993, *Gendered Anthropology*, London, Routledge.

Varandan, G., 1994, *Child Labour and Women Workers*, New Delhi, Ashish Publication.

Walter, L., 2003, *The Greenwood Encyclopedia of Women's Issues World Wide Asia and Oceania*, London (CT), Greenwood Press Westport.

Yadav, L. B., 2000, *Readings in Social and Labour Welfare*, Vol. 3., New Delhi, Anmol Publications Pvt. Ltd.

Zaheeruddin, 1985, *Labour Welfare Laws and Employment Conditions in India*, New Delhi, Deep and Deep Publications.

II. Articles in books

Abraham, P., 1991. "The Working Girl Children: A Case Study of Children of Match Industries at Sivakasi", in R. N. Pati (ed.), *Rehabilitation of Child Labourers in India*, New Delhi, Ashish Publishing House.

Ali, N., 1987, "Child Labour in the Carpet Industry of Kashmir", in M. Gupta and K. Voll (eds), *Young Hands at Work*, New Delhi, Atma Ram.

Banerjee, 1988, 'Small and Large Units—Symbiosis or Matsyanyaya?', in K. B. Suri (ed.), *Small Scale Enterprises in Industrial Development: The Indian Experience*, New Delhi, Sage Publication.

Beachy, V., 1978, "Women and Production: A Critical Analysis of Some Sociological Theories of Women's Work", in A. Kuhn and A. M. Wolpe (eds), *Feminism and Materialism: Women and Modes of Production*, London, Routledge and Kegan Paul.

Bequela, A., 1986, "Child Labour: A Frame Work for Policies and Programmes", in *Child Labour: A Briefing Manual*, Geneva, International Labour Organisation.

Bhatt, E., 1994, "From Survival to Self-reliance: The Experience of the Self Employed Women's Association (SEWA)", in M. Fatima (ed.), *Poverty in the 1990s: The Responses of Urban Women*, Paris, UNESCO and International Social Science Council, pp. 275–285.

Bromley, R., 1982, "Working in the Streets: Survival Strategy, Necessity or Unavoidable Evil?", in A. Gilbert, J. Hardoy and R. Ramirez (eds), *Urbanisation in Contemporary Latin America*, New York, John Wiley.

Castells, M., and A. Portes, 1989, "World Underneath: The Origins, Dynamics, and Effects of the Informal Economy", in A. Portes, M. Castells and L. A. Benton (eds), *The Informal Economy: Studies in Advanced and Less Advanced Developed Countries*, Baltimore (MD), John Hopkins University Press.

David, N., 1996, "Unorganised Women Workers: Problems and Prospects", in S. N. Tripathy (ed.), *Unorganised Women Labour in India*, New Delhi, Discovery Publishing House.

Devi, D. R., and K. R. Kapadia, 1985, "Prevalence of Child Labour in India: A Secondary Data Analysis", in U. S. Naidu (ed.), *Child Labour and Health: Problems and Prospects*, Bombay, Tata Institute of Social Sciences.

Dholakia, R. H., 1992, "Wage Differentials Between Sexes in India: An Explanation", in A. N. Sharma and S. Singh (eds), *Women and Work Changing Scenario in India*, New Delhi, Indian Society of Labour Economics and B.R. Publishing Corporation.

Durvasula, R., 1992, "Occupational Health Information's Systems in India", in M. R. Reich and T. Okubo (eds), *Protecting Workers Health in the Third World, National and International Strategies*, New York, Auburn House.

Feldman, S., 1992, "Crisis, Islam and Gender in Bangladesh: The Social Construction of a Female Labor Force", in B. Lourdes and S. Feldman (eds), *Unequal Burden: Economic Crises, Persistent Poverty, and Women's Work*, Boulder (CO), Westview Press, pp. 105–130.

Gibson, A., 1994, "Fortress or Easy Street: The Impact of Emerging Trade Structures on Globalization and Developing Countries", in S. Neelamegham (ed.), *Competing Globally*, New Delhi, Allied Publishers.

Gupta, M., 1987, "Child Labour: A Harsh Reality", in M. Gupta and K. Voll (eds), *Young Hands in Work: Child Labour in India*, New Delhi, Atma Ram.

Kasturi, L., 1990, "Poverty, Migration and Women's Status", in V. Majumdar (ed.), *Women Workers in India*, New Delhi, Chanakya Publications, pp. 3–169.

Kumar, R. (ed.), (1988), *Child Development in India*, Vol. 1., New Delhi, Ashish Publishing House.

Leslie, J., 1989, "Women's Work and Child Nutrition in the Third World", in J. Leslie and Michael Paolisso (eds), *Women Work and Child Welfare in the Third World*. Boulder (CO), Westview Press.

Manoshi, M., 1987, "Women's Work: Gains Analysis of Women's Labour in Daily Production", in A. M. Singh and A. Kelles-Viitanen (eds), *Invisible Hands, Women in Home Based Production*, New Delhi, Sage Publication, pp. 109–143.

Mehta, A. K., 1999, "Globalization and the Third World", in Raj Mohan Sethi (ed.), *Globalization, Culture and Women's Development*, New Delhi, Rawat Publications, pp. 55–76.

Mencher, J., 1987, "Women's Work and Poverty: Women's Contribution to HouseHold Maintenance in Two Regions of South India", in D. Deoyer and J. Bruce (eds), *A Home Divided: Women and Income Control in the Third World*, Stanford (CA), Stanford University Press.

Murray, C. J. L., and L. C. Chen, 1994, "Understanding Morbidity Change", in L. C. Chen, A. Kleinman and N. C. Ware (eds), *Health and Social Change in International Prospects*, Boston (MA), Harvard School of Public Health.

Padmavathi, D., and V. L. Ramamohan, 1999, "Technological Dichotomy: The Story of Women Quarry Workers", in R. M. Sethi (ed.), *Globalization, Culture and Women's Development*, New Delhi, Rawat Publications, pp. 146–163.

Pande, R., 2007a, "Role of Women in Indian Agriculture—A Historical Perspective", in A. Sahida and L. K. Sami (eds), *Indian Women in Development Perspective*, New Delhi, Anmol Publication, Pvt. Ltd, pp. 66–96.

Pande, R., 2007b, "Women's Work in the Beedi Industry in India", in R. Pande, S. Nalini and R. Mahalingam (eds), *Women in Nation Building—A Multidimensional Perspective*, Hyderabad, Panchajanya Publications, pp. 7–34.

Parker, J., J. Arrowsmith and A. Boyd, 2017, "Papua New Guinea: Work and Care in a Subsistence Economy", in M. Baird, M. Ford and E. Hill (eds), *Women, Work and Care in the Asia-Pacific*, Sydney, Routledge.

Rao, R., and S. Hussain, 1987, "Invisible Hands: Women in Home Based Production in the Garments Export Industry in Delhi", in M. Singh and A. Kelles-Viitanen (eds), *Invisible Hands, Women in Home Based Production*, New Delhi, Sage Publication, pp. 51–67.

Rao, V., G. Radhaiah and V. Narayana, 1990, "How Poor Can Help the Poor", in P. V. Sukhatme (ed.), *Statistics in Health and Nutrition*, Hyderabad, National Institute of Nutrition, Indian Council of Medical Research.

Sandhu, A. N., and A. Singh, 1986, "Socio-economic Aspects of Child Labour in India", in D. N. Saraf (ed.), *Social Policy, Law and Protection of Weaker Sections of Society*, New Delhi, Eastern.

Sankaran, K., 2006, "Women, Work and Empowerment", in A. Gandhi (ed.), *Women Work, Health and Empowerment*, New Delhi, Aakar Books, pp. 54–63.

Sebastian, A., 1979, "Child Migrants and Child Migrant Labour", in P. C. Saxena and T. Kanithar (eds), *Demography and Socio-economic Aspects of the Child in India*, Bombay, Himalaya.

Sharma, B. K., and N. Mittar, 1990, "Child Labour in India: An Anatomy", in B. P. Singh and M. Shukla (eds), *Children at Work; Problems and Policy Options*, New Delhi, B.R. Publishing.

Sukhatme, P. V., 1990, "How Poor Can Help the Poor", in V. Rao, G. Radhaiah and V. Narayana (eds), *Statistics in Health and Nutrition*, Hyderabad, National Institute of Nutrition, Indian Council of Medical Research.

Tanwar, R., 1999, "Women and Falling Incomes: The Impact of Cash Economy in Rural India", in R. M. Sethi (ed.), *Globalization, Culture and Women's Development*, New Delhi, Rawat Publications, pp. 129–145.

Varshney, A., 2001, "Mass Politics or Elite Politics? Indian Economic Reforms in Comparative Perspective", in J. Sachs, A. Varshney and N. Bajaj (eds), *India in the Era of Economic Reforms*, New Delhi, Oxford University Press.

III. Journal articles

Abraham, A., 1980, "Beedi workers of Bombay", *Economic and Political Weekly*, Vol 15, No. 44, pp. 1881–1882.

Acharya, P., 1982, "Child Labour", *Seminar* (27th), July, pp. 18–21.

Aggarwala, A. N., 1949, *Indian Labour Problems*, Allahabad, Indian Research Association.

Aggarwala, R. C., 1983, "Child Welfare Today and Tomorrow", *Yojna*, July 15.

Aghi, M. B. and M. Gopal, 2001, "Exploiting Women and Children–India's Beedi Industry", *Lifeline*, Vol. 6, pp. 8–10.

Ali, L., 1997, "Unorganised Labour and the Legislature Measures for their Welfare", *Social Action*, Vol. 47, No. 2, April–June.

Allen, A. M., C. Onken and D. Hatsukami, 2014, "Women and Smoking: The Effect of Gender on the Epidemiology, Health Effects, and Cessation of Smoking", *PubMed Central*, Vol. 1, pp. 53–60. https://www.ncbi.nlm.nih.gov/pmc/articles/PMC4871621/ Accessed 10th August, 2020.

Anand, M., 2006, "Women's Work: Visible Work, Invisible Hands", *Women's Link*, Vol. 12, No. 4, October-December, Social Action Trust, New Delhi.

Apte, M., 1979, "Priority Needs of Children in India", *The Indian Journal of Public Administration*, Vol. 25, No. 3.

Arora, D., 1999, "Structural Adjustment Program and Gender Concerns in India", *Journal of Contemporary Asia*, Vol. 29, No. 3, pp. 328–361.

Arora, S., 1987–1988, 'Meeting Migrant Women Labourers', *Main Stream*, Vol. 26, No. 15, p. 58.

Avachat, A., 1978, "Beedi Workers of Nipani", *Economic and Political Weekly*, Vol. 13, No. 29, pp. 1176–1178; Vol. 13, No. 30, pp 1203–1205.

Bagwe, A. N., R. A. Bhisey and R. B. Govekar, 1992, "Toxic Effects of Exposure to Tobacco Among Beedi Rollers", *Toxicology Letters,* Vol. 22, No. 6, pp. 1205–1206.

Bagwe, A. N., and R. A. Bhisey, 1995, "Occupational Exposure to Unburnt Bidi Tobacco Elevates Mutagenic Burden Among Tobacco Processors", *Carcinogenesis*, Vol. 16, No. 5, pp. 1095–1099.

Balagopal, K. R., and M. Kodandram, 1982, "Forever 'Disturbed': Peasant Struggle of Sircilla-Vemulawada", *Economic and Political Weekly,* Vol. 17, No. 48, Nov. 27, pp. 1897–1901.

Banerjee, N., 1999, "Can Markets Alter Gender Relations?" *Gender, Technology and Development*, Vol. 3, No. 1, pp. 103–122.

Banerjee, S., 1980, "Children Without Childhood", *Economic and Political Weekly*, Vol. 15, No. 23.

Basharat, H., 2002, "Sexual Harassment of Women at Work Place: A Socio-Legal Study of Srinagar City with Special Reference to Hospitals and Educational Institutions", *Kashmir University Law Review*, Vol. VIII.

Basu, A. M., and K. Basu, 1991, "Women's Economic Roles and Child Survival: The Case of India", *Health Transition Review*, Vol. 1, pp. 83–101.

Beevi, F. A., 2014, "Problems and Prospects of the Unorganised Sector in Kerala: Reference to Sales Women in Textiles", *Abhinav National Monthly Refereed Journal of Research in Commerce & Management*, Vol. 3, No. 9, pp. 35–39.

Best, J., 1979, "Economic Interests and the Vindication of Deviance: Tobacco in Seventeenth Century Europe", *Sociological Quarterly*, Vol. 20(Spring), pp. 171–182.

Bhalla, S., 1989, "Technological Change and Women Workers: Evidence From the Expansionary Phase in Haryana Agriculture", *Economic and Political Weekly*, October 28, WS, pp. 67–78.

Bharati, N. P., and R. Kesari, 2014, "Child Labour in Unorganized sector in India", *New Man International Journal of Multidisciplinary Studies*, Vol. 1, No. 12, December, pp. 248–252.

Bhati, J. B., and D. V. Singh, 1987, "Women's Contribution to Agricultural Economy in Hill Regions of North West India", *Economic and Political Weekly*, Vol. 22, No. 17, April 25. New Delhi, pp. ws7–ws11.

Bhatty, Z., 1985, "Economic Role and Status of Women—A Case Study of Women in the Beedi Industry in Allahabad", *Maunshi*, No.27, pp. 29–32.

Bhisey, R. A., and A. N. Bagwe, 1995, "Occupational Exposure to Unburnt Beedi Tobacco Elevates Mutagenic Burden Among Tobacco Processors", *Carcinogenesis*, Vol. 16, No. 5, pp. 1095–1099.

Biradar, R. R., and S. T. Bagalkoti, 2001, "Changing Facets of Employment in Rural India: Emerging Issues and Challenges", *Indian journal of Agricultural Economics,* Vol. 56, No. 3, July–September, pp. 538–552.

Boeke, J. H., 1953, "Economics and Economic Policy of Dual Societies", New York: International Secretariat, Institute of Pacific Relations, *International Affairs*, Vol. 30, No. 2, April 1954, pp. 259–260.

Brandt, A. M., 1990, "The Cigarette, Risk, and American Culture", *Dædalus*, Vol. 119, No. 4, pp. 155–176.

Brita, B., 1979, "Women, Food and Technology", *Economic and Political Weekly*, Vol. XIV, No. 47.

Burnham, J. C., 1989, "American Physicians and Tobacco Use: Two Surgeons General, 1929 and 1964", *Bulletin of the History of Medicine*, Vol. 63, No. 1, pp. 1–31.

Burney, L. E., 1958, "Lung Cancer and Excessive Cigarette Smoking. Statement by Surgeon General Leroy E. Burney of the Public Health Service, Department of Health, Education, and Welfare, July 12, 1957. CA", *A Bulletin of Cancer Progress*, Vol. 8, No. 3, p. 44.

Chakravarty, D., 2004, "Expansion of Markets and Women Workers Case Study of Garment Manufacturing in India", *Economic and Political Weekly*, November 6.

Chauhan, P. S., 1997, "Gender Issue in Labour", *Award Digest Journal of Labour Legislation,* Vol. XXIII, No. 1–6, January–June.

Chitra, N., 2015, "A Descriptive Study on Problems of Women Workers in Construction Industry at Tiruchirappalli", *IOSR Journal of Humanities and Social Science*, pp. 46–52.

Choudry, P., 1993, "Women Worker in Rural Haryana", *Economic and Political Weekly*, No. 25, December.

Costa, R., 1989, "Exploited Children in a Bangladesh Bidi Industry", *Child Workers in Asia*, Vol. 5, No. 3, pp. 10–11.

Dalela, S. C., 1979, "No Time to Play or Dream", *Social Welfare*, 8–9 November.

Das, B., and B. Bharat, 2004, "Women Workers in the Unorganised Sector: A Human Right Perspective", *Cochin University Law Review,* Mar and June, 27 (1 and 2).

Das, S. K., and R. A. Pande, 2000, "Better deal for beedi workers", *Occupational Environment Health*, Vol. 109, No. 3, pp. 23–25.

Datt, R. 2007, "Unorganised Sector and Informalisation of the Indian Economy", *The Indian Journal of Labour Economics*, Vol. 50, No. 4, pp. 775–792.

Desai, S., and D. Jain, 1994, "Maternal Employment and Changes in Family Dynamics: the Social Context of Women's Work in Rural South India", *Population and Development Review*, Vol. 20, pp. 115–133.

Deshpande, S., and L. K. Deshpande, 1992, "New Economic Policy and Female Employment", *Economic & Political Weekly*, Vol. 27, No. 41, pp. 2248–2252.

Dev, J. M., 2006, "Female Work Participation and Child Labour: Occupational Dataform NFHS", *Economic and Political Weekly*, August.

Dewan, R., 1999, "Gender Implications of the 'New' Economic Policy: A Conceptual Overview", *Women's Studies International Forum*, Vol. 22, No. 4, pp. 425–429.

Dharmalingam, A., 1993, "Female Beedi Workers in a South Indian Village", *Economic and Political Weekly*, July 3–10.

Dikshit, R. P., and S. Kanhere, 2000, "Tobacco Habits and Risk of Lung, Oropharyngeal and Oral Cavity Cancer: A Population Based Case-control Study in Bhopal, India", *International Journal of Epidemiology*, Vol. 29, No. 8, pp. 609–614.

Dillow, G. L., 1981, "Thank You for Not Smoking: The Hundred Year War Against the Cigarette", *American Heritage*, Vol. 32, No. 2, pp. 94–107.

Dyson, T., and M. Moore, 1983, "On Kinship Structure, Female Autonomy, and Demographic Behaviour in India", *Population and Development Review*, Vol 3, pp. 35–60.

Elson, D., 1982, "Differentiation of Children's Labour in the Capitalist Labour Market", *Development and Change,* Wiley Online Library, International Institute of Social Studies, The Hague. https://doi.org/10.1111/j.1467-7660.1982.tb00132.x

Ernster, V. L., 1985, "Mixed Messages for Women: A Social History of Cigarette Smoking and Advertising", *New York State Journal of Medicine*, Vol. 85, No. 7, pp. 335–340.

Ezzati, M., S. J. Henley, M. J. Thun and A. D. Lopez, 2005, "Role of Smoking in Global and Regional Cardiovascular Mortality", *Pub Med. Gov*, Vol. 112, No. 4, pp. 489–497, https://pubmed.ncbi.nlm.nih.gov/16027251/ Accessed 10th August, 2020.

Fernandes, W., and G. Menon, 1987, *Tribal Women and Forest Economy*, New Delhi, Indian Social Institute.

Ghosh, J., 2002, "Globalization, Export-Oriented Employment for Women and Social Policy: A Case Study of India", *Social Scientist,* Vol. 30, No. 11/12, pp. 17–60.

Ghosh, J., 1994, "Gender Concerns in Macro – Economic Policy", *Economic and Political Weekly*, Vol. 29, No. 18, pp. ws2–ws4.

Gill, T., 1989, "Case of Famine Monitoring: A Gender Perspective", *Economic and Political Weekly*, October 28, pp. ws91–95.

Gopal, M., 2006, "Gender Ageing and Social Security", *Economic and Political Weekly*, Vol. XLI, No. 42, October 21.

Gopal, M., 1999, "Disempowered Despite Wage Work: Women Workers in Beedi Industry", *Economic and Political Weekly*, Vol. 34, pp. 16–17.

Gowda, Y. S., R. Sidde and R. Indira, 1987, "Women Workers in Agarbathi Industry: A Study", *Indian Journal of Social Work*, October.

Gulati, L., and G. Mitu, 1997, "Female Labour in the Unorganised Sector: The Brick Worker Revisited", *Economic and Political Weekly*, Vol. 32, p. 96.

Gupta, P. C., 1984, "Mortality Experience in Relation to the Tobacco Chewing and Smoking Habits From a Ten Year Follow Up Study in Ernakulum District, Kerala", *International Journal of Epidemiology*, Vol. 13, pp. 184–187.

Gupta, S. D., R. Gupta, A. Zafar, D. K. Mangal and R. Sharma, 1983, "Control of Anemia Among Pregnant Women by Iron Supplementations", *Indian Journal of Public Health*, No. 27.

Hart, K., 1973, "Informal Income Opportunities and Urban Employment in Ghana", *Journal of Modern African Studies*, Vol. 11, No. 1, pp. 61–89. http://dx.doi.org/10.1017/S0022278X00008089

Heyzer, N., 1989, "Asian Women Wage-Earners: Their Situation and Possibilities for Donor Intervention", *World Development,* Vol. 17, No. 17, pp. 1109–1123.

Isabelle, G., B. Augendra and V. G. Parthasarthy, 2007, "Labour in Brick Kilns: A Case Study in Chennai", *Economic and Political Weekly,* February 17.

Jain, D., and S. Desai, 1995, "The Women Worker and Her Child", *Institute of Social Studies,* Dossier No. 4, Bangalore.

Jayadevan, C. M., 1996, "Casualisation of Work-force in India: An Analysis of Spatial Variations", *Indian Journal of Labour Economics,* Vol. 39, No. 4.

Jeyaranjan, J., and P. Swaminathan, 1999, "Resilience of Gender Inequalities: Women and Employment in Chennai', *Economic and Political Weekly*, April 17–24.

Jigging, J., 1986, "Gender Related Impacts and the Work of the International Agricultural Center", *Consultative Group on International Agricultural Research (CGIAR)*, The World Bank, No. 17, pp. 2–21. https://cgspace.cgiar.org/bitstream/handle/10947/582/study17.pdf Accessed 4th June, 2022.

John, R. M., R. K. Rao, M. G. Rao, J. Moore, R. S. Deshpande, J. Sengupta, S. Selvaraj, F. J. Chaloupka and P. Jha, 2010, *The Economics of Tobacco and Tobacco Taxation in India*, Paris, France, International Union Against Tuberculosis and Lung Disease.

Joshi, K., M. Robins, Venu Parashramlu and K. Mallikarjunaih, 2013, "An Epidemiological Study of Occupational Health Hazards Among Bidi Workers of Amarchinta, Andhra Pradesh", *Journal of Academic and Industrial Research*, Vol. 1, No. 9, pp. 561–564.

Kabeer, N., K. Milward and R. Sudarshan, 2013, "Organising Women Workers in the Informal Economy", *Gender & Development*, Vol. 21, No. 2, pp. 249–263, https://doi.org/10.1080/13552074.2013.802145

Kannan, K. P., R. Srivastava and A. Sengupta, 2006, "Social Security for Unorganised Sector", *Economic and Political Weekly*, Vol. XLI, No. 32, August 12.

Kaur, S., H. K. Verma, J. Singh, S. K. Dash and S. K. Kansal, 2017, "Knowledge Level of Women Dairy Farmers about Various Farming Practices in Border Area of Punjab", *Journal of Animal Research*, Vol. 7, No. 6, pp. 1051–1059.

Krishnaraj, M., 1992, "Women Craft Workers as Security for Family Subsistence", *Economic and Political Weekly*, Vol. 27.

Kumar, K., 1991, "Banning Child Labour", *Economic and Political Weekly*, Vol. 26, No. 52, p. 2983.

Kuruvila, M., S. Mukhi, P. Kumar, G. Rao, K. S. Sridhar and M. S. Kotian, 2002, "Occupational Dermatoses in Beedi Rollers", *Indian Journal of Dermatology, Venereology and Leprology*, Vol. 68, pp. 10–12.

Lum, K. L., J. R. Polansky, R. K. Jackler and S. A. Glantz, 2008, "Signed, Sealed and Delivered: "big tobacco" in Hollywood, 1927–1951", *Tobacco Control*, Vol. 17, pp. 313–323.

Mahimkar, M. B., and R. A. Bhisey, 1995, "Occupational Exposure to Bidi Tobacco Increases Chromosomal Aberrations in Tobacco Processors", *Mutation Research*, Vol. 334, pp. 39–144.

Maloney, W. F., 1999, "Does Informality Imply Segmentation in Urban Labour Markets? Evidence from Sectoral Transitions in Mexico", *World Bank Economic Review*, Vol. 13, No. 2, pp. 275–302. https://www.jstor.org/stable/3990099 Accessed 2nd June, 2022.

Mehta, P., 1985, "We Are, Made to Mortgage Our Children—Interviews With Women Beedi Workers of Vellore", *Maunshi*, Vol. 22, pp. 14–17.

Mitra, S., 2006, "Problems of Female Employment in Urban India, Analysis of NSS Data (1983 to 1999–2000)", *Economic and Political Weekly*, Vol. XLI, No. 48, December 2.

Mittal, S., M. Apoorva and R. Rengappa, 2008, "Ocular Manifestations in Beedi Industry Workers", *Indian Journal of Ophthalmology*, Vol. 56, pp. 319–322.

Mohandas, M., 1980, "Beedi Workers in Kerala: Conditions of Life and Work", *Economic and Political Weekly*, Vol. 15, No. 36, pp. 1517–1523.

Murthy, K. G., and J. T. Rani, 1983, "Wages of Child Labour", *Yojana*, Vol. 27, No. 18, pp. 12–14.

Muna, K., 2015, "Unorganised Workers: A Core Strength of Indian Labour Force: An Analysis", *International Journal of Research in Business Studies and Management*, Vol. 2, No. 12, December, pp. 44–56.

Nadagoudar, S. V., 2002, "Social Security for Workers in the Unorganised Sector", *Cochin University Law Review*, Vol. XXVI, March and June, No. 1 and 2.

Nakkeeran, S. K., and S. B. Pugalendhi, 2010, "A Study on Occupational Health Hazards Among Women Beedi Rollers in Tamilnadu, India", *International Journal of Current Research*, Vol. 11, No. 1 (5 December 2010), pp. 117–122.

Namasivayam, N., and S. Vijayakumar, 2004, "A Study on Socio-Economic Factors Influencing Employment of Women Workers in Petrol Pumps at Madurai City", *The PRP Journal of Human Rights*, July–September, Vol. 3.

Nandal, S., 2006a, "Women Workers in Unorganised Sector: A Study on Construction Industry in Haryana", *International Journal of Development Issue,* Vol. 5 No. 2, pp. 119–120.

Nandal, S., 2006b, "Women in Informal Economy: A Case Study of Construction Workers in Haryana", *Social Action Trust*, Vol. 12, No. 4, October–December, New Delhi.

Neupane, T. P., 1987, "A Reality Behind the Problems", *Voice of Child Workers* (Nepal), pp. 24–25.

Nihila, M., 1999, "Marginalisation of Women Workers Leather Tanning Industry in Tamil Nadu", *Economic and Political Weekly*, Vol. 34, No. 16 and 17, April.

Nomani, M. Z. M., 1996, "Health, Environment and Industrial Relation: Emerging Judicial Trends in India", *The Academy Law Review*, Vol. 20, pp. 1, 2.

Noronha, E., and R. N. Sharma, 1999, "Displaced Workers and Withering of Welfare State", *Economic and Political Weekly*, Vol. 34, No. 23, June 5.

Pande, R., 2019, "Globalisation and Women's Work in the Beedi Industry", *Studia Historiae Oeconomicae, The Journal of Adam Mickiewicz University*, Vol. 37, No. 1, pp. 191–221.

Pande, R., 2008, Women and Children Workers in the Old City of Hyderabad, India, *Intersections: Gender and Sexuality in Asia and the Pacific: Women Workers and Traders and the Globalisation Agenda in the Asian Context*, Guest editor Barbara Hartley Issue 17, June.

Pande, R., 2006, "Gender Concerns in Rural Settlement-looking at Sustainable Agriculture", *Journal of Development Alternatives and Area study*, San Antonio, Texas, USA, Vol. 25, No. 3, September, pp. 63–86.

Pande, R., 2003, "Girl Child Rights and Labour Exploitation in the Beedi Industry," *Indian Journal of Human Rights,* Vol. 7, No. 1 and 2, January–December, pp. 52–73.

Pande, R., 2001a, "Health issues of Women and Children—A Study of the Beedi Industry", *Women's Link,* Vol. VII, No. 2, pp. 8–16.

Pande, R., 2001b, "The Social costs of Globalization: Restructuring Developing World Economies", *Journal of Asian Women's Studies,* Vol. 10, December, Japan, Kitakyushu Forum, pp. 1–14.

Pande, R., 2000, "Globalization and Women in the Agricultural Sector", *International Feminist Journal of Politics,* Vol. 2, No. 3, Routledge, London, pp. 409–412.

Pande, R., 1999, "Structural Violence and Women's Health: Work in the Beedi Industry of India", *Proceedings of WHO Global Symposium on Violence and Health*, Kobe, Japan, pp. 192–205.

Parvathi, S., 1999, "Perspective Rules of Extension Workers to Carry Post Harvest Technologies to Farm Women", *Indian Journal of Social Work*, April.

Patel, R. K., 1993, "Present Status and Promise of Dairying in India", *Indian Dairyman*, Vol. 45, No. 7, pp. 276–308.

Perry, C. L., 1999, "The Tobacco Industry and Underage Youth Smoking: Tobacco Industry Documents From the Minnesota Litigation", *Archives of Pediatrics & Adolescent Medicine,* Vol. 153, No. 9, pp. 935–941. https://jamanetwork.com/journals/jamapediatrics/fullarticle/347724 Accessed 11th August, 2020.

Pillai, J. K., and V. Bhasin, 2007, "Study of Short Stay Homes Managed by All India Women's Conference", *Social Welfare,* Vol. 53, No. 12, March.

Prakasamma, M., 1993, *Women's Employment as Empowerment and Exploitation: The Case of Beedi Making Women*, Mimeographed Paper, Research Paper No. 80, Takemi Program, Harvard school of public health, Boston.

Prakash, B., and U. Vyas, 2013, "Association Between Occupational Tobacco Exposure of Health Hazards in Women Laborers of Bidi Industry of Ajmer", *International Journal of Pharma Medicine and Biological Sciences*, Vol. 2, No. 1.

Prugl, E., and I. Tinker, 1997, "Microentrepreneurs and Home workers, Convergent Categories", *World Development*, Vol. 25, No. 9, pp. 1471–1482.

Rajeev, M., 2006, "Contract Labour in Karnataka, Emerging Issues and Options", *Economic and Political Weekly*, Vol. XLI, No. 21, May 27.

Rajni, V., 2007, "Casual Labour Contracts of Agricultural Labourers in East and West Uttar Pradesh", *Economic and Political Weekly,* January 13.

Raju, S., 2006, "Locating Women in Social Development", *India Social Development Report* (1st edition).

Ramakrishna, S., 1987, "Child Labour in India Industries", *Alpha*, Vol. 24, No. 15, pp. 2–3.

Randeria and Yagnik, 2008, "Holiday From Labour Laws", *Economic and Political Weekly*, October.

Ranjitsingh, A. J. A., and C. Padmalatha, 1995, "Occupational Illness of Beedi Rollers in South India", *Environment Economics*, Vol. 13, No. 4, pp. 875–887.

Rao, E. K., 2006. "Role of Women in Agriculture: A Micro Level Study", *Journal of Global Economy, Research Centre for Social Sciences*, Mumbai, India, Vol. 2, No. 2, pp. 107–118, June.

Rao, P. V., 1990, "Childhood Disability in Andhra Pradesh", *Social Change*, Vol. 20, No. 3, pp. pp. 52–57.

Rao, V. M., D., Rajasekhar and J. Y. Suchitra, 2006, "Unorganized Workers, Deprivation, Social Security Needs, Policy Implications", *Economic and Political Weekly*, Vol. XLI, No. 19, May 13.

Reddy, T. C., S. V. Udaykumar and R. Tamilselvi, 1991, "Some Structural Determinants of Union Participation Among Women Workers", *Social Action*, April–June.

Robinson, W. I., and J. Harris, 2000, "Towards a Global Ruling Class? Globalization and the Transnational Capitalist Class", *Science & Society*, Vol. 64, No. 1 (Spring), pp. 11–54.

Rustagi, P., 1997, "Women Employment in the Unorganised Sector: Some Issues", *Social Action,* Vol. 47, No. 2, April–June (1997).

Sajama, A. M., 1979, "Child Labour in Indian Industries", *The Indian Journal of Social Work*, Vol. 40, No. 3, pp. 345–352.

Salway, S., S. Rahman and S. Jesmin, 2003, "A Profile of Women's Work Participation Among the Urban Poor of Dhaka", *World Development*, Vol. 31, No 5, pp. 881–901.

Saradamoni, K, 1987, 'Labor, Land and Rice Production: Women's Involvement in Three States", *Economic and Political Weekly,* Vol. 17, No. 52, pp. ws2–ws6.

Sarika, P., and R. Pandya, 2017, "Problems of Women in Unorganized Sector—A Study on Home Based Women Workers and Domestic Women Workers in Vadodara", *International Journal of Applied Home Science,* Vol. 4, No. 7–8, July & August, pp. 593–610.

Saxena, A., 2004, "Women Workers in Unorganised Sector: Inequity and Discrimination", *Social Action,* Vol. 54, October–December.

Sen, G., 1999, "Engendering Poverty Alleviation: Challenges and Opportunities", *Development and Change*, Vol. 30, Institute of Social Studies, Oxford, pp. 685–692.

Sethuraman, S. V., 1976, "The Urban Informal Sector: Concept, Measurement and Policy", *International Labour Review,* Vol. 114, No. 1.

Sharma, A. M., 1979, "Child Labour in India Industries", *The Indian Journal of Social Work*, Vol. 40, No. 3, pp. 545–552.

Sharma, V., 2004, "Constitutional Provisions Relating to Women and International Instrument on Rights of Women", *Aligarh Law Journal*, Vol. XVI and VII.

Sharma, M., and U. Varjani, 1989, "Women's Work Is Never Done: Dairy Development and Health in the Lives of Rural Women in Rajasthan", *Economic and Political Weekly,* April 29, WS, pp. 38–44.

Shatrugna, V., N. Soundarajan, P. Sundaraiah and L. Raman, 1990, "Backpain, the Feminine Affliction", *Economic and Political Weekly*, Vol. 25, No. 17, pp. WS2–WS6. http://www.jstor.org/stable/4396219

Shobha, V., 1992, "Female Agricultural Labourers and Rural Development", *Mainstream.*

Shukla, T., 1989, "Rural Nonagricultural Employment", *Economic and Political Weekly,* Vol. 24, No. 35–36, pp. 1993–1995.

Sidde, Y., S. Gowda and R. Indira, 1987, "Women Workers in Agarbatthi Industry—A Study", *Indian Journal of Social Work,* 48, Oct.

Singh, D. P., 2003, "Living Conditions of Women Workers in Brick Kilns: Reflecting the Agenda for Social Work Intervention," *Indian Journal of Social Work*, July, Vol. 64, No. 3.

Singh, I. J., 1979, "A Study of Morbidity Pattern in Rural Community", *Health and Population Perspectives and Issues,* No. 2, pp. 193–206.

Singh, M., 1992, "Enforcement of Equal Remuneration Act, 1976 and Status of Women Workers: Myth and reality", *Indian Journal of Industrial Relations,* Vol. 27, No. 33.

Singh, G., S. P. Shyam and P. R. Bhardwaj, 1994, "Structural Adjustment and Female Workers", *Mainstream*, Vol. 32, No. 14.

Singh, M. D., and G. Pony, 2004, "Sexual Victimization of Women in India", *Indian Socio-Legal Journal, An International Journal of Legal Philosophy, Law and Society,* Vol. XXX, No. 1.

Sinha, M. L., 1994, "Conditions of Women Workers in the Brick Kilns", *Man in India,* Vol. 74, No. 1, March.

Srinivasulu, K., 1997, "Impact of Liberalisation on Beedi Workers", *Economic and Political Weekly*, Vol. 32, No. 11, March 15–21, pp. 515–517.

Srivastava, R. C., 2004, "Sexual Harassment of Women at the Workplace", *Labour Law Journal*, Vol. III, October.

Srivastava, S. C., 2001, "Impact of the Supreme Court Decision on Contract Labour", *Journal of the Indian Law Institute*, Vol. 43, p. 4.

Sundan, L., 1984, "Sociological Aspects of Child Labour", *Indian Journal of Pediatrics*, Vol. 51, No. 413, pp. 665–668.

Sudarshan, R., and R. Kaur, 1999, "The Tobacco Industry and Women's Employment: Old Concerns and New Imperatives", *The Indian Journal of Labour Economics*, Vol. 42, No. 4.

Surbhi, K., and P. K. Sethy, 2014, "Working and Living Conditions of Workers in Unorganized Sector—A Review of Literature", *Online International Interdisciplinary Research Journal,* Vol. IV, No. II, March–April.

Swaminathan, M., 2000, "Structural Adjustment and Food Subsidy. Selected Country Experiences", in *Weakening Welfare. The Public Distribution of Food in India*, New Delhi, LeftWord, pp. 64–77.

Swami, S., A. N. Suryakar and R. V. Katkam, 1995, "Absorption of Nicotine Induces Oxidative Stress Among Beedi Workers", *Toxicology Letters*, Vol. 18, No. 2, pp. 259–265.

Taneja, A., 2003, "Human Rights of Working Women Under Various Legislations", *Indian Bar Review*, Vol. XXX, p. 4.

Tewary, S., 2004, "Equal Pay for Equal Work—How Far it is Recognised as a Fundamental Right", *Labour Law Journal*, Vol. III, October.

Thakur, D., and Chandar, M., 2006, "Gender Based Differential Access to Information Among Livestock Owners and its Impact on House Hold Milk Production in Kangra District of Himachal Pradesh", *Indian Journal of Dairy Science*, Vol. 59, No. 6, pp. 401–404.

Thippaiah, P., 1989, "Women Workers in Urban Unorganised Sector", *Social Welfare*, May.

Tokman, V., 1978, "An Exploration into the Nature of the Informal-Formal Sector Relationship", *World Development*, Vol. 6, No. 9/10.

Tripathi, P. K., 1972, "Some Insights into Fundamental Rights", *Indian Journal of Politics.*

Umadevi, B., M. Swarna, P. Padmavathi, A. Jyothi and P. P. Reddy, 2003, "Cytogenetic Effects in Workers Occupationally Exposed Tobacco Dust", *Mutation Research/Genetic Toxicology and Environmental Mutagenesis*, Vol. 535, No. 2, pp. 147–154.

Unni, J., 1989, "Changes in Women's Employment in Rural Areas 1961–83", *Economic and Political Weekly*, April 29, WS, pp. 23–31.

Unni, J., and G. Raveendran, 2007, "Commentary on Growth of Employment (1993–94 to 2004–05): Illusion of Inclusiveness", *Economic and Political Weekly*, January 20.

Upadhyaya, S., 1997, "Gender Under the Indian Constitution", *Award Digest Journal of Labour Legislation,* Vol. XXIII, No. 1–6, January–June.

V. B., 1993, "Maternal Education, Female Labour Force Participation and Child Mortality: Evidence from the Indian Census", *Health Transition Review*, Vol. 3, pp. 171–189.

Verma, N. M. P., and R. Bano, 1998, "Determinants of Women Workers Participation: Notes on Some Interdisciplinary Controversies", *Indian Journal of Industrial Relations*, Vol. 34, No. 1, July.

Verma, S. K., and D. Dutta, 1988, "Personality Profiles of Grass Root Level Women Workers: Some Reflections for Action", *Social Action,* April–June.

V. G. 1984, "Tendu Leaf Labourers in Telangana: Working Conditions and Struggles", *Economic and Political Weekly,* Vol. 19, No. 46, November 17, pp. 1941–1943.

Visuthas, J. J., 1985, "Women Beedi Workers of Vellore", *Social Welfare*, Vol. 31, No. 11, pp. 26–27.

Ware, H., 1984, "Effects of Maternal Education, Women's Roles and Child Care on Child Mortality", *Population and Development Review*, 10(Supplement), pp. 191–214.

Wessel, C. A., 1924, "The First Sixty Billions Are the Hardest for Cigarette Industry", *Printers' Ink*, Vol. 126, No. 5, pp. 3–6, 137–46.

William, I. R., and J. Harris, 2000, "Towards a Global Ruling Class? Globalization and the Transnational Capitalist Class", *Science & Society*, Vol. 64, No. 1 (Spring, 2000), pp. 11–54.

IV. Commissioned papers and reports

Annual Report, 2018–19, Government of Telangana, Department for Women, Children, Disabled & Senior Citizens, https://www.telangana.gov.in/PDFDocuments/Telangana-Women-Children-Disabled-and-Senior-Citizens-Department-Annual-Report-2018-19.pdf Accessed 10th October, 2019.

Annual Report, 1972, International Crop Research Institute for Semi-Arid Tropics, Patancheru, Hyderabad, India.

Baxi Upendra, 1985, "State, Seths and Sikhsa—The Saga of Sahemma", paper presented at the Asian Regional Conference on Women and the Household, New Delhi (WSDC, DV).

Carr, M., and M. Chen, 2002, *Globalization and the Informal Economy: How Global Trade and Investment Impact on the Working Poor,* Working Paper on the Informal Economy Working No. 1 INTEGRATION. Geneva: International Labour Office.

Census of India. Registrar General of India.

Central Statistical Organisation/India, 2001, *Expert Group on Informal Sector Statistics (Delhi Group), Report of the Fifth Meeting* (New Delhi, 19–21 September 2001).

Chant, S., and C. Pedwell, 2008, *Women, Gender and the Informal Economy: An Assessment of ILO Research and Suggested Ways Forward, Discussion Papers Are Preliminary Documents Circulated to Stimulate Debate and Obtain Comments.* International Labour Organization.

Chatterjee, M., 1988, *Both Gender and Age Against Them,* Mimeo Report, NIPCCD, New Delhi.

Chaudhry, K., 2000, Multisectoral and Intersectoral Approach to National Tobacco Control. Paper commissioned by the World Health Organization on the occasion of The WHO International Conference on *Global Tobacco Control Law: Towards a WHO Framework Convention on Tobacco Control,* 7–9 January, New Delhi, India.

Chief Labour Commissioner, 1965, *The Payment of Bonus Act, 1965,* https://clc.gov.in/clc/acts-rules/payment-bonus-act-0#Short%20title, %20extent%20and%20application Accessed 14th June, 2022.

Chowdhruy, K., 2000, Multisectoral and Intersectoral Approach to National Tobacco Control. Paper commissioned by the World Health Organization on the occasion of The WHO International Conference on *Global Tobacco Control Law: Towards a WHO Framework Convention on Nipani Organize,* New Delhi, Kali for women. *Tobacco Control,* 7–9 January, New Delhi, India.

Das, S. K., 2000, DG, Labour Welfare, Ministry of Labour, *report prepared for ILO,* October.

Economic Survey 2017–18, Ministry of Finance, New Delhi, Press Information Bureau, Government of India, https://timesofindia.indiatimes.com/realtime/Economic_Survey_2017_18.pdf Accessed 14th September, 2020.

Economic Survey 2015–16, Ministry of Finance, New Delhi, Government of India.

Farhham A, 2013, E-cigarette Sales to hit $1 Billion. *ABC News*, July 31.

Gender and Poverty in India, 1991, *A World Bank Country Study*, Washington.

Government and the Economics of Tobacco Control, 1999, *Development in Practice. Curbing the Epidemic*, Washington (DC), A World Bank Publication.

Government of India, 1993, *Economic Reforms: Two Years After and the Tasks Ahead*, New Delhi, Ministry of Finance.

Human Development Report, 1999, New York, Oxford University Press.

Human Development Report, 1995, *UNDP*. New York: Oxford University Press, Principle coordinator, Mahbub ul Haq.

ILC, 2019, *International Labour Standards Department*, Conference Committee on the Application of Standards: Record of Proceedings, 21st October.

ILO, 2018, *Women and Men in the Informal Economy: A Statistical Picture*, 3rd ed., Geneva, International Labour Office. https://www.ilo.org/wcmsp5/groups/public/---dgreports/---dcomm/documents/publication/wcms_626831.pdf Accessed 6th June, 2022.

ILO, 2017, *Global Estimates of Child Labour: Results and Trends, 2012–2016*, Geneva, International Labour Office.

ILO, 2015, *World Report on Child Labour, Paving the Way to Decent Work for Young People*, Geneva, International Labour Office.

ILO, 2007, *ABC of Women Workers' Rights and Gender Equality*, 2nd ed., Geneva, International Labour Office.

ILO, 2002, *Women and Men in the Informal Economy: A Statistical Picture*, Geneva, ILO. Written by Marty Chen and Joann Vanek using multi-country data analyzed by Jacques Charmes and country studies by Debbie Budlender, Peter Buwembo, Nozipho Shabala, Jeemol Unni, Marge Guerrero, Rodrigo Negrete, Françoise Carré, and Joaquin Herranz, Jr. Geneva, ILO.

ILO, 1995, Women Work More, But are Still Paid Less, ILO/95/22, Press release | 25 August 1995, https://www.ilo.org/global/about-the-ilo/newsroom/news/WCMS_008091/lang--en/index.htm Accessed 26th March, 2020.

ILO, 1984, *International Labour Organisation, Towards an Action Programme on Child Labour*, Technical Commission.

ILO, 1972, *Employment, Income and Equality: A Strategy for Increasing Productive Employment in Kenya*, Geneva, International Labour Office.

ILO-IPEC, Y. Diallo, Alex Etienne and F. Mehran, 2013, *Global Child Labour Trends 2008 to 2012. ILO International Programme on the Elimination of Child Labour (IPEC)*, Geneva, International Labour Office.

International Labour Office, 2002a, *Decent Work and the Informal Economy; Report of the Director-General;* International Labour Conference, 90th Session; Report VI. Geneva, Switzerland: International Labour Office.

Isaac, T., T. M. Richard, W. D. Franke and P. Raghavan, 1998, "Government of Madras report, 1947", *Democracy at work in an Indian Cooperative: The story of Kerala Dinesh Beedi*, Ithaca (NY), Cornell University Press. R Ayyar, Bench: Rajagopalan, R Ayyar. https://indiankanoon.org/doc/68600/ Accessed 12th October, 2018.

Jain, Devaki and Sonalde Desai, 1995, "The Women Worker and Her Child", *Institute of Social Studies,* Dossier No. 4, Bangalore.

Jeemoi, U., and R. Uma, 2005, *Impact of Recent Policies on Home Based Work in India*. Discussion paper Series, 10, Human Development Resource Centre, UNDP, India.

John, R. M., R. K. Desai, M. G. Rao, J. Moore, R. S. Deshpande, J. Sengupta, S. Selvaraj, F. J. Chaloupka and P. Jha, 2010, *The Economics of Tobacco and Tobacco Taxation in India*, Paris, France, International Union Against Tuberculosis and Lung Disease.

Kameshwari, J., and R. Pande, 1992, Mimeo Report, *Crèches in the Organized and Unorganized Sectors in Secunderabad and Hyderabad*, Department of women and child welfare, Government of India, New Delhi.

Madras High Court, 1961, Abdur Rahim vs State of Madras (Secretary, on 21 January, 1960) IILLJ 213 Madras, 29th March, 2020.

Mendelievich, Elias, 1979, "Child Labour at Work", *International Labour Review*, Vol. 118, No. 5, September–October, Geneva, International Labour Organization, pp. 557–568.

National Agriculture Policy, 1998, *Confederation of Indian Industry*, Chandigarh, Agro-Tech

NCEUS, 2007, *Report on Conditions of Work and Promotion of Livelihoods in the Unorganised Sector,* New Delhi, National Commission for Enterprises in the Unorganised Sector, https://msme.gov.in/sites/default/files/Condition_of_workers_sep_2007.pdf Accessed 13th September, 2020.

NSSO, 2014, 2011–12 Unit Level Data, 68th Round, Employment Unemployment Survey, National Sample Survey Office—Ministry of Statistics and Programme Implementation(MOSPI), Government of India (GOI), New Delhi.

NSO, 2019, 2017–18 Unit Level Data, Periodic Labour Force Survey, National Statistical Office, NSSO Ministry of Statistics and Program Implementation, New Delhi, Government of India.

Ratnam, C., and S. Venkata, 2006, "Social Security in the Organised Sector", *India Social Development Report.*

Report of Committee on Child Labour, 1979, New Delhi, Government of India.

Report, ILO, 1984, International Labour Organisation, *Towards an Action Programme on Child Labour,* Technical Commission.

Rodyers, G., and G. Standings, 1981, "Economic Roles of Children in Low Income Countries", *International Labour Review,* Vol.120, I, Jan-Feb.

Shimkhada, R., and J. W. Peabody, 2003, "Tobacco Control in INDIA", *Bulletin of the World Health Organ*, Vol. 81, pp. 48–52.

Shram Shakti, 1988, *Report of the National Commission on Self-Employed Women and Women in the Informal Sector,* New Delhi, Publication Division, Government of India, Patiala House, June.

Socioeconomic Outlook Reports, 2017–2020, Government of Telangana, Planning Department, https://www.telangana.gov.in/PDFDocuments/Telangana-Socio-Economic-Outlook-2020.pdf Accessed 5th May, 2020.

Stanford Research Into the Impact of Tobacco Advertising, http://tobacco.stanford.edu/tobacco_main/index.php Accessed 12th September, 2020.

Statistical Year Book 2017, Directorate of Economics and Statistics. Hyderabad: Government of Telangana, http://ecostat.telangana.gov.in/PDF/PUBLICATIONS/Statistical_Year_Book_2017.pdf, Accessed 5th May, 2020.

Statistical Year Book 2015, Directorate of Economics and Statistics. Hyderabad: Government of Telangana, https://www.telangana.gov.in/PDFDocuments/Statistical-Year-Book-2015.pdf Accessed 10th October, 2018.

Srivastava, A., 2000, The Role and Responsibility of Media in Global Tobacco Control. Paper commissioned by the World Health Organization on the Occasion of The WHO International Conference on Global Tobacco Control Law: *Towards a WHO Framework Convention on Tobacco Control*, 7–9 January, New Delhi, India.

Tamang, D., 1990, Indigenous Forest Management Systems in Nepal: A Review: Research Report Series—HMG Ministry of Agriculture, Nepal/Winrock International, Policy Analysis in Agriculture and Related Resource Management, No. 12.

TARI, 2019, Thought Arbitrage Research Institute (TARI) on behalf of the Assocham, *The Economic Times*, June 5th.

The India Economic Survey, 2015/2016, https://www.thehinducentre.com/resources/article8285564.ece Accessed 13th September, 2020.

Towards Equality, 1974, Report on the Committee on the Status of women, Ministry of Education and Social Welfare, New Delhi, Government of India.

UNICEF, 1986, *The Report on Child Labour*, United Nations Organisation.

WCTU, 1884, *Woman's Christian Temperance Union*, St. Louis, Missouri Convention.

WHO, World Health Report, World Health Organization, https://www.who.int/whr/media_centre/factsheet2/en/ Accessed 25th March, 2020.

WHO FCTC, 2003, Framework Convention on Tobacco Control, https://apo.who.int/publications/i/item/9241591013 Accessed 14th May, 2022.

Women and men in India, 1996–97, Central Statistical Organization, Department of Statistics, Ministry of Planning and program implementation, Government of India.

V. Newspapers and magazines

Barse Sheela, 1986, "Crafting Keys with Calloused Hands", *Indian Express*, July 29, 1986.

Barse Sheela 1986, "Glass Factories of Firozabad-I: Children Playing with Fire", *Indian Express*, April 5.

Barse Sheela, 1986, "Glass Factories of Firozabad-II: Fleeting of Hapless Labour", *Indian Express*, April 6.

Barse Sheela, 1986, "Glass Factories of Firozabad-III: Nelson's Eye to Workers Safety", *Indian Express*, April 7.

Chaturvedi, M., 1980, "Child Labour: The Shame of a Nation", *The Illustrated Weekly of India*, 20–26 July, pp. 12–13.

Hirji, Z., 2000, "Toil and Trouble: The Beedi Workers of Jelligude", *Lifeline*, Vol. 3, March 2000, p. 11–12.

Jain, S. M., 1979, "Law and the Child in India", *The Indian Journal of Public administration*, Vol. XXV, No. 3, July–September.

Joshi, K., M. R., P. Venu and K. Mallikarjunaih, 2013, "An Epidemiological Study of Occupational Health Hazards Among Bidi Workers of Amarchinta, Andhra Pradesh", *Journal of Academic and Industrial Research*, Vol. 1, No. 9, pp. 561–564.

Junod, S. W., 1997, "Early Tobacco Regulation: Myth and Reality", *FDLI Update*, Vol. 4, p. 6, 8.

Juyal, B. N., 1991, "The Problem of Child Labour: Worsening With Growth?" *People's Action*, Vol. 6, No. 1, pp. 3–7.

Menon, S., 1979, "Sivakasi—The Little Japan of India", *The Time of India*, New Delhi, 7th October.

Mukesh, R., 2019, "Child Labour in India: Violators Go Scot-free as Only 25% Cases Reach Conviction", *India Today*, 12th June.

Rai, U., 1986, "Controversy Hounds Child labour", *The Times of India*, August 9th.

Rodyers, G. and G. Standings, 1981, "Economic Roles of Children in Low Income Countries", *International Labour Review*, Vol. 120, I, January–February.

Ray, R., 1998. *South Asia drug demand reduction report*. UNDCP Regional Office for South Asia.

Sen, A. K., 1999, "Marlboro, Camel, Rothmans Make Way for Bidis", *Deccan Chronicle*, Monday, 20th September.

Singh, U., and N. A. Vijay Avinashilingam, 2005, "Need for Women Extension Workers in Agriculture", *Employment Newspaper*, 29 October–4 November.

Sunil, K. P., 1991a, "Children of a Lesser God", *The Illustrated Weekly of India*, 30 November–6 December.

Sunil, K. P., 1991b, "Dreams Die Young", *The Illustrated Weekly of India*, 22–24 February, pp. 30–31.

TARI, 2019, "Thought Arbitrage Research Institute (TARI) on behalf of the Assocham", *The Economic Times*, 5 June.

Thomas, E. C., 2005a, "Job Guarantee for the Rural Poor", *Employment Newspaper*, 15–21 October.

Thomas, E. C., 2005b, "Protection of the Rights of Women", *Employment Newspaper*, p. 1218.

VI. Thesis

Maheshwari Prakash Condition of Labour in the Beedi Industry Chandra, in Central India, Agra University, Agra, 1962, Thesis.

Pujari Gobardhan, A Study of Beedi Workers in Orissa University of Delhi, Delhi, 1970, Thesis.

VII. Web resources

Camel, 1935, R. J. Reynolds *Tobacco Company*, http://tobacco.stanford.edu/tobacco_main/images.php?token2=fm_st149.php&token1=fm_img4496.php&theme_file=fm_mt018.php&theme_name=Sm Accessed 12th September, 2020.

Census data, Office of the Registrar General & Census Commissioner, India. Ministry of Home Affairs, Government of India. https://censusindia.gov.in/census.website/about/contact Accessed 10th June, 2022.

Cook, R., 2022, Ranking of Countries That Produce the Most Tobacco, October, 26th. https://beef2live.com/story-ranking-countries-produce-tobacco-263-212893 Accessed 14th May, 2022.

Heckewelder, J., 1818, *History, Manners and Customs of the Indian Nations Who Once Inhabited Pennsylvania*, The Historical society of Pennsylvania, USA. https://www.gutenberg.org/files/50350/50350-h/50350-h.htm#:~:text=Heckewelder%2C%20in%201818%2C%20published%20under, and%20in%201822%20he%20prepared Accessed 12th September, 2020.

Hussmanns, R., 2001, Defining and Measuring Informal Employment, Bureau of Statistics, Geneva, Switzerland International Labour Office, https://www.ilo.org/public/english/bureau/stat/download/papers/meas.pdf Accessed 25th March, 2020.

International Labour Office, The Regulatory Framework and the Informal Economy, Geneva, https://www.ilo.org/wcmsp5/groups/public/---ed_emp/---emp_policy/documents/publication/wcms_210445.pdf Accessed 25th March, 2020.

ILO, 1995, Women Work More, But are Still Paid Less, ILO/95/22, Press Release | 25 August 1995, https://www.ilo.org/global/about-the-ilo/newsroom/news/WCMS_008091/lang--en/index.htm, Accessed 26th March, 2020.

Lucky Strike, 1930, http://tobacco.stanford.edu/tobacco_main/index.php Accessed 12th September, 2020.

Ministry of Statistics and Programme Implementation, Government of India. https://mospi.gov.in/ Accessed 18th June, 2022.

NCEUS, http://www.wiego.org/informal_economy_law/country-study-india

Save the Children, 2016, Statistics of Child Labour in India State Wise, https://www.savethechildren.in/articles/statistics-of-child-labour-in-india-state-wise#:~:-text=It%20is%20not%20surprising%20that, Report%20on%20Child%20Labour%20 2015).&text=According%20to%20Census%20data Accessed 16th September, 2020.

Shimkhada, R., and J. W. Peabody. "Tobacco Control in India", *Bull World Health Organ*, Vol. 81, pp. 48–52.

Stanford Research into the impact of Tobacco Advertising, http://tobacco.stanford.edu/tobacco_main/index.php Accessed 12th September, 2020.

The Child Labour (Prohibition and Regulation) Act, 1986, https://labour.gov.in/sites/default/files/act_3.pdf Accessed 27th March, 2020.

The Domestic Workers' Welfare & Social Security Act, 2010, http://bslsa.bih.nic.in/PDF/acts16/domestic_worker_welfare_and_social_security_act_2010.pdf. Accessed 25th March, 2020.

The Unorganised Workers' Social Security Act, 2008, Act No. 33 of 2008 (30th December) http://legislative.gov.in/sites/default/files/A2008-33.pdf. Accessed 20th January, 2020.

Tobacco in India, http://www.fao.org/3/y4997e/y4997e0h.htm#TopOfPage%20 Accessed 12th September, 2020.

Sengupta, Arjun chairperson of the National Commission on Enterprises in the Unorganised/Informal Sector, Union Ministry of labour and employment, Government of India, http://www.medcindia.org/cgi-bin/Oct07/Indian%20Review.HTM Accessed 17th March, 2008.

UN-Habitat, "Monitoring the Implementation of the Goal of the United Nations Millennium Declaration on Improving the Lives of Slum Dwellers", http://www.unhabitat.org/downloads/docs/1672_90752_K0473689_6addd1.pdf, Accessed 24th March, 2008. To avoid introducing too many concepts the terms "shelter deprivation" and "slums" are used to when describing the same phenomenon.

Universal Leaf Tobacco, 2013, UN Trade database. http://www.universalcorp.com/UniversalLeaf Accessed 16th May, 2022.

World Health Organization, 2015, WHO Framework Convention on Tobacco Control, Geneva, Switzerland, https://www.who.int/fctc/WHO_FCTC_summary.pdf Accessed 7th August, 2020.

World Health Report, World Health Organization. https://www.who.int/whr/media_centre/factsheet2/en/ Accessed 25th March, 2020.

VII. Telugu books

Giri Nagabhushanam, 1990, Beedi Kaaluthunna Bhatukulu (Telugu), Tarakam Bojja (ed.), Hyderabad, Hyderabad Book Trust Publication.

PART C

Appendix

APPENDIX 1

MAP OF TELANGANA WITH THE THREE REGIONS

Armoor, Balkonda, and Nizamabad and Hyderabad Urban areas

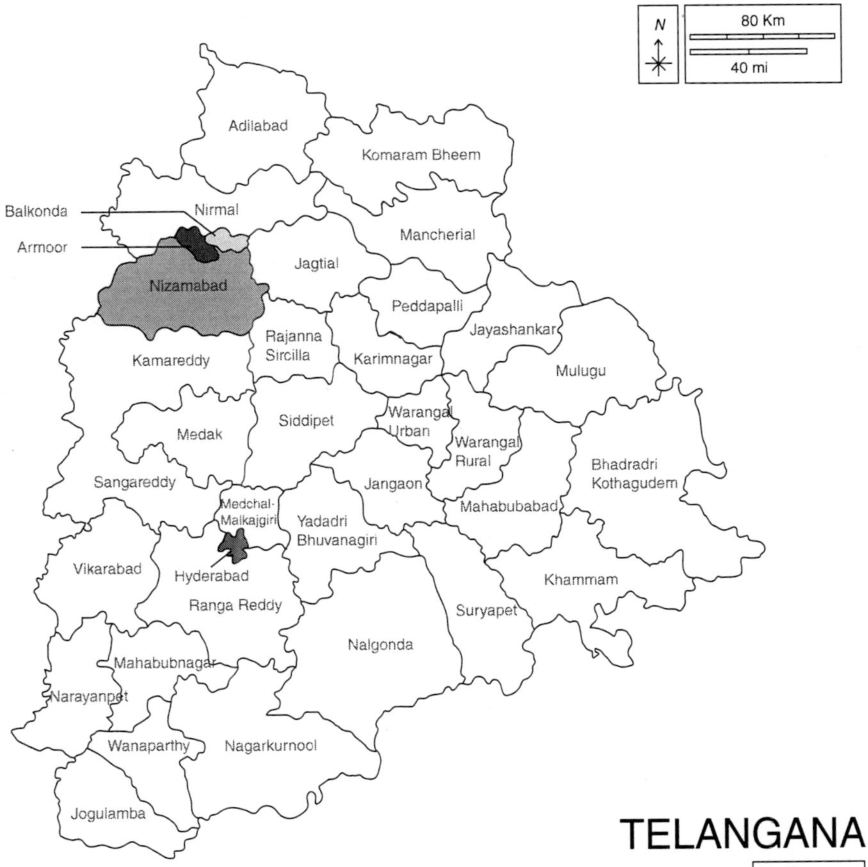

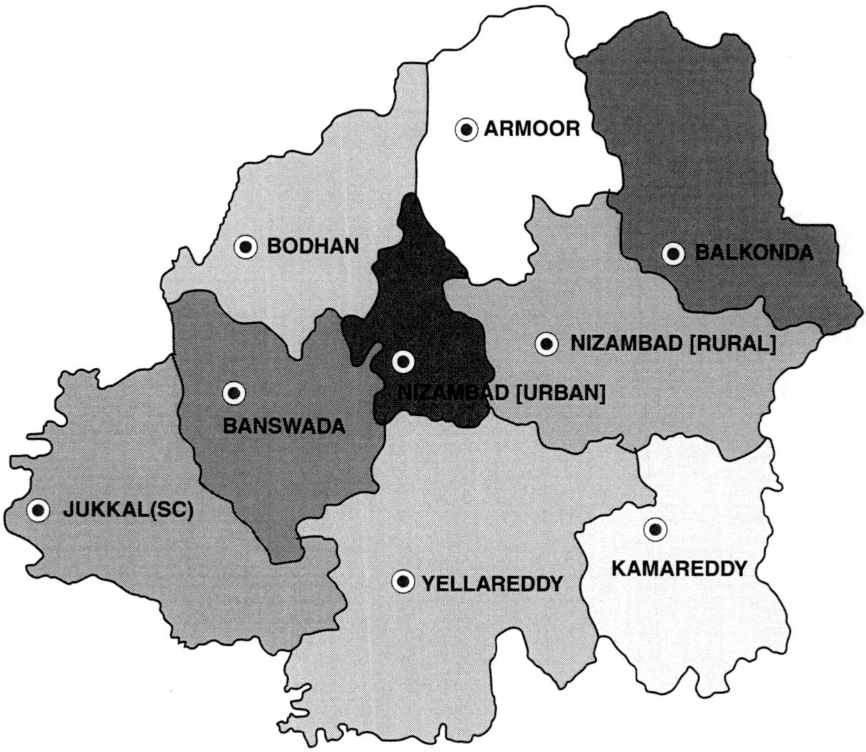

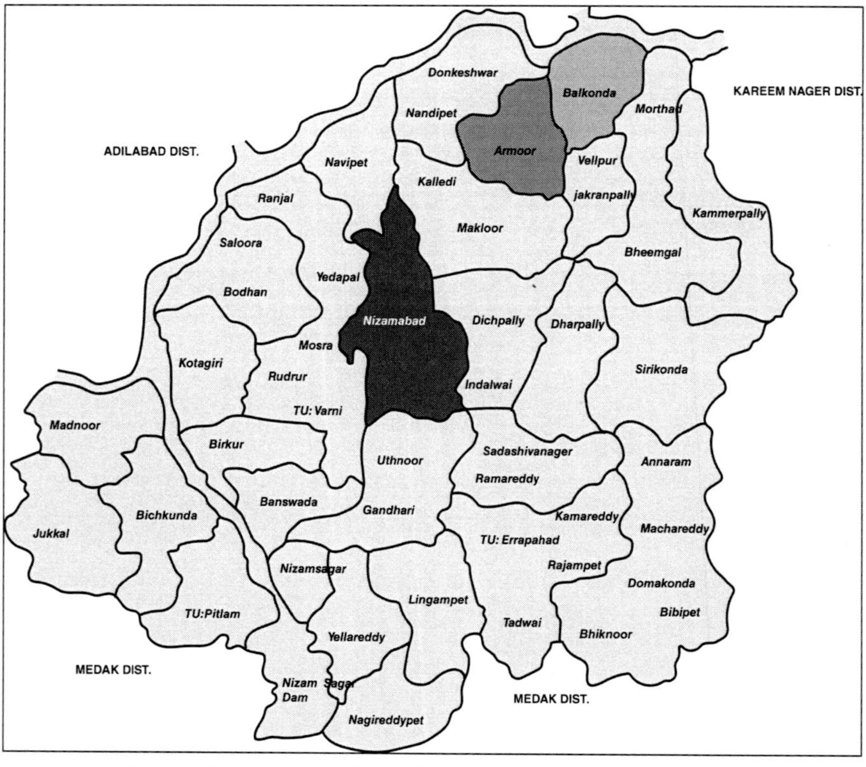

Source: https://www.telangana.gov.in/about/districts/nizamabad
http://nizamabad-district.blogspot.com/2012/12/nizamabad-dist-map.html
https://d-maps.com/carte.php?num_car=117973&lang=en

APPENDIX 2

A LIST OF FEW BEEDI FACTORIES IN TELANGANA

1. Major Chaap Beedi Company
   Address: Barni Road, Nizamabad Ho, Nizamabad-503001

2. Langar Beedi Company
   Address: Hyderabad Road, Pragathi Nagar, Nizamabad-503001

3. Kurla Beedi Factory
   Address: Door No. 10-1-105, Sriji Bhavan, Shivaji Nagar, Nizamabad-503001, beside Pochi Lingiya Temple

4. B.S. Parikh & Co. Beedi Factory
   Address: Kisan Nagar, Kissannagar, Nizamabad-503218

5. Patel Jivrajbhai Bidi Works
   Address: Pangra B, Mahalaxmi Nagar, Bank Colony, Nizamabad, Telangana-503230

6. Charbhai Bidi Works
   Address: 6-3-582, beside Zilla Parishad, Gandhi Tata Nagar, Khairtabad, Hyderabad, Telangana-500004

7. Beedi Making Company
   Address: Nizamabad, Telangana-503111

8. Radha Lakshmi Beedi Factory
   Address: Unnamed Road, Kisan Nagar, Telangana-503217

9. C.J. Patel & Co – Beedi Company
   Address: Kisan Nagar, Telangana-503218

10. A.A. Saquib Beedi Manufacturers Allauddin
    Address: Akkannapet-Lingapur Rd, Telangana-502115

11. Mohan Seth Ginni Beedi Factory
    Address: Brahmapuri, Nirmal, Telangana-504106

12. Dhantal Beedi Works, Manufacturing Unit
    Address: Village, Donkal, Telangana-503311

13. Lokam Limbadri Beedi Factory
    Address: Near Kothbadi, Neela, Telangana-503235

14. Modern Beedi Factory UMS
    Address: Armoor, Telangana-503224

15. Armoor Desai Beedi Factory
    Address: Armoor, Telangana-503224

16. G. Venkatram Beedi Kharkana
    Address: Seetharam Nagar Colony, Sitha Ram Nagar, Anand Nagar, Telangana-503001, India

17. Thakur Savdekar Beedi Kharkana
    Address: Arsapally, Nizamabad, Telangana-503001

INDEX

For Product Safety Concerns and Information please contact our EU representative GPSR@taylorandfrancis.com Taylor & Francis Verlag GmbH, Kaufingerstraße 24, 80331 München, Germany